LAPHAM'S
QUARTERLY

The disaster takes care of everything.
                    —Maurice Blanchot, 1980

Lot and His Daughters, by Albrecht Dürer, c. 1496.

www.laphamsquarterly.org

Volume 9, No. 2. www.laphamsquarterly.org. Lapham's Quarterly (ISSN 1935-7494) is published four times yearly (December, March, June, September) by the American Agora Foundation, 116 E. 16th Street, 8th Floor, New York, NY 10003. Periodicals postage paid at New York, NY, and additional mailing offices. Copyright © 2016 American Agora Foundation, Inc. All Rights Reserved. Nothing shown may be reproduced in any form without obtaining the permission of the creators and of any other person or entity that may have copyright ownership. Printed in Canada.
For newsstand sales inquiries, please contact newsstand@circmonster.com.
Subscriber Services. Subscription: 1 year, $60; in Canada, $70; in all other countries, $100. All payments in U.S. dollars. Direct all inquiries, address changes, subscription orders, etc., to: email: customerservice@laphamsquarterly.us; telephone: 877-890-3001; mail: Lapham's Quarterly, PO Box 8564, Big Sandy, TX 75755. Editorial and Business Office: 116 E. 16th Street, 8th Floor, New York, NY 10003. Postmaster: Send changes of address to Lapham's Quarterly, PO Box 8564, Big Sandy, TX 75755.

LAPHAM'S
QUARTERLY

DISASTER

Introductory

Voices in Time

PREMONITION

Voices in Time

Voices in Time

AFTERMATH

Breathless, southern Edwards County, Kansas, by Larry Schwarm, 2008.

Voices in Time

Further Remarks

ESSAYS

DEPARTMENTS

Serpent carrying off the child Opheltes,
Roman jasper gemstone, first century BC to third century.

Many of the passages in this issue have been abbreviated without the use of ellipses; some punctuation has been modified, and while misspellings have been corrected, archaic grammar and word usage remains unchanged. The words are faithful to the original texts.

ART, PHOTOGRAPHY, AND ILLUSTRATIONS

Cover: Tragic mask of a king, late Hellenistic terra cotta, first century BC.

IFC: *Lot and His Daughters*, by Albrecht Dürer, c. 1496.

5: *Breathless*, by Larry Schwarm, 2008.

6: Serpent carrying off the child Opheltes, first century BC to third century.

12: Panel of *The Last Judgment* triptych, by Hieronymus Bosch, late fifteenth century.

15: Baghdad under attack by U.S.-led coalition forces, March 21, 2003.

18: *The Good Samaritan*, by George Frederick Watts, 1850.

22: "A Harvest of Death, Gettysburg, Pennsylvania," July 1863. Photograph by Timothy H. O'Sullivan.

24: *Aristocracy Two*, by David LaChapelle, 2014.

27: Fireman carrying a child pulled from the overturned *SS Eastland*, Chicago, 1915. Photograph by Jun Fujita.

29: Tourists react to approaching tsunami, Thailand, 2004.

32: Ice calving into Disenchantment Bay, Alaska, 1986. Photograph by Chris Johns.

35: *The Destruction of the House of Job and the Theft of his Herd by the Sabians*, by Bartolo di Fredi, 1356.

38: Hiroshima after the atomic bomb, 1945. Photograph by the U.S. Air Force.

40: Shia, wooden lacquered mask, India, nineteenth century.

41: Various disasters, from *A Rod for Runaways*, by Thomas Dekker, 1625.

42: *State of the Union*, by John Brosio, 2011.

45: Neville Chamberlain and Adolf Hitler shaking hands, 1938.

47: Mother comforting her son, Pakistan, 2005. Photograph by Paula Bronstein.

51: Battle between Roman and Germanic armies, detail of the Portonaccio sarcophagus, Rome, c. 180.

53: Locust swarms, Iran, 1952. Photograph by Erich Lessing.

54: *The Expulsion from Paradise*, by Franz von Stuck, c. 1890.

57: Devastation following a cyclone, India, 1999. Photograph by Raghu Rai.

59: Boy killed by falling masonry, School of Giotto, fourteenth century.

63: *The Kent Fire*, by Théodore Gudin, 1828.

65: Helmet mask, Côte d'Ivoire, nineteenth or early twentieth century.

66: *Miners' Wives*, by Ben Shahn, c. 1948.

69: *Cape Coral #1, Lee County, Florida, USA, 2012*, by Edward Burtynsky.

71: *A Deluge*, by Leonardo da Vinci, c. 1517.

73: *Displaced*, by Manuel Cunjamá, 2000.

74: Human remains from a mass grave, Iraq, 2003. Photograph by Marco Di Lauro.

77: *The Destruction of the Temple of Jerusalem*, by Francesco Hayez, 1867.

78: *Rope Out*, by Mitch Dobrowner, 2014.

83: Suicide attack, Pakistan, 2007. Photograph by John Moore.

84: *The Horrors of War*, by Peter Paul Rubens, c. 1638.

87: Celestial fire destroying the army of Satan, miniature from a thirteenth-century edition of the Book of Revelation.

89: *Pain Is Universal but So Is Hope*, by Liset Castillo, 2007.

92: *Erimo Cape, 1976*, by Fukase Masahisa, 1976.

95: Toxic clouds and ash, Japan. Photograph by Hiroshi Hamaya.

96: Drawing from *Stereoscope*, by William Kentridge, 1998–99.

99: Goddess Durga slaying Mahishasura, Nepal, fourteenth century.

103: Family members after a flooded shaft trapped 153 miners, China, 2010.

104: Iceberg that purportedly sank the *Titanic*, 1912. Photograph by Hope Chapin.

107: *Gustav Klimt's The Kiss (Freedom Graffiti)*, by Tammam Azzam, 2013.

108: *Funeral Honors Rendered to Titian After His Death at Venice During the Plague of 1576*, by Alexandre Hesse, 1833.

111: Refugees, Democratic Republic of Congo, 2008. Photograph by Jim Goldberg.

113: "Monumental Chaos," by Mitchell Krog, 2011.

114: *The Temptation of Saint Anthony*, by Herri met de Bles, c. 1550.

117: *Illustrated Legends of the Kitano Tenjin Shrine*, Japan, late thirteenth century.

119: *Circulation Desk*, by Lori Nix, 2012.

120: "West Memphis, Arkansas. After the Flood," by Eugene Richards.

123: *Dust Storm, Fifth Avenue*, by John Sloan, 1906.

124: Camels before an oil fire, Kuwait, 1991. Photograph by Steve McCurry.

127: *Widow*, by Alexandre Antigna, 1849.

128: Train wreck at the Gare Montparnasse, Paris, 1895.

130: Meteorite. SEM micrograph by Edward Kinsman.

133: *Flight of Sultan Bahadur*, by Abu'l Fazl, sixteenth century.

134: *Pogroms*, c. 1915.

137: David Bowie in *Merry Christmas, Mr. Lawrence*, 1983.

139: *The Prairie Burial*, by William Ranney, 1848.

140: Struggling against a typhoon, Vietnam, 2000. Photograph by John Vink.

143: "An Abandoned Farm," by Arthur Rothstein, 1936.

144: A scene from *Deep Impact*, directed by Mimi Leder, 1998.

146: Men being attacked by bees, Attic amphora, c. 540 BC.

149: Flood victims, Goza, Pakistan, 2010. Photograph by Daniel Berehulak.

150: The *Lusitania* after being torpedoed, 1915.

153: *Gaza Border*, by Rina Castelnuovo, 2009.

155: Monju Bosatsu, Japan, mid-to-late fourteenth century.

159: Market Street after the San Francisco earthquake, 1906.

161: *The Thin Red Line*, by Robert Gibb, 1881.

162: *The Flood*, by Hans Baldung, 1516.

165: Comforting a wounded friend, Syria, 2012. Photograph by Edouard Elias.

166: Relief depicting battle, Thebes, c. 1400 BC.

168: *A Sudden Appearance Out of the Sea of a Race of Amphibious Monsters, Capable of Sweeping Men Out of Existence*, by Warwick Goble, 1900.

171: *Stalemate*, by Richard Mosse, 2011.

173: *The Rescue*, by Maurice Poirson, c. 1880.

176: *The Burning of the Houses of Lords and Commons, October 16, 1834*, by Joseph Mallord William Turner, c. 1835.

179: *The Horseman*, by Honoré Fragonard, c. 1770.

181: *Admirable Act of Valor: Stoker Saves Girl near Ancona by Lying Over Her Under an Oncoming Train*, by Achille Beltrame, 1909.

182: *What More Can One Do?*, by Francisco de Goya, c. 1815.

185: "A Man in Four Million," 1946.

186: Typhoon Haiyan approaching Vietnam, 2013.

193: *Amoco Cadiz* sinking, 1978. Photograph by Jean Gaumy.

194: *Battle on the Bridge*, by Arnold Böcklin, 1892.

197: *Barbarians Marching to the West*, by Max Ernst, 1937.

200: Dancers in *The Peaceful City*, by Ambrogio Lorenzetti, 1338–1340.

203: *Triumph of Death*, by Félix Nussbaum, 1944.

206: Evacuation of a dead gorilla, Democratic Republic of Congo, 2007. Photograph by Brent Stirton.

216: Production still for *Oedipus Rex*, directed by Pier Paolo Pasolini, 1967.

219: *Little Hope*, by Paul Klee, 1938.

IBC: World Trade Center, New York City, September 11, 2001. Photograph by Steve McCurry.

Among the Contributors

In her 2009 book, *A Paradise Built in Hell*, essayist **Rebecca Solnit** (1961–) probed five disasters in depth, focusing on communities that arise in the face of crisis. "Sometimes as the emergencies are resolved," she has said, "people seem to have a different sense of what is possible, for themselves personally, and for their society."

Born in Bulgaria, **Elias Canetti** (1905–1994) was a Sephardic Jew who grew up speaking Ladino. He lived with his parents in Manchester and Vienna before receiving his doctorate in chemistry at the University of Vienna in 1929. He wrote *Crowds and Power* in England, where he moved in 1938. In 1981 Canetti was awarded the Nobel Prize for literature.

Annie Dillard (1945–) was born in Pittsburgh but wrote her best-known work, 1974's *Pilgrim at Tinker Creek*, about her explorations of Virginia's Roanoke Valley. "It is a young writer's book in its excited eloquence and its metaphysical boldness," she wrote in 2007. "Fools rush in."

Thomas Mann called the German novelist **Ernst Jünger** (1895–1998) "an ice-cold playboy of barbarism." Jünger published his first novel, *Storm of Steel*, in 1920, and his last, *A Dangerous Encounter*, in 1985. He also gained worldwide recognition as an entomologist, collecting beetles while in the trenches during World War I.

As a writer, **Evan S. Connell** (1924–2013) was unwilling to take on academic assignments or speaking engagements. For many years, the author of *Mrs. Bridge* worked as a counselor for the California State Unemployment Office in San Francisco.

At the age of twenty-one **Ibn Battuta** (1304–c. 1368) left his home in Tangiers on a pilgrimage to Mecca. He decided to keep traveling, visiting Delhi and Beijing before returning to Morocco in 1353. Battuta's personality, notes novelist James Buchan, "is a war between contradictory impulses of mysticism and worldliness."

After spending eleven months in Auschwitz, **Primo Levi** (1919–1987) returned to his native Turin to work as a chemist in a paint factory. In 1975 Levi published a memoir, *The Periodic Table*. Twelve years later, he committed suicide in the apartment he had lived in—with "involuntary interruptions"—since his birth.

The Belarusian writer **Svetlana Alexievich** (1948–) has made her career by interviewing Soviet citizens who were victims of war and calamity. "When I was in Afghanistan during the Soviet war," she said upon receiving her Nobel Prize for literature in 2015, "I heard how quickly man sheds culture, and a monster emerges. The beast is revealed."

The French philosopher **Paul Virilio** (1932–) was drafted into the army and spent six months fighting in the Algerian war of independence, attaining the rank of sergeant. Upon completion of his military service, he studied phenomenology at the Sorbonne with Maurice Merleau-Ponty.

The Christian historian **Paulus Orosius** (c. 385–c. 420) went to Hippo in 414 to meet St. Augustine. Two years later Augustine asked Orosius to write a historical apology of Christianity, which became *Seven Books of History Against the Pagans*, one of the first world histories by a Christian.

The Greek poet **C.P. Cavafy** (1863–1933) maintained a small library in his home in Alexandria, consisting of some three hundred volumes. One friend referred to his collection of books as containing "unmentionable novels by unknown and forgotten writers." Notable exceptions were the works of Marcel Proust and Georges Simenon.

Since 1999 **Elizabeth Kolbert** (1961–) has been a staff writer for *The New Yorker*. For the past decade, she has focused on writing about the effects of global warming. "It may seem impossible to imagine that a technologically advanced society could choose, in essence, to destroy itself," Kolbert writes, "but that is what we are now in the process of doing."

In 1934 the writer **Gertrude Stein** (1874–1946) returned to America after living in Paris for thirty years. She arrived in Chicago on November 7, after her first ever airplane trip. Following a dinner party at the University of Chicago, two homicide detectives took Stein and her partner, Alice Toklas, for a ride around the city in their squad car.

On the night of August 27, 1260, a mob of followers from an opposing Buddhist sect gathered at the hermitage of the monk **Nichiren** (1222–1282) in an attempt to murder him. It is said that an old white monkey took Nichiren by the hand and led him into the forest to safety.

As a young boy **Lucian** (125–180) showed a talent for making wax figures. He was apprenticed to his uncle, a sculptor, but broke a piece of marble on his first day at work, and was beaten for it. Lucian soon thereafter left home to study rhetoric.

Ayi Kwei Armah (1939–) completed his studies at Ghana's Achimota School in 1958. When Vice President Richard Nixon visited Ghana in 1957, he mixed up his speeches, and offered Achimota a scholarship intended for students at another school. As a result of Nixon's blunder, Armah received a full scholarship to the Groton School in Massachusetts.

Thomas Bernhard (1931–1989) published his first novel, *Frost*, in 1963. Its unrelentingly pessimistic prose met with many detractors. "Don't people have any sense of humor or what?" Bernhard later wrote. "It always makes me laugh, even today. Whenever I am bored or there is some sort of tragic period, I open a book of mine. That will most likely get me to laugh."

Born Kurt Eric Suckert in Tuscany to a German father and Italian aristocratic mother, writer **Curzio Malaparte** (1898–1957) chose as his nom de plume a mischievous inversion of Bonaparte. Starting in 1939, he designed and built Casa Malaparte on the isle of Capri; his house figured prominently in Jean-Luc Godard's 1963 film *Contempt*, starring Brigitte Bardot.

Survival of the Fittest

Six mass extinctions

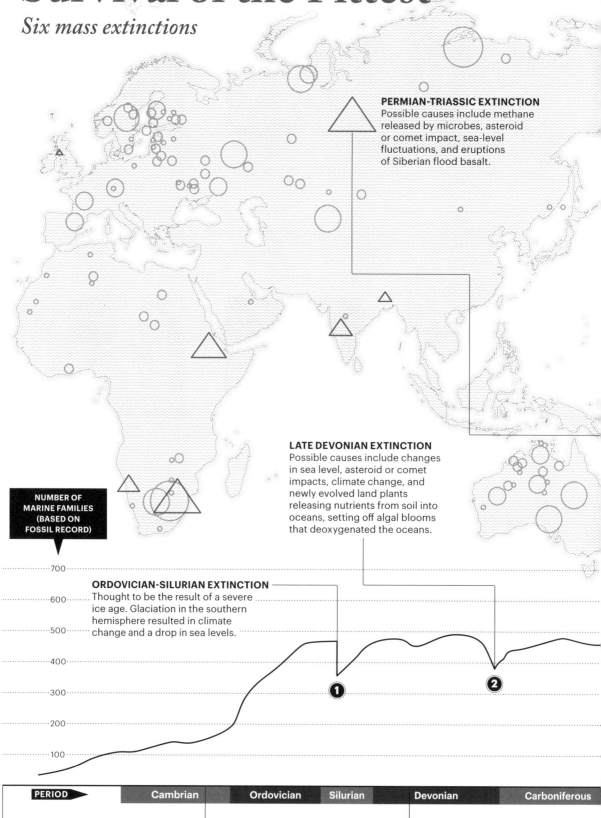

PERMIAN-TRIASSIC EXTINCTION
Possible causes include methane
released by microbes, asteroid
or comet impact, sea-level
fluctuations, and eruptions
of Siberian flood basalt.

LATE DEVONIAN EXTINCTION
Possible causes include changes
in sea level, asteroid or comet
impacts, climate change, and
newly evolved land plants
releasing nutrients from soil into
oceans, setting off algal blooms
that deoxygenated the oceans.

**NUMBER OF
MARINE FAMILIES
(BASED ON
FOSSIL RECORD)**

ORDOVICIAN-SILURIAN EXTINCTION
Thought to be the result of a severe
ice age. Glaciation in the southern
hemisphere resulted in climate
change and a drop in sea levels.

700
600
500
400
300
200
100

1
2

| PERIOD ▶ | Cambrian | Ordovician | Silurian | Devonian | Carboniferous |

600 MILLION YEARS AGO   500 M   400 M

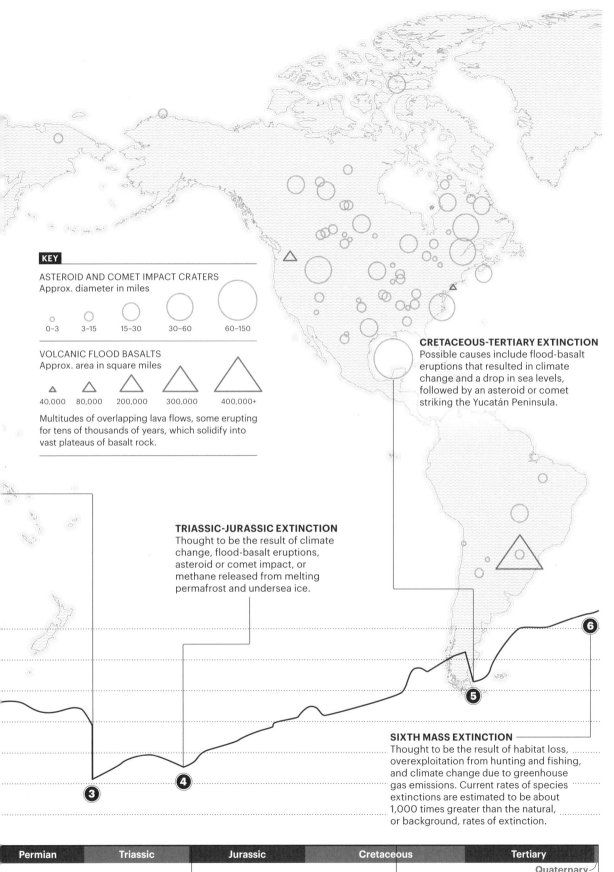

KEY

ASTEROID AND COMET IMPACT CRATERS
Approx. diameter in miles

0–3   3–15   15–30   30–60   60–150

VOLCANIC FLOOD BASALTS
Approx. area in square miles

40,000   80,000   200,000   300,000   400,000+

Multitudes of overlapping lava flows, some erupting
for tens of thousands of years, which solidify into
vast plateaus of basalt rock.

CRETACEOUS-TERTIARY EXTINCTION
Possible causes include flood-basalt
eruptions that resulted in climate
change and a drop in sea levels,
followed by an asteroid or comet
striking the Yucatán Peninsula.

TRIASSIC-JURASSIC EXTINCTION
Thought to be the result of climate
change, flood-basalt eruptions,
asteroid or comet impact, or
methane released from melting
permafrost and undersea ice.

SIXTH MASS EXTINCTION
Thought to be the result of habitat loss,
overexploitation from hunting and fishing,
and climate change due to greenhouse
gas emissions. Current rates of species
extinctions are estimated to be about
1,000 times greater than the natural,
or background, rates of extinction.

Permian	Triassic	Jurassic	Cretaceous	Tertiary

Quaternary

00 M   200 M   100 M   PRESENT DAY

Map by Haisam Hussein

SHOCK AND AWE

by Lewis H. Lapham

Catastrophe is our bedtime story.
—Don DeLillo

*'Tis not contrary to reason to prefer the
destruction of the whole world to the scratching
of my finger.*
—David Hume

Nor is it contrary to reason to prefer the sight of a raging inferno or restless typhoon to the view of a worm in one's apple or a fly in the soup. The spectacle of disaster—real and imagined, past, present, and imminent—is blockbuster box office, its magnitude measured by the number of dead and square miles of devastation, the cost of property, rates of insurance, long-term consequences, short-form shock and awe.

Ground zero in all instances is the eye of both beholder and storm, some disasters therefore more disastrous than others—my first lesson learned as an apprentice reporter for the *San Francisco Examiner* in the autumn of 1957, posted to the press room in Oakland to stand watch for blood in the streets. First thing of a morning I telephoned every police station and emergency room in Contra Costa and Alameda counties to ask if anything of interest had turned up overnight—multiple homicide, heavy-metal highway accident, five-alarm fire. The worth of the story was graded by color: banner headline on page one if the victims were white; if not, three paragraphs on page twenty-eight.

Times change, and with them the markets in human interest and grief. We live surrounded by terror alerts projected on myriad screens, late-breaking reports of the Four Horsemen of the Apocalypse in full stride at all points of the compass—corpses of unarmed black men on the streets of Chicago and Cleveland, jihadists

Center panel of *The Last Judgment* triptych, by Hieronymus Bosch, late fifteenth century.

massacring innocents in Palmyra and Paris, disease in Bahia, flood in Missouri, birds flying north to extinction, the economy headed south to oblivion, nuclear weapons falling into the hands of despots, carbon despoiling the atmosphere, ice abandoning the poles, drought in California, famine in South Sudan, seas rising offshore Miami and Mumbai, civil war in the Congo, concealed weapons walking around in plain sight in Texas, Syrian migrants at the gates of Vienna and Berlin, drug addicts littering the lawns of Bel Air, the end of the world coming soon to your neighborhood cineplex, this year *The Revenant* starring Leonardo DiCaprio, recovered from his going down on the *Titanic*, up for an Academy Award.

Fear of the future is a long-abiding shadow on the horizon of the American dream (present in the years prior to the Civil and Spanish American wars as in those leading to the year 2000), but since the 9/11 pouring out of God's wrath on the Manhattan temples of mammon it has moved steadily up the media leader boards into the red zones of near-hysteria. The directors of Hollywood disaster movies shoot scenes from the Book of Revelation (*Patmos*, page 52), dress their sets with dead children, cries of anguish, pillars of smoke, dote lovingly on blood-soaked deserts east and west of Suez.

The Hollywood field commanders poolside in Beverly Hills might not know the difference between Arab and Turk, or how much to tip the parking attendant to valet the tank, but dystopia they recognize as a travel destination no farther away than next week's atrocity in Charleston or San Bernardino. Their holiday entertainments come wrapped in ribbons of critical acclaim—"nervously plausible future," "glorious bummer that lifts you to the rafters, transporting you with the greatness of its filmmaking."

And with the greatness of what else? Together with headline and prize-winning photograph the images of disaster come wrapped in a sermon or sales pitch. To whom is the message addressed? With what beast in view? How and why a bedtime story?

The questions raised in this issue of *Lapham's Quarterly* follow from a speculation floated by Adam Smith in 1759 in his *Theory of Moral Sentiments* (*Glasgow*, page 136). The author of *The Wealth of Nations*, like David Hume a son of the Scottish Enlightenment, concerned himself not only with the divisions of labor but also with the distribution of man's humanity to man:

> Let us suppose that the great empire of China, with all its myriads of inhabitants, was suddenly swallowed up by an earthquake, and let us consider how a man of humanity in Europe, who had no sort of connection with that part of the world, would be affected upon receiving intelligence of this dreadful calamity.

Due consideration leads Smith to observe that a man of humanity in eighteenth-century Europe would "express very strongly his sorrow for the misfortune of that unhappy people," make many "melancholy reflections upon the precariousness of human life...and when all this fine philosophy was

Baghdad under attack by U.S.-led coalition forces, March 21, 2003.

over," go comfortably to sleep with the conclusion that the loss of millions of Chinese was a no "more real disturbance" than "if he was to lose his little finger tomorrow." Smith presumably had in mind the response among the intellectual gentry in Glasgow to the Lisbon earthquake of 1755, which swallowed up sixty thousand Portuguese but in Scotland didn't excite much of an effort to relieve the suffering of an unknown multitude. Smith takes comfort in the happier reflection that a man of humanity, no matter how or where placed, never would willingly sacrifice a hundred million of his unseen brethren to forestall or prevent a "paltry misfortune to himself…Human nature startles with horror at the thought, and the world, in its greatest depravity and corruption, never produced such a villain as could be capable of entertaining it."

Smith's generous view of his fellow man, consistent with the one embraced by Jean-Jacques Rousseau's social contract, persuades him that it is not the "feeble spark of benevolence" in the human heart that prompts men to aid and abet one another in the throes of disaster. It is the recognition of their being part of the collective and therefore immortal life of mankind that induces "a more powerful affection" than self-love, which is always small-minded, grasping, and sordid. The stronger feeling draws men to "the love of what is honorable and noble, of the grandeur and dignity and superiority of our own characters."

This issue of *Lapham's Quarterly* bears witness to the truth of Smith's happier reflection—the art of Ambrogio Lorenzetti and Achille Beltrame, the report of King Charles II joining the common effort to smother the great London fire of 1666, nurse Helen Repa's unbidden response to the tragedy engulfing

844 people aboard the excursion boat *Eastland* overturned at its dock on the Chicago River in 1915 (page 123), the testimony of the nineteenth-century American philosopher and Harvard professor William James (*Palo Alto, CA*, page 141), and the American essayist Rebecca Solnit (*Halifax*, page 182).

Solnit's observations are drawn from her book *A Paradise Built in Hell*, published in 2009 as a summation of her encounters with people caught in the hurricane coming ashore on the Gulf Coast in 2005, clearing the wreckage of the 9/11 attack on New York, stranded in the rubble of the earthquake that devastated Mexico City in 1985. At ground zero in all instances Solnit finds "the prevalent human nature in disaster is resilient, resourceful, generous, empathic, and brave." When she asks people about the disasters they have lived through she is struck by their "retrospective basking" in the joy arising from their immersion in a suddenly formed community of unselfish motive and purpose, free of their loneliness and fear because granted in the face of calamity "a glimpse of who else we ourselves may be and what else our society could become."

William James was teaching at Stanford when earthquake and fire overwhelmed San Francisco in 1906; like Solnit he finds among those present (on day one in Palo Alto, a few days later in the ruined city) "cheerfulness," "a tendency more toward nervous excitement than toward grief," and "not a single whine or plaintive word." From sympathetic friends back east James soon received letters "ringing with anxiety and pathos"; they convinced him of "what I have always believed, that the pathetic way of feeling great disasters belongs rather to the point of view of people at a distance than to the immediate victims." Sentiment is a privilege reserved for spectators in galaxies far, far away, tormented by their opinions of things, not by the things themselves.

If a great catastrophe is not announced in the morning, we feel a certain void: "There is nothing in the papers today," we sigh.
—Paul Valéry, c. 1930

The distance between James in California and his friends at Harvard was the distance between the earthquake in Lisbon and the fine-feathered gentry in Glasgow. Smith recoiled from the prospect of a distance even greater if human suffering could be reduced to bloodless abstraction, but he couldn't conceive of a world producing such villainy.

The Industrial Revolution could. Machines don't startle with horror; neither does money. Nor does the sensibility shaped to regard their joint enterprise (the working of Smith's "invisible hand") as the new and improved presence of God. Prior to the invention of the steam engine and spinning jenny the villain in man's heart didn't lack for depravity—Caesar's legions in Gaul exterminated over a million barbarians; Tamerlane's Mongols massacred entire populations of cities throughout Persia and Mesopotamia. But the twentieth century was born blessed with the creatively annihilating energies of free-market capitalism, capable of yielding not only the wealth of nations but also the means of their utter destruction—Henry Ford's motorcars and Heinrich Himmler's crematoria, the building of Hoover Dam and the dropping of atomic bombs. The century opened with warfare upgraded from sport to industry, the manufacture of death setting new records by employing an efficient division of labor—the killing done with machines, the dying by human beings.

Further downstream from the nineteenth-century coal mines and cavalry officers—along with the climate-changing rise of greenhouse gases into the once-upon-a-time clear blue sky—the consumer consciousness of disaster undergoes further distancing between the eye of beholder and storm as a result of consequences also unforeseen by Smith but noted by Marshall McLuhan: "We become what we behold," that we shape our tools and thereafter our tools shape us; by the Swiss novelist Max Frisch, technology "is the knack of so arranging the world that we don't have to experience it"; and by the French philosopher Simone Weil, "It is the thing that thinks and the man who is reduced to the state of a thing."

McLuhan's *Understanding Media* accounts for the extension of the nineteenth-century Industrial Revolution into the twentieth-century communications revolution. The epistemological shift from words in print to icons on screen establishes a new aesthetic and political order in which the image is substance, the medium the message; war is an advertising campaign, a bomb a figure of speech.

Robert S. McNamara, U.S. secretary of defense, explicitly defined the bombing raids helping to eventually dispose of three million civilians in Cambodia and Vietnam as a means of communication—dispatches intended to win the hearts and minds of the Vietcong to an appreciation of America's goodness and greatness. Among staff officers at the Pentagon, the four-color spreads of explosion overhead Phnom Penh and Hanoi came to be known as "bomb-o-grams."

It is an easy thing for one whose foot is on the outside of calamity to give advice and to rebuke the sufferer.
—*Aeschylus, c. 460 BC*

The NATO alliance adopted a similar approach to the bombardment of Belgrade in March 1999. The targets were chosen for rhetorical rather than tactical reasons, as were the cities in Germany (among them Hamburg and Dresden) terror-bombed by British and American air forces during World War II under instruction from Winston Churchill to make no distinction between civilian and military targets because the mission was to remind the German people of their being on the wrong side of history.

Like presidents Ronald Reagan and George H.W. Bush, President Clinton understood foreign policy as a Hollywood action picture. During the filming of *Dark Moon over Belgrade* (sequel to Reagan's *Sands of Grenada* and Bush's *Storm in the Desert*), his military spokesmen appeared at podiums every night in Brussels or Washington to say the NATO aircraft had enjoyed another glorious day of filmmaking in Yugoslavia. The uniformed publicists displayed maps and video highlight reels, counted sorties, apologized for the odd cruise missile wandering off into Bulgaria or finding a hospital instead of a bridge, reaffirmed their faith in democracy and the rule of law. Later in the program the camera angle shifted to the mountains of Macedonia, where network news correspondents culled the herd of refugees for those with prime-time stories to tell. Here was Saimir, whose three sons had been beheaded, and there was

The Good Samaritan (detail), by George Frederick Watts, 1850.

Besjana, who had been raped by fourteen Serbian soldiers in Peć, and over here, just behind the tractor, we have little Besim, age nine, who watched his father and mother burn to death in a barn.

The Bush administration's 2003 invasion of Iraq (code name, "Operation Iraqi Freedom"; tactic, "shock and awe"), conceived by Secretary of Defense Donald Rumsfeld and Vice President Dick Cheney as the playing of a video game, deployed twenty-four-hour montages akin to a Super Bowl halftime show. The fireworks displays were deftly intercut and cross-promoted, the correspondent aboard an aircraft carrier handing the microphone across a split screen to the correspondent in a Bradley Fighting Vehicle, two- and three-star generals parading to and fro on Tom Brokaw's reviewing stand, computer animations of the hostile terrain presented in the manner of golf-course graphics illustrating the perils of the PGA tour.

Journalists on duty at the Pentagon pronounced the assault worthy of Napoleon, the tanks in the desert reminding them of George Patton and Erwin Rommel, the battle of Basra analogous to the defense of Stalingrad. The rave reviews never squared with the facts on the ground. Proofs of a fierce Iraqi resistance were nowhere to be seen.

Like the Super Bowl halftime shows, the capture of Baghdad inspired heroic feats of merchandising, not only on the part of the Pentagon and the White House but also for home-front consumer products. The triumphant framing of the camera shots in old, romantic Baghdad sponsored a flurry of applications for the trademark "Shock and Awe" from makers of women's underwear and men's cologne, the manufacturers of bubble-making wands and dollhouse furniture, ski boots, teddy bears, mouse pads, cigars, yo-yos, and inflatable bathtub toys.

Whether presented as entertainment or news, the spectacle of disaster seen from a safe distance demands nothing from the eye of the beholder other than the duty of ritual observance. Words in print require the active presence of a reader's imagination. The camera does not: like the moon acting upon the movement of the tides, it calls forth collective surges of emotion that rise and fall with as little apparent meaning as the surf breaking on the beach at Santa Monica. Consciousness becomes pattern recognition rather than the forming of a thought, the networking of brands—many hundreds of them in the course of an afternoon's shopping and an evening's programming—all we know or need to know.

The constant viewer learns to read the signs as advertisements for reality, weightless and without consequence, returning once again to the 24/7 news cycle as surely as the swallows to Capistrano—what was seen last week certain to be seen this week, then again next week, next month, and next year—the familiar face masks reworked and rearranged in other settings for other football or bombing seasons; other Coca-Cola commercials and presidential elections. Rerun the same show often enough and in the benumbed mind of the constant viewer it serves as sedative and bedtime story.

The evening news hour begins with glimpses of the big, bad wolf just in from London or Boston, then the camera cuts away to the reassuring smiles of the Geico lizard, State Farm insurance, Southwest Airlines, L'Oréal, and Mercedes-Benz. The message is overt and covert. Obey the law, follow instructions, watch your mouth, speak nicely to the police officer, and you go to the Virgin Islands on your American Express card. Disobey the law, neglect your prescription drugs, speak rudely to the police, and you go to Kings County Hospital in a body bag.

Behold the world for what it is, a raging of beasts and a writhing of serpents, and know that the war on terror will be with us until the end of our days. Get used to it; harden thy resolve; America is everywhere besieged by monsters that must be destroyed—by any and all means necessary, no matter how costly or barbaric. And yes, Virginia, there is an answer to Adam Smith's disturbing question—to prevent a paltry misfortune to oneself not only is it possible, it's also prudent to sacrifice as many of our fellow human beings as circumstances require. The UN Security Council in 1990 imposed harsh economic sanctions on Iraq in order to send a stern message to Saddam Hussein. When Madeleine Albright, then U.S. ambassador to the United Nations, was asked in an interview on *60 Minutes* whether she had considered the resulting death of over 500,000

Iraqi children (of malnutrition and disease for lack of medicine and baby food), she said, "We think the price is worth it."

Together with an estimated $2 trillion, President George W. Bush sacrificed the lives of nearly 5,000 American soldiers and 165,000 Iraqi civilians to prevent America from being harmed by Saddam Hussein's nonexistent weapons of mass destruction. The cost–benefit analysis emerged from the administration's doctrine of forward deterrence and preemptive strike, a policy predicated on the notion that if any nation anywhere in the world presumed even to begin to think of challenging America's supremacy (moral, military, cultural, and socioeconomic) America reserved the right to strangle the impudence at birth—to bomb the peasants or the palace, block the flows of oil or bank credit. Michael Ledeen, foreign-policy adviser to the Bush White House and Freedom Scholar at the Foundation for Defense of Democracies, put the policy in its clearest perspective: "Every ten years or so, the United States needs to pick up some crappy little country and throw it against the wall, just to show the world we mean business."

Nuclear weapons and TV have simply intensified the consequences of our tendencies, upped the stakes.
—*David Foster Wallace, 1993*

Fortunately for the faint-hearted among us we can throw crappy little countries over cliffs or up against walls because our technologies protect us in cocoons of virtual reality. They allow us to be tormented, if tormented we must be, by sentiments. Good for a moment of silence and a pause that refreshes the conscience, sentiments are one mouse click away from our little finger tapping the Facebook icons. We can sit ten rows back at the neighborhood movie palace within the cinematic equivalent of a federal witness-protection program. Safe behind popcorn boxes, we can cast a moist eye at the sight of a dismembered Palestinian teenager or a butchered African elephant, ward off the fear of death by picturing it as a Quentin Tarantino cartoon.

A product of Smith's invisible hand (joint venture of money and machine), the *danse macabre* surrounding us on-screen reduces human beings to things—broken toys, smashed dollhouse furniture, scattered debris knowing not how or why it was destroyed. Too far removed or arriving too late on the scene, the camera doesn't grasp the human response in the eye of the storm, what Solnit discovered to be the joyful "measure of otherwise neglected desires, desires for public life and civil society, for inclusion, purpose, and power."

The discovery accorded with Solnit's own experience during the Loma Prieta earthquake of 1989, surprised to find herself in "an intensely absorbing present," as was almost everybody else she ran across in the San Francisco Bay Area. People without orders or centralized organization stepped up to meet the needs of the moment, directing traffic at blacked-out intersections, cooking meals in the street, gladly and gratefully inducted—as was Helen Repa on the Chicago River and the first responders to Hurricane Katrina, many of them traveling thousands of miles to reach their unknown but fellow human beings—into what the French novelist Albert Camus called "the only indisputable human solidarity—our solidarity against death."

The response is normal everyday practice among people who come together in the face of calamity. It is common among soldiers in combat, doctors and patients in operating rooms, strangers becoming neighbors at the scene of the accident, people anywhere and everywhere engaged at ground zero in what Sigmund Freud identified as the struggle between Eros, the instinct of life, and Thanatos, the instinct of death. Civilization Freud defines (*Vienna*, page 44) as a process in the service of Eros, "whose purpose is to combine single human individuals, and after that families, then races, peoples and nations, into one great unity, the unity of mankind." And it is "this battle of the giants"—for the life of the human species—"that our nursemaids try to appease with their lullaby about heaven."

The nursemaids in charge of our fairy-tale media regard mankind as too sinful and weak to preserve the living substance of anything without their advice and consent. The cameras fielded by CNN and Disney cast ordinary people on the set of disaster as frightened rabble or dangerous

Life is to be lived, not controlled; and humanity is won by continuing to play in face of certain defeat.
—*Ralph Ellison, 1952*

mob, desperate mothers cowering in panic, the anarchist poor looting a Walmart. The story is false, but the images establish the markets in fear. They convey to the constant viewer the sense of his or her helplessness while at the same time promoting the need for more heavily armed law enforcement, more security apparatus, stronger defense budgets, more bubble-wand magic technology.

The spectacle of disaster as Old Testament trauma sells newspapers, but the drug of fear—administered in increasingly heavy dosages over prolonged periods of time—produces a harmful side effect among natives both foreign and domestic. Humans too long imprisoned by society in its dehumanized extensions, knowing themselves downgraded to things, turn for relief to the dream of apocalypse that solves all the problems, takes out the whole world, and with it all the flies in the soup. To prophets secure in the knowledge that only the wicked shall perish, Armageddon is a consummation devoutly to be wished. Let the Lord make manifest his disgust with the sins of mankind and so loose upon earth the redeeming flood and purifying fire, and the host of the damned will drown in sewers of their foul and pestilent blood.

Such is the bright hope and fond expectation of the Islamic terrorist acronym ISIS (*Syria*, page 119) that locates itself in "the prophetic end time" and wages what it bills as the "final battle" between forces of darkness (the American capitalist world order) and armies of the light (the start-up Muslim caliphate) with postings on the Internet of images up to the standards of Jerry Bruckheimer and Ridley Scott.

The champions of Western civilization make a bad mistake by deploring the mind and method of jihad as medieval and barbaric. The techniques and the objectives are modern. From whom do we suppose that jihadists learn to appreciate the value of high explosive as vivid speech if not from the example of the U.S. Air Force overhead Vietnam, Serbia, and Iraq? The organizers of the 9/11 attacks on Manhattan clearly not only understood the ethos of globalized finance capitalism but also the idiom of the American news and entertainment media. Their production values were akin to those of *Independence Day*; the spectacle of the

World Trade Center collapsing in ruins was rated by the New York film and social critics as "awe inspiring," "never to be forgotten," "shatteringly emotional."

The sense of living in the prophetic end time has been running around in the American consciousness for the past twenty-five years, on the disheartened political left as on the ferocious political right. The final battle of Armageddon furnished the climax for the Left Behind series of sixteen neo-Christian fables that have sold more than 65 million copies to date, presumably to Rush Limbaugh's dittoheads and future members of the Tea Party. The coauthors of the books, Tim LaHaye and Jerry B. Jenkins, offer their hatred of man as testimony to their love of God, and devote many fondly worded pages to the wholesale slaughter of intellectuals in New York, politicians in Washington, and homosexuals in Los Angeles. Their language is of a piece with the film footage in Mel Gibson's *Passion of the Christ* or the videos just in of an ISIS beheading.

At the higher levels of academic and political discourse the 1990s brought forth many best-selling books and articles announcing the destruction of worlds. Two of the early terror alerts appeared within a few weeks of each other in the autumn of 1989—"The End of History?" by Francis Fukuyama and "The End of Nature" by Bill McKibben. Both authors assign the sad endings of their tales to the worthlessness of human beings. Fukuyama, a State Department policy intellectual, foresaw a future owned and operated by machines, human courage, imagination, and idealism replaced by economic calculation and the endless solving of technical problems. "In the post-historical period," he wrote, "there will be neither art nor philosophy, just the perpetual caretaking of the museum of human history."

McKibben, a principled environmentalist, listed what were then less familiar effects of forthcoming climate change—endless drought, boiling oceans, dying forests, extinct species—and didn't take the trouble to conceal his disgust for humans beings. Man is vile, a hideous many-headed beast ceaselessly replicating itself, spewing pollution into the innocent atmosphere and the blameless sea. From time to time the word *human* occurs in one of McKibben's sentences, and his association is invariably with something foul—a stinking automobile, an ugly condominium, a noisy chainsaw.

The dream of apocalypse is being carried into this year's presidential election campaign by two leading candidates for the Republican nomination, both of them so angry at the prospect of a future not made in their own image that they have resolved to destroy it. To "Make America Great Again," Donald Trump proposes to annihilate every last one of its competitors and enemies, to savage ISIS, quarantine Mexicans, bankrupt the Chinese. Ted Cruz promises to "strap on the full armor of God" and carpet-bomb the Syrian desert to find out whether "sand can glow in the dark." They talk the talk of holy jihad, but when I try to see them walking the walk, I remember a 1970 newspaper story about a nineteen-year-old moviegoer and heir to great wealth intent upon cleansing the world of its impurities. From an expensive New York tailor he had acquired the look of the old American West—frock coat, wide-brimmed hat, string tie—and from Abercrombie & Fitch a pair of pearl-handled six-guns. Deeply impressed by *Butch Cassidy and the Sundance Kid* he showed up on a Saturday night in a bar on Long Island, not far from F. Scott Fitzgerald's setting for *The Great Gatsby*, demanding a duel with the local drug dealer. The bartender, not being set up for that sort of thing, persuaded the young gentleman to wait in the parking lot. Because the scene never showed up on the evening news, I'm free to imagine it, and so in my mind's eye I still see it—a Siegfried among pickup trucks in the neon half-light between a supermarket and a bowling alley, his hands held above his guns in the chivalrous fashion traditional on the streets of Deadwood and Dodge. Sometimes I wonder what he was thinking, what beast he had in view. He never saw the local police. They weren't in the mood to take chances, and they killed him with rifles at long-range.

The story would be funnier if it wasn't another long-term consequence of the Industrial Revolution that Adam Smith didn't foresee. The difference between ground zero in the eye of beholder and storm becomes not only a matter of distance but also of fantasy. Let the machines do the work and the workmen lose sight of their own consciousness. Like Rumsfeld and Cheney and Bush before them, Trump and Cruz neither know nor care to know the difference between reality and virtual reality. What they know is what they see on TV and in the movies. Their enemies are reflections of their own fear. Like the friends of William James on the Harvard faculty, they have sentiments; their tweets, whining and plaintive, ring with "anxiety and pathos." Like the prophet Isaiah, they envision calamity from a galaxy far, far away—Trump from a golf club terrace, Cruz from a boardroom at Goldman Sachs—and they picture the end of the world as bright Hollywood explosions under cover of which the faithful and saved (themselves in company with Isaiah and Sylvester Stallone) shall find their way home to Palm Beach and Houston. The longing for Armageddon is confession of weakness and counsel of despair, not an attitude one hopes to find on the other end of a phone in command of an atomic bomb.

"A Harvest of Death, Gettysburg, Pennsylvania," July 1863. Photograph by Timothy H. O'Sullivan.

PREMONITION

2004: Greenland

ELIZABETH KOLBERT SEES THE END OF A WORLD

Swiss Camp is a research station that was set up in 1990 on a platform drilled into the Greenland ice sheet. Ice flows like water, only more slowly, and, as a result, the camp is always in motion: in fifteen years it has migrated by more than a mile, generally in a westerly direction. Every summer the whole place gets flooded, and every winter its contents solidify. The cumulative effect of all this is that almost nothing at Swiss Camp functions anymore the way it was supposed to. To get into it, you have to clamber up a snowdrift and descend through a trapdoor in the roof, as if entering a ship's hold or a space module. The living quarters are no longer habitable, so now everyone at the camp sleeps outside, in tents. (The one assigned to me was, I was told, the same sort used by Robert Scott [page 167] on his ill-fated expedition to the South Pole.) By the time I arrived at the camp, in late May, someone had jackhammered out the center of the workspace, which was equipped with some battered conference

tables. Under the tables, where, under normal circumstances, you would stick your legs, there were still three-foot-high blocks of ice. Inside the blocks, I could dimly make out a tangle of wires, a bulging plastic bag, and an old dustpan.

Konrad Steffen, a professor of geography at the University of Colorado, is the director of Swiss Camp. A native of Zurich, Steffen speaks English in the lilting cadences of *Schweizendeutsch*. He is tall and lanky, with pale blue eyes, a graying beard, and the unflappable manner of a cowboy in a western. When Steffen planned Swiss Camp—he built much of the place himself—it was not with global warming in mind. Rather, he was interested in meteorological conditions on what is known as the ice sheet's "equilibrium line." Along this line, winter snow and summer melt are supposed to be precisely in balance. But in recent years "equilibrium" has become an increasingly elusive quality. During the summer of 2002, for example, melt occurred in areas where liquid water had not been seen for hundreds, perhaps thousands, of years. The following winter there was an unusually low snowfall, and in the summer of 2003 the melt was so great that around Swiss Camp five feet of ice was lost.

When I arrived at the camp, the 2004 melt season was already underway. This, to Steffen, was a matter of both intense scientific interest and serious practical concern. A few days earlier one of his graduate students and a postdoc had driven out on snowmobiles to service some weather stations closer to the coast. The snow there was warming so fast that they had had to work until five in the morning, and then take a long detour back to avoid getting caught in the quickly forming rivers. Steffen

Human history becomes more and more a race between education and catastrophe.
—*H.G. Wells, 1920*

wanted to complete everything that needed to be done ahead of schedule, in case everyone had to pack up and leave early. My first day at Swiss Camp he spent fixing an antenna that had fallen over in the previous year's melt. It was bristling with equipment, like a high-tech Christmas tree. Even on a relatively mild day on the ice sheet, which this was, it never gets more than a few degrees above freezing, and I was walking around in a huge parka, two pairs of pants plus long underwear, and two pairs of gloves. Steffen, meanwhile, was tinkering with the antenna with his bare hands. He had spent the last fourteen summers at Swiss Camp, and I asked him what he had learned during that time. He answered with another question.

"Are we disintegrating part of the Greenland ice sheet over the longer term?" he asked.

Greenland, the world's largest island, is nearly four times the size of France—840,000 square miles—and, except for its southern tip, lies entirely above the Arctic Circle. The first Europeans to make a stab at settling it were the Norse, under the leadership of Erik the Red, who, perhaps deliberately, gave the island its misleading name. In the year 985 he arrived with twenty-five ships and nearly seven hundred followers. (Erik had left Norway when his father was exiled for killing a man, and then was himself exiled from Iceland for killing several more.) The Norse established two settlements: the Eastern Settlement, which was actually in the south, and the Western Settlement, which was to the north. For roughly four hundred years, they managed to scrape by, hunting, raising livestock, and making occasional logging expeditions to the coast of Canada. But then something went wrong. The last written record of them is an Icelandic affidavit regarding the marriage of Thorstein Ólafsson and Sigridur Björnsdóttir, which took place in the Eastern Settlement on the "Second Sunday after the Mass of the Cross" in the autumn of 1408.

More than 80 percent of Greenland is covered by ice. Locked into this enormous glacier is 8 percent of the world's freshwater supply. Except for researchers like those at Swiss Camp, no one lives on the ice, or even ventures out onto it very often. (The edges are riddled with crevasses large enough to swallow a dogsled or, should the occasion arise, a five-ton truck.)

Like all glaciers, the Greenland ice sheet is made up entirely of accumulated snow. The most recent layers are thick and airy, while the older layers are thin and dense, which means that to drill through the ice is to descend backward in time, at first gradually, and then much more rapidly. A hundred and thirty-eight feet down, there is snow that fell during the time of the American Civil War; 2,500 feet down, snow from the time of the Peloponnesian Wars; and 5,350 feet down, snow from the days when the cave painters of Lascaux were slaughtering bison. At the very bottom, 10,000 feet down, there is snow that fell on central Greenland before the start of the last ice age, more than 100,000 years ago.

As the snow is compressed, its crystal structure changes to ice. (Two thousand feet down, there is so much pressure on the ice that a sample drawn to the surface will, if mishandled, fracture and in some cases even explode.) But in most other respects the snow

Fireman Leonard E. Olson carrying a child pulled from the overturned SS *Eastland*, Chicago, 1915. Olson later received the Lambert Tree Award for valor. Detail of a photograph by Jun Fujita.

remains unchanged, a relic of the climate that first formed it. In the Greenland ice there is nuclear fallout from early atomic tests, volcanic ash from Krakatoa, lead pollution from ancient Roman smelters, and dust blown in from Mongolia on ice age winds. Every layer also contains tiny bubbles of trapped air, each of them a sample of a past atmosphere.

As a continuous temperature record, the Greenland ice cores stop providing reliable information right around the start of the last glaciation. Climate records pieced together from other sources indicate that the previous interglacial, which is known as the Eemian, was somewhat warmer than the present one, the Holocene. They also show that sea levels during that time were at least fifteen feet higher than they are today. One theory attributes this to a collapse of the West Antarctic ice sheet. A second holds that meltwater from Greenland was responsible. All told, the Greenland ice sheet holds enough water to raise sea levels worldwide by twenty-three feet. Scientists at NASA have calculated that throughout the 1990s the ice sheet, despite some thickening at the center, was shrinking by twelve cubic miles per year.

James Hansen, the NASA official who directed one of the initial 1970s studies on the effects of carbon dioxide, has argued that if greenhouse-gas emissions are not controlled, the total disintegration of the Greenland ice sheet could be set in motion in a matter of decades. Although the process could take centuries to fully play out, once begun it would become self-reinforcing, and hence virtually impossible to stop. In an article published in the journal *Climatic Change* in February 2005, Hansen, who is now the head of the Goddard Institute for Space Studies, wrote that he hoped he was wrong about the ice sheet, but added, "I doubt it."

As it happened, I was at Swiss Camp just as the global-warming disaster movie *The Day After Tomorrow* was opening in theaters. One night Steffen's wife called on the camp's satellite phone to say that she had just taken the couple's two teenage children to see it. Everyone had enjoyed the film, she reported, especially because of the family connection.

The fantastic conceit of *The Day After Tomorrow* is that global warming produces global freezing. At the start of the film, a chunk of Antarctic ice the size of Rhode Island suddenly melts. (Something very similar to this actually happened in March 2002, when the Larsen B ice shelf collapsed.) Most of what follows—an instant ice age, cyclonic winds that descend from the upper atmosphere—is impossible as science but not as metaphor.

For the whole time I was at Swiss Camp, it was "polar day," and so the sun never set. Dinner was generally served at ten or eleven P.M., and afterward everyone sat around a makeshift

132: Luoyang

DRAGON BALLS

In the first year of the Yangjia reign period Zhang Heng invented an "earthquake weathercock."

It consisted of a vessel of fine cast bronze, resembling a wine jar, and having a diameter of eight *chi* [six feet].

It had a domed cover, and the outer surface was ornamented with antique seal characters and designs of mountains, tortoises, birds, and animals.

Inside there was a central column capable of lateral displacement along tracks in eight directions, and so arranged that it would operate a closing and opening mechanism.

Outside the vessel there were eight dragon heads, each one holding a bronze ball in its mouth, while around the base there sat eight corresponding toads with their mouths open, ready to receive any ball that the dragons might drop.

The toothed machinery and ingenious constructions were all hidden inside the vessel, and the cover fitted down closely all around without any crevice.

When an earthquake occurred the dragon mechanism of the vessel was caused to vibrate so that a ball was vomited out of a dragon mouth and caught by the toad underneath. At the same instant a sharp sound was made that called the attention of observers.

Now although the mechanism of one dragon was released, the seven other heads did not move, and by following the azimuthal direction of the dragon that had been set in motion one knew the direction from which the earthquake shock had come. When this was verified by the facts there was found an almost miraculous agreement between the observations made with the apparatus and the news of what had actually happened.

Nothing like this had ever been heard of before since the earliest records of the *Shujing*.

On one occasion one of the dragons let fall a ball from its mouth though no perceptible shock could be felt. All the scholars at the capital were astonished at this strange effect occurring without any evidence of an earthquake to cause it. But several days later a messenger arrived bringing news of an earthquake in Longxi. Upon this everyone admitted the mysterious power of the instrument. Thenceforth it became the duty of the officials of the Bureau of Astronomy and Calendar to record the directions from which the earthquakes came.

Fan Ye, *from the* Book of the Later Han. *Three hundred years after Zhang Heng's invention of the seismograph, historian Fan Ye described it in this account using only 196 Chinese characters. The works of Zhang, who was born in 78, also included lyric poetry, a water clock, a star catalogue, and an extensive calculation of the value of pi. Only scant descriptions of his "Instrument for Earthquake" were preserved, and many scholars, including John Milne, the British geologist who translated Fan Ye's account into English in 1883, failed to recreate it. Finally, in 2005, Chinese scientists completed a working replica.*

Foreign tourists on the exposed seabed reacting as the first of six tsunamis approaches Railay Beach, Thailand, 2004.

table in the kitchen, talking and drinking coffee. (Because it weighs a lot and is not—strictly speaking—necessary, alcohol was in short supply.) One night I asked Steffen what he thought conditions at Swiss Camp would be like in the same season a decade hence. "In ten years the signal should be much more distinct, because we will have added another ten years of greenhouse warming," he said.

Jay Zwally, a NASA scientist working in the area, interjected, "I predict that ten years from now we won't be coming this time of year. We won't be able to come this late. To put it nicely, we are heading into deep doo-doo."

Either by disposition or by training, Steffen was reluctant to make specific predictions, whether about Greenland or, more generally, about the Arctic. Often he prefaced his remarks by noting that there could be a change in atmospheric-circulation patterns that would dampen the rate of temperature increase or even—temporarily, at least—reverse it entirely. But he was emphatic that "climate change is a real thing."

"It's not something dramatic now—that's why people don't really react," he told me. "But if you can convey the message that it will be dramatic for our children and our children's children—the risk is too big not to care." The time, he added, "is already five past midnight."

On the last night that I spent at Swiss Camp, Steffen took the data he had downloaded off his weather station and ran them through various programs on his laptop to produce the mean temperature at the camp for the previous year. It was, it turned out, the highest of any year since the camp was built. When Steffen announced this to the group around the kitchen table, no one seemed the slightest bit surprised.

That night dinner was unusually late. On the return trip of another pole-drilling expedition, one of the snowmobiles had caught on fire and had to be towed back to camp. When I finally went out to my tent to go to bed, I found that the snow underneath it had started to melt, and there was a large puddle in the middle of the floor. I went back to the kitchen to get some paper towels and tried to mop it up. But the puddle was too big, and eventually I gave up.

From Field Notes from a Catastrophe. *A* New Yorker *staff writer since 1999, Kolbert wrote a three-part series for the magazine called "The Climate of Man," which later became* Field Notes. *She won a Pulitzer Prize for her 2014 book,* The Sixth Extinction, *about the man-made mass extinction currently underway. "I don't subscribe to the We'll Be Fine school of thought," Kolbert said in a 2015 interview about an article she wrote on the threat of rising sea levels to Miami and Miami Beach. "Surviving and being fine are very different things."*

Chronicles of Disasters Foretold

Prognostication is complicated work

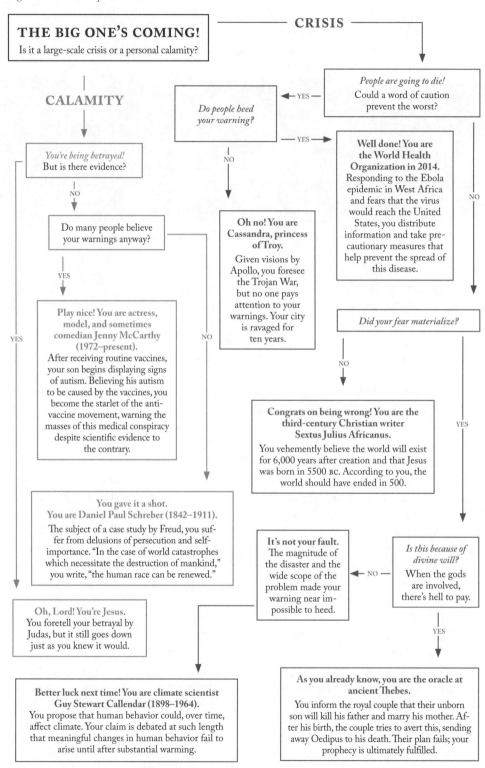

THE BIG ONE'S COMING!
Is it a large-scale crisis or a personal calamity?

CRISIS

CALAMITY

Do people heed your warning?

People are going to die!
Could a word of caution prevent the worst?

— YES →

— YES →

NO

You're being betrayed!
But is there evidence?

NO

Do many people believe your warnings anyway?

YES

YES

NO

Oh no! You are Cassandra, princess of Troy.

Given visions by Apollo, you foresee the Trojan War, but no one pays attention to your warnings. Your city is ravaged for ten years.

Well done! You are the World Health Organization in 2014.
Responding to the Ebola epidemic in West Africa and fears that the virus would reach the United States, you distribute information and take precautionary measures that help prevent the spread of this disease.

NO

Did your fear materialize?

NO

Play nice! You are actress, model, and sometimes comedian Jenny McCarthy (1972–present).
After receiving routine vaccines, your son begins displaying signs of autism. Believing his autism to be caused by the vaccines, you become the starlet of the anti-vaccine movement, warning the masses of this medical conspiracy despite scientific evidence to the contrary.

Congrats on being wrong! You are the third-century Christian writer Sextus Julius Africanus.
You vehemently believe the world will exist for 6,000 years after creation and that Jesus was born in 5500 BC. According to you, the world should have ended in 500.

YES

You gave it a shot.
You are Daniel Paul Schreber (1842–1911).
The subject of a case study by Freud, you suffer from delusions of persecution and self-importance. "In the case of world catastrophes which necessitate the destruction of mankind," you write, "the human race can be renewed."

It's not your fault.
The magnitude of the disaster and the wide scope of the problem made your warning near impossible to heed.

— NO —

Is this because of divine will?
When the gods are involved, there's hell to pay.

Oh, Lord! You're Jesus.
You foretell your betrayal by Judas, but it still goes down just as you knew it would.

YES

Better luck next time! You are climate scientist Guy Stewart Callendar (1898–1964).
You propose that human behavior could, over time, affect climate. Your claim is debated at such length that meaningful changes in human behavior fail to arise until after substantial warming.

As you already know, you are the oracle at ancient Thebes.
You inform the royal couple that their unborn son will kill his father and marry his mother. After his birth, the couple tries to avert this, sending away Oedipus to his death. Their plan fails; your prophecy is ultimately fulfilled.

C. 425 BC: Attica

BRING 'EM ON

Timon of Athens: O Zeus, god of friends, strangers, comrades, the hearth, lightning, and oaths; gatherer of the clouds, thunderer—and whatever else the wild-eyed poets call you (particularly when they're stumped by their meter—with all your names strung out you're a big help to a verse that's short; you plug the gaps in the rhythm). Well, Zeus, where's your crashing lightning and rolling thunder and blazing, flashing, terrifying thunderbolt now? It's become painfully clear that this is all nonsense, just poetic hot air—the only crash and roar is the sound of the words. That far-famed, far-flying, ever-ready missile of yours has somehow or other fizzled out; it's stone cold; it hasn't a spark of wrath left in it to descend on the heads of wrongdoers. As a matter of fact, anyone out to try his hand at perjury would get more of a scare from an old candle stump than the flame of that all-consuming thunderbolt of yours. You look so much like a mere person just wagging a torch that sinners aren't the least bit afraid of the fire and smoke; the worst hurt they think they can get is a messy smudge of soot. That's why Salmoneus had the nerve to set himself up as a rival thunderer—a perfectly logical thing to do, considering what a cocksure hothead he was and how slow-burning your anger is. Why shouldn't he have? You're as fast asleep as if you'd taken a narcotic; you don't hear the perjurers or notice the wrongdoers; your eyes are bleary and can't focus on what's going on; your ears are as deaf as any dotard's. When you were young and hot-tempered and in the bloom of your anger, you carried on against the wicked and the violent. You never gave them a moment's peace in those days: the thunderbolt was always in action and the aegis in motion; the thunder rolled, and the lightning flashed so thick and fast it seemed to come in volleys. Quakes tossed the earth like a salad, to use the vernacular; snow came down in bucketfuls, and the hailstones were like rocks. The rain pelted fast and furious, each drop a river. Why, back when Deucalion was alive, in the twinkling of an eye such a flood took place that everything was swamped and only one vessel, some sort of ark, barely came through; it grounded on a peak of Parnassus carrying human seed with its spark of life so that greater wickedness could be propagated on earth. Well, you're reaping the reward of your laziness: men don't sacrifice to you any longer or wear garlands in your honor—someone may do it as an afterthought during the Olympic Games, but he hardly thinks of it as an obligation; he's just helping to keep an old tradition alive.

Why listen to me? I can only predict epidemics and plagues.
—Larry Kramer, 1992

Little by little, my King of the Gods, they're making a second Cronus of you and shoving you off your throne. I won't bother mentioning how many times they've robbed your temple by now. But some have even laid hands on your very image at Olympia—and you, Almighty Thunderer, didn't have the energy to unleash the bloodhounds or call out your neighbors so they could help you catch the criminals while still packing up for the getaway. The noble Destroyer of the Giants and Master of the Titans sat still, his fifteen-foot thunderbolt motionless in his hand, while his golden locks were clipped from his head. Well, Your Highness, when are you going to stop being so careless and indifferent to all this? When are you going to punish such wrongdoing? How much fire and flood do you think you'll need to deal with this rampaging human insolence?

Lucian, *from "Timon." Born around 120, Lucian was apprenticed to a sculptor in his native Syria and became a successful rhetorician in Italy and Gaul before beginning his writing career in Athens around 160. William Shakespeare drew inspiration from Lucian's dialogue for* Timon of Athens; *Ben Jonson took the idea that Helen "launched a thousand ships" from his* Dialogues of the Dead.

c. 1875: Walnut Grove, MN

GRIM REAPING

The light was queer. It was not like the changed light before a storm. The air did not press down as it did before a storm. Laura was frightened, she did not know why.

She ran outdoors, where Pa stood looking up at the sky. Ma and Mary came out too, and Pa asked, "What do you make of that, Caroline?"

A cloud was over the sun. It was not like any cloud they had ever seen before. It was a cloud of something like snowflakes, but they were larger than snowflakes, and thin and glittering. Light shone through each flickering particle.

There was no wind. The grasses were still and the hot air did not stir, but the edge of the cloud came on across the sky faster than wind. The hair stood up on Jack's neck. All at once

he made a frightful sound up at that cloud, a growl and a whine.

Plunk! Something hit Laura's head and fell to the ground. She looked down and saw the largest grasshopper she had ever seen. Then huge brown grasshoppers were hitting the ground all around her, hitting her head and her face and her arms. They came thudding down like hail.

The cloud was hailing grasshoppers. The cloud *was* grasshoppers. Their bodies hid the sun and made darkness. Their thin, large wings gleamed and glittered. The rasping whirring of their wings filled the whole air and they hit the ground and the house with the noise of a hailstorm.

Laura tried to beat them off. Their claws clung to her skin and her dress. They looked at her with bulging eyes, turning their heads this way and that. Mary ran screaming into the house. Grasshoppers covered the ground,

Pillar of ice from Hubbard Glacier calving into Disenchantment Bay, Alaska, 1986. The glacier formed a dam that temporarily turned Russell Fjord into a fast-rising lake, threatening the area's wildlife and salmon fisheries. Photograph by Chris Johns.

there was not one bare bit to step on. Laura had to step on grasshoppers and they smashed squirming and slimy under her feet.

Ma was slamming the windows shut, all around the house. Pa came and stood just inside the front door, looking out. Laura and Jack stood close beside him. Grasshoppers beat down from the sky and swarmed thick over the ground. Their long wings were folded and their strong legs took them hopping everywhere. The air whirred and the roof went on sounding like a roof in a hailstorm.

Then Laura heard another sound, one big sound made of tiny nips and snips and gnawings.

"The wheat!" Pa shouted. He dashed out the back door and ran toward the wheat field.

The grasshoppers were eating. You could not hear one grasshopper eat, unless you listened very carefully while you held him and fed him grass. Millions and millions of grasshoppers were eating now. You could hear the millions of jaws biting and chewing.

Pa came running back to the stable. Through the window Laura saw him hitching Sam and David to the wagon. He began pitching old, dirty hay from the manure pile into the wagon as fast as he could. Ma ran out, took the other pitchfork, and helped him. Then he drove away to the wheat field and Ma followed the wagon.

Pa drove around the field, throwing out little piles of stuff as he went. Ma stooped over one, then a thread of smoke rose from it and spread. Ma lit pile after pile. Laura watched till a smudge of smoke hid the field and Ma and Pa and the wagon.

Grasshoppers were still falling from the sky. The light was still dim because grasshoppers covered the sun.

Ma came back to the house, and in the closed lean-to she took off her dress and her petticoats and killed the grasshoppers she shook out of them. She had lit fires all around the wheat field. Perhaps smoke would keep the grasshoppers from eating the wheat.

Ma and Mary and Laura were quiet in the shut, smothery house. Carrie was so little that she cried, even in Ma's arms. She cried herself to sleep. Through the walls came the sound of grasshoppers eating.

The darkness went away. The sun shone again. All over the ground was a crawling, hopping mass of grasshoppers. They were eating all the soft, short grass off the knoll. The tall prairie grasses swayed and bent and fell.

"Oh, look," Laura said, low, at the window.

They were eating the willow tops. The willows' leaves were thin and bare twigs stuck out. Then whole branches were bare and knobby with masses of grasshoppers.

"I don't want to look anymore," Mary said, and she went away from the window. Laura did not want to look anymore either, but she could not stop looking.

The hens were funny. The two hens and their gawky pullets were eating grasshoppers with all their might. They were used to stretching their necks out low and running fast after grasshoppers and not catching them. Every time they stretched out now, they got a grasshopper right then. They were surprised. They kept stretching out their necks and trying to run in all directions at once.

"Well, we won't have to buy feed for the hens," said Ma. "There's no great loss without some gain."

The green garden rows were wilting down. The potatoes, the carrots, the beets and beans were being eaten away. The long leaves were eaten off the cornstalks, and the tassels, and the ears of young corn in their green husks fell covered with grasshoppers.

There was nothing anybody could do about it.

Laura Ingalls Wilder, *from* On the Banks of Plum Creek. *Wilder became a schoolteacher in the Dakota Territory at the age of fifteen in 1882 and began her writing career in 1910 as the poultry columnist for the* St. Louis Star Farmer. *Visiting her journalist and novelist daughter in San Francisco in 1915, she wrote that she wanted "to do a little writing" with her "to get the hang of it a little better so I can write something perhaps I can sell." Wilder published the first of her nine "Little House" novels in 1932 at the age of sixty-five.*

c. 1880: Gila River Valley

Earth Maker took some clay in his hands, mixed it with his own sweat, and formed it into two figures—a man and a woman. He breathed life into them and they began to walk around. They lived. They had children. They peopled the land. They built villages.

At a time when there were already numbers of people living, Szeukha, Earth Maker's son, dwelled in the valley of the Gila River. Near him lived a famous seer who could foretell the future.

What quarrel, what harshness, what unbelief in each other can subsist in the presence of a great calamity when all the artificial vesture of our life is gone and we are all one with each other in primitive mortal needs?
—George Eliot, 1860

One night while this seer slept, someone came to speak to him, making a great noise at his door. The seer woke up and looked out. Silhouetted against the light of the moon was a big bird standing in the doorway. It was the great eagle, who said, "Wake up! Stir yourself! You're a seer; you're a healer. Don't you know that a great flood is coming?"

"I know nothing about a flood," said the seer, laughing at the eagle. "Go away and let me sleep."

The great eagle came three times more to warn the seer, who ridiculed and scolded him. "Don't bother me, bird of misfortune. We all know what kind of person you are. You roam the villages in the shape of an old woman, and afterward some girls and children have disappeared and are never seen again. We don't want you around here."

"You'd better believe what I'm telling you," said the great eagle. "This whole valley will be flooded. Everything will be destroyed."

"You're a liar," said the seer.

"And you're a seer who sees nothing," said the great eagle.

The bird flew away, and hardly had he gone when a tremendous thunderclap was heard, the loudest there has ever been. Even children in the womb heard it. It began thundering continuously as great flashes of lightning lit up the sky. When morning came the sun remained hidden behind dark clouds, and there was only twilight, gray and misty. Then the earth trembled and there was a great roar of something immense moving. The people saw a sheer green wall advancing toward them, filling the valley from one side to the other. At first they did not know what it was, and then they realized that it was a wall of green water. Destroying everything in its path, it came like a huge beast, a green monster, rushing upon them foaming, hissing, in a cloud of spray. It engulfed the seer's house and carried it away with the seer, who was never seen again. Then the water fell upon the villages, sweeping away homes, people, fields, and trees. The flood swept the valley clean as with a broom. Then it rushed on beyond the valley to wreak havoc elsewhere.

When the next day dawned there was nothing alive except Szeukha, Earth Maker's son, floating on a lump of pine resin. The waters abated a little, and his strange craft bumped into a mountain above the Salt River. He stepped ashore and lived for a while in a cave on that mountain. The cave is still there, and so are some of the tools and weapons that Earth Maker's son used.

Now, Szeukha was going up to fight the great eagle. He was furious at this bird, who, he thought, had caused the great flood. Szeukha took wood from different kinds of trees and made a ladder. He leaned it against the cliff atop which the great eagle had his home, and the ladder reached into the clouds. Szeukha climbed it, found the great eagle, and fought him. It was a big fight and lasted a long time, for both Szeukha and the great eagle were powerful and had strong magic. But Szeukha was more powerful, his

The Destruction of the House of Job and the Theft of his Herd by the Sabians, by Bartolo di Fredi, 1356.

magic more potent, and at last he killed the great eagle.

Looking around, Szeukha saw the corpses and bones of all the people the great eagle had abducted and killed. He brought them all back to life, fed and clothed them, and told them to spread out and repeople the land. Inside the great eagle's house he found a woman and her child alive. The eagle had stolen her from a village and taken her for his wife. Szeukha fed and clothed her and the child also and sent them on their way. The woman was pregnant at the time, and she became the mother and begetter of the Hohokam people, from whom the Pimas are descended.

A Pima folk tale. Other versions of this tale disagree on the eagle's culpability: one claims the eagle was wrongly blamed for the flood, another that he hated man and flooded the land after tiring of the taste of human flesh. The Pima of southern Arizona are believed to be descended from the ancient Hohokam (a name that means "those who have gone before"), who created a vast system of irrigation canals for farming.

c. 1897: Russia

DEVIL OF DESTRUCTION

[*A country house on a terrace. In front of it a garden. In an avenue of trees, under an old poplar, stands a table set for tea, with a samovar. It is three o'clock in the afternoon of a cloudy day.*]

Astrov: I should be really delighted if you would come to see me someday with Miss Sophia. My estate is small, a little more than eighty acres, but if you are interested in such things I should like to show you a nursery and seedbed whose like you will not find within a thousand miles of here. My place is surrounded by government forests. The forester is old and always ailing, so I superintend almost all the work myself.

Yelena: I have always heard that you were very fond of the woods. Of course one can do a great deal of good by helping to preserve them, but does that work not interfere with your real occupation? You are a doctor, after all.

Astrov: God alone knows what a man's real occupation is.

Yelena: And do you find it interesting?

Astrov: Yes, very.

Voynitsky: [*sarcastically*] Oh, extremely!

Yelena: You're still young, not over thirty-six or thirty-seven, I should say, and I suspect that the woods don't interest you as much as you say they do. Nothing but tree after tree—I should think you would find them monotonous.

Sophia: No, the work is very interesting. Dr. Astrov watches over the old woods and sets out new forests every year, and he has already received a diploma and a bronze medal. If you'll listen to what he can tell you, you'll agree with him entirely. He says that forests are the ornaments of the earth, that they teach mankind to understand beauty and attune his mind to lofty sentiments. Forests temper a stern climate, and in countries where the climate is milder, less strength is wasted in the battle with nature, and the people are kind and gentle. The inhabitants of such countries are handsome, tractable, sensitive, graceful in speech and gesture. Their philosophy is joyous, art and science blossom among them, their treatment of women is full of exquisite nobility—

Voynitsky: [*laughing*] Bravo! Bravo! All that's very pretty, but it's also unconvincing. So, my friend [*to Astrov*], you must let me go on burning firewood in my stoves and building my sheds of planks.

Astrov: You can burn peat in your stoves and build your sheds of stone. Oh, I don't object, of course, to cutting wood from necessity, but why destroy the forests? The woods of Russia are trembling under the blows of the ax. Millions of trees have perished. The homes of the wild animals and birds have been desolated; the rivers are shrinking, and many beautiful landscapes are gone forever. And why? Because men are too lazy and stupid to stoop down and pick up their fuel from the ground. [*To Yelena*] Am I not right, Madame? Who but a stupid barbarian could burn so much beauty in his stove and destroy that which he cannot make? Man is endowed with reason and the power to create, so that he may increase that which has been given him, but until now he has not created, but demolished. The forests are disappearing, the rivers are running dry, the wildlife is exterminated, the climate is spoiled, and the earth becomes poorer and uglier every day. [*To Voynitsky*] I see irony in your look; you don't take what I am saying seriously, and—and—after all, it may very well be nonsense. But when I pass village forests that I have preserved from the ax, or hear the rustling of the young trees set out with my own hands, I feel as if I had had some small share in improving the climate, and that if mankind is happy a thousand years from now I'll have been a little bit responsible for their happiness. When I plant a little birch tree and then see it budding into young green and swaying in the wind, my heart swells with pride

Left Behind

Objects that survived catastrophe

Herculaneum bread
A loaf of bread dating to 79 was found by archaeologists in an oven in Herculaneum, near Pompeii; the oven had protected the simple flour-and-yeast loaf from the volcanic explosion. In 2013 the British Museum published a recipe for the bread on its website—though its recommendation was to "leave to rest for one hour" instead of two millennia.

Hiroshima tree
A 320-year-old bonsai tree, protected by a concrete wall, passed unscathed through the 1945 bombing of Hiroshima by the United States. In 1976 the tree was included in a bicentennial gift to the U.S., where it is now on display at the National Arboretum. Its history was unknown until 2001, when the original owner's grandsons traveled to Washington, DC, and told the story. "We really don't play up the idea of its surviving Hiroshima," said a curator at the arboretum. "It's just a fact of life."

Chicago Water Tower
One of the few Chicago structures to survive the Great Fire of 1871, the tower was almost demolished a number of times in the twentieth century. On a visit to the Windy City in 1882, Oscar Wilde called it "a castellated monstrosity with pepperboxes stuck all over it."

Titanic cracker
A Spillers & Bakers hardtack biscuit from a *Titanic* survival kit was left in one of the lifeboats brought on board the *Carpathia* during rescue. A *Carpathia* passenger who was on his honeymoon found and saved it; he and his wife passed it down as a family keepsake until, in 2015, the biscuit sold at auction for $23,000.

Tanauan Jesus statue
In 2013 Typhoon Haiyan ravaged the Philippines, leaving thousands dead and destroying many towns in the predominantly Catholic country. But in the coastal town of Tanauan, one landmark survived entirely: a giant statue of Jesus dressed in white robes.

Chelsea Jeans window display
After the September 11, 2001, attacks, an intact display from an apparel store situated one block from the World Trade Center was moved piece by piece (including the dust and debris covering it), to be exhibited at the New-York Historical Society. "Here I am, trying to preserve what I normally clean off," said a conservator. The display is now at the September 11 Memorial Museum.

---

and I—I must be off. Probably it's all nonsense, anyway. Goodbye.

[*Astrov and Sophia go into the house. Yelena and Voynitsky walk over to the terrace.*]

Yelena: You have behaved shockingly again. Really, your behavior is too petty.

Voynitsky: If you could only see your face, the way you move! Oh, how tedious your life must be, absolutely tedious.

Yelena: It is tedious, yes, and boring! How well I understand your compassion! As Astrov said just now, see how you thoughtlessly destroy the forests, so that there will soon be none left. So you also destroy mankind, and soon loyalty and purity and self-sacrifice will have vanished with the woods. Why cannot you look calmly at a woman unless she is yours? Because, the doctor was right, you are all possessed by a devil of destruction; you have no mercy on the woods or the birds or on women or on one another.

Voynitsky: I don't like your philosophy.

Anton Chekhov, *from* Uncle Vanya. *Chekhov published his first story at age twenty in 1880 and his first book in 1884, the same year he graduated with a medical degree from Moscow University and contracted tuberculosis. "The sun and the skies and the forests and the rivers and the creatures—all this is created, adapted, adjusted to each other. Each is at work and knows its place. And all this is doomed to perish," Chekhov wrote in his story "The Pipe" a decade before he published* Uncle Vanya.

1260: Japan

POLICY BRIEF

A traveler came to lament: "We see many signs in heaven and on earth of famine and plague. The whole country is filled with misery. Horses and cows die on the roadsides and so do men, and there is no one to bury them. Half the population is stricken, and no house goes unscathed.

"Hence many minds turn to religion. Some comfort themselves with the thought that disease is but a short-lived phenomenon, that old age and death are but fantasies. Others say, 'The seven troubles come merely as a matter of rotation, and soon will be succeeded by the seven forms of prosperity.' With this thought they set themselves to the details of countless ceremonies. Others, again, enter into ecstatic meditation, and contemplate the truth free from all care. Some write the names of the seven gods of luck on pieces of paper, and affix these papers by the hundreds to the doorposts of their houses.

"In other parts of the country, the lords are in fear. They remit taxes and govern their people with benevolence. But no matter what men do, famine and plague still rage. There are beggars everywhere, and unburied corpses line the roads.

"Now, when we see sun, moon, and stars go on in their courses, when the three treasures of Buddhism continue to be respected, and when kings rule peaceably, we know that the world is not about to come to an end. But look around at the misery. Look at the decay of Buddhism. What do you think causes all this?"

The master answered: "This is just what I've been contemplating. I see that our thoughts run in the same channels. Pray forgive me if I enlarge on this topic. When a man embraces the Buddhist religion he expects that his religion

Hiroshima after the dropping of the atomic bomb in August 1945. Photograph by the U.S. Air Force.

will be a way to obtain enlightenment. But at the present day neither does the power of the gods manifest itself, nor are there any signs of men attaining enlightenment. When I look around, my foolishness fills me with doubts about the future. When I look to the sky, I am filled with resentment. When I contemplate the earth, I see matter for earnest thought. But when I come to examine things more closely in light of the scriptures, I find that the whole world rebels against what is right. Men have universally become slaves of evil. Not only have the good deities left the country, but even the sages abandon it and refuse to come back. Evil spirits and demons have come to take their places, and calamities and sorrows have befallen us. We cannot help speaking of these matters. We can only fear them."

The traveler inquired: "I am not the only one who bemoans the sorrows of our empire and the miseries of my country. But I have never heard anyone suggest that the gods and sages were forsaking the country, and that demons and evil spirits have taken their places. Please tell me what scriptural proof you have for your statement?"

The master responded: "The proofs are many and varied. In the Golden Light Sutra it is said: Although this sutra exists in the land, it has no proper power or influence, for the people are backsliders at heart. They do not wish to hear it read. They do not offer it worship, respect, or reverence. For this reason, both we and our families and all the hosts of heaven have lost our proper dignity and power. Men close their ears to the deep mysteries of the sutra, and get out of the current of the stream of true Buddhism. These men cherish the causes of evil. They injure men and angels. They fall into the river of life and death, and wander from the road to nirvana. Therefore, World-Honored One, we, the four heavenly kings, and all our followers, seeing these things taking place, shall forsake that country and cease to act as its protectors. Not only shall we forsake the king, but all good deities that are the guardians of the land will depart from it. Once this forsaking is accomplished, many calamities will befall this land, and it will lose its dignity and self-respect. Its people will lose their virtuous minds and become criminals and malefactors. They will rage against one another. They will slander one another. They will even wag their tongues against the innocent. There will be plagues and comets. Two suns will appear simultaneously in the sky, with disturbed courses. Two-colored rainbows, black and white, will be

Woe-hurricanes beat ever at the gate.
—John Keats, 1818

seen with distressful omens. There will be falling stars and earthquakes, and voices will come forth from wells. Storms and hurricanes will occur out of season. There will be constant famines, and rice will perish in its tender shoots. Bandits will invade the country from foreign lands and plunder it. The inhabitants will suffer all sorts of evils. Peace and comfort will not be found there.

"These sutra states the case clearly, and there is no doubt as to its meaning. But men's ears are deaf and their eyes are blind. They believe in the corrupt teaching because they want to believe it. They have lost the power to distinguish between truth and falsehood. In short, the whole world has departed from Buddha and the sutras, and no one desires to protect them. It is no wonder that the good deities and sages have forsaken the land, and that evil spirits and heretics have brought about calamities and distress."

Nichiren, *from "Establishing Righteousness to Secure the Peace of Nations." Born in 1222 in eastern Japan, Nichiren became a Buddhist monk at fifteen. In 1260, in response to the earthquakes, epidemics, and discord ravaging Japan, Nichiren submitted this treatise to national authorities claiming that only adherence to the Lotus Sutra could stabilize the country; for this he was exiled. Pardoned in 1262, he was soon exiled again for making similar assertions. After his death in 1282, Nichiren's school grew to become among the most popular of modern-day Buddhism.*

1960: Buenos Aires

ACTS OF MAN

The images in dreams, wrote Coleridge, figure forth the impressions that our intellect would call causes; we do not feel horror because we are haunted by a sphinx, we dream a sphinx in order to explain the horror that we feel. If that is true, how might a mere chronicling of its forms transmit the stupor, the exultation, the alarms, the dread, and the joy that wove together that night's dream? I shall attempt that chronicle, nonetheless; perhaps the fact that the dream consisted of but a single scene may erase or soften the essential difficulty.

The place was the College of Philosophy and Letters; the hour, nightfall. Everything (as is often the case in dreams) was slightly different; a slight magnification altered things. We chose authorities; I would speak with Pedro Henríquez Ureña, who in waking life had died many years before. Suddenly, we were dumbfounded by a great noise of demonstrators or street musicians. From the Underworld, we heard the cries of humans and animals. A voice cried: *Here they come!* And then: *The gods! The gods!* Four or five individuals emerged from out of the mob and occupied the dais of the auditorium. Everyone applauded, weeping; it was the gods, returning after a banishment of many centuries. Looming larger than life as they stood upon the dais, their heads thrown back and their chests thrust forward, they haughtily received our homage. One of them was holding a branch (which belonged, no doubt, to the simple botany of dreams); another, with a sweeping gesture, held out a hand that was a claw; one of Janus' faces looked mistrustfully at Thoth's curved beak. Perhaps excited by our applause, one of them, I no longer remember which, burst out in a triumphant, incredibly bitter clucking that was half gargle and half whistle. From that point on, things changed.

It all began with the suspicion (perhaps exaggerated) that the gods were unable to talk. Centuries of a feral life of flight had atrophied

Shia, devourer of men, wooden lacquered mask, Arunachal Pradesh, India, nineteenth century.

that part of them that was human; the moon of Islam and the cross of Rome had been implacable with these fugitives. Beetling brows, yellowed teeth, the sparse beard of a mulatto or a Chinaman, and beastlike dewlaps were testaments to the degeneration of the Olympian line. The clothes they wore were not those of a decorous and honest poverty, but rather of the criminal luxury of the Underworld's gambling dens and houses of ill repute. A carnation bled from a buttonhole; under a tight suit coat one could discern the outline of a knife. Suddenly, we felt that they were playing their last trump, that they were cunning, ignorant, and cruel, like aged predators, and that if we allowed ourselves to be swayed by fear or pity, they would wind up destroying us.

We drew our heavy revolvers (suddenly in the dream there were revolvers) and exultantly killed the gods.

Jorge Luis Borges, *"Ragnarök." Born in 1899, Borges lived in Europe during World War I before returning to his native Argentina. In Scandinavian mythology, Ragnarök is the doom of the gods, the event that precipitates the end of the cosmos, and it includes a battle between Thor and the sea serpent Midgarthormr. "Its inconceivable shadow will loom / high above the pale world on the day / of high wolves and splendid agony / of a twilight without name," wrote Borges in his poem "Midgarthormr." "Toward dawn I saw it all in nightmare." He died in 1986 at the age of eighty-six.*

1982: New York City

IN A NEW YORK MINUTE

One way to begin to grasp the destructive power of present-day nuclear weapons is to describe the consequences of the detonation of a one-megaton bomb, which possesses eighty times the explosive power of the Hiroshima bomb, on a large city, such as New York. Burst some 8,500 feet above the Empire State Building, a one-megaton bomb would gut or flatten almost every building between Battery Park and 125th Street, or within a radius of four and four-tenths miles, or in an area of sixty-one square miles, and would heavily damage buildings between the northern tip of Staten Island and the George Washington Bridge, or within a radius of about eight miles, or in an area of about two hundred square miles. A conventional explosive delivers a swift shock, like a slap, to whatever it hits, but the blast wave of a sizable nuclear weapon endures for several seconds and can surround and destroy whole buildings. People, of course, would be picked up and hurled away from the blast along with the rest of the debris. Within the sixty-one square miles, the walls, roofs, and floors of any buildings that had not been flattened would be collapsed, and the people and furniture inside would be swept down onto the street. As far away as ten miles from ground zero pieces of glass and other sharp objects would be hurled about by the blast wave at lethal velocities. In Hiroshima, where buildings were low and, outside the center of the city, were often constructed of light materials, injuries from falling buildings were often minor. But in New York, where the buildings are tall and are constructed of heavy materials, the physical collapse of the city would certainly kill millions of people. The streets of New York are narrow ravines running between the high walls of the city's buildings. In a nuclear attack the walls would fall and the ravines would fill up. The people in the buildings would fall to the street with the debris of the buildings, and the

Various disasters afflicting London, woodcut from *A Rod for Runaways*, by Thomas Dekker, 1625.

State of the Union, by John Brosio, 2011. Oil on canvas, 41 x 66 inches.

people in the street would be crushed by this avalanche of people and buildings. At a distance of two miles or so from ground zero winds would reach four hundred miles an hour, and another two miles away they would reach 180 miles an hour. Meanwhile, the fireball would be growing, until it was more than a mile wide, and rocketing upward, to a height of over six miles. For ten seconds it would broil the city below. Anyone caught in the open within nine miles of ground zero would receive third-degree burns and would probably be killed; closer to the explosion, people would be charred and killed instantly. From Greenwich Village up to Central Park, the heat would be great enough to melt metal and glass. Readily inflammable materials, such as newspapers and dry leaves, would ignite in all five boroughs (though in only a small part of Staten Island) and west to the Passaic River, in New Jersey, within a radius of about nine and a half miles from ground zero, thereby creating an area of more than 280 square miles in which mass fires were likely to break out.

If it were possible (as it would not be) for someone to stand at Fifth Avenue and Seventy-Second Street (about two miles from ground zero) without being instantly killed, he would see the following sequence of events. A dazzling white light from the fireball would illumine the scene, continuing for perhaps thirty seconds. Simultaneously, searing heat would ignite everything flammable and start to melt windows, cars, buses, lampposts, and everything else made of metal or glass. People in the street would immediately catch fire, and would shortly be reduced to heavily charred corpses. About five seconds after the light appeared the blast wave would strike, laden with the debris of a now nonexistent midtown. Some buildings might be crushed, as though a giant fist had squeezed them on all sides, and others might be picked up off their foundations and whirled uptown with the other debris. On the far side of Central Park, the West Side skyline would fall from south to north. The four-hundred-mile-an-hour wind would blow from south to north, die down after a few seconds, and then blow in the reverse direction with diminished intensity. While these things were happening, the fireball would be burning in the sky for the ten seconds of the thermal pulse. Soon huge, thick clouds of dust and smoke would envelop the scene, and as the mushroom cloud rushed overhead (it would have a diameter of about twelve miles) the light from the sun would be blotted out, and day would turn to night. Within minutes, fires, ignited both by the thermal pulse and by broken gas mains, tanks of gas and oil, and the like, would begin to spread in the darkness, and a strong, steady wind would begin to blow in the direction of the blast. As at Hiroshima, a whirlwind might be produced, which would sweep through the ruins, and radioactive rain, generated under the meteorological conditions created by the blast, might fall. Before long the individual fires would coalesce into a mass fire, which, depending largely on the winds, would become either a conflagration or a firestorm. In a conflagration prevailing winds spread a wall of fire as far as there is any combustible material to sustain it; in a firestorm a vertical updraft caused by the fire itself sucks the surrounding air in toward a central point, and the fires therefore converge in a single fire of extreme heat. A mass fire of either kind renders shelters useless by burning up all the oxygen in the air and creating toxic gases, so that anyone inside the shelters is asphyxiated, and also by heating the ground to such high temperatures that the shelters turn, in effect, into ovens, cremating the people inside them. In Dresden, several days after the firestorm raised there by Allied conventional bombing, the interiors of some bomb shelters were still so hot that when they were opened the inrushing air caused the contents to burst into flame. Only those who had fled their shelters when the bombing started had any chance of surviving. (It is difficult to predict in a particular situation which form the fires will take. In actual experience, Hiroshima suffered a firestorm and Nagasaki suffered a conflagration.)

In this vast theater of physical effects all the scenes of agony and death that took place at Hiroshima would again take place, but now involving millions of people rather than hundreds of thousands. Like the people of Hiroshima, the people of New York would be burned, battered, crushed, and irradiated in every conceivable way. The city and its people would be mingled in a smoldering heap. And then, as the fires started, the survivors (most of whom would be on the periphery of the explosion) would be driven to abandon to the flames those family members and other people who were unable to flee, or else to die with them. Before long, while the ruins burned, the processions of injured, mute people would begin

> 'Tis no discomfort in the world to fall,
> When the great crack not crushes one, but all.
> —Robert Herrick, 1648

their slow progress out of the outskirts of the devastated zone. However, this time a much smaller proportion of the population than at Hiroshima would have a chance of escaping. In general, as the size of the area of devastation increases, the possibilities for escape decrease. When the devastated area is relatively small, as it was at Hiroshima, people who are not incapacitated will have a good chance of escaping to safety before the fires coalesce into a mass fire. But when the devastated area is great, as it would be after the detonation of a megaton bomb, and fires are springing up at a distance of nine and a half miles from ground zero, and when what used to be the streets are piled high with burning rubble, and the day (if the attack occurs in the daytime) has grown impenetrably dark, there is little chance that anyone who is not on the very edge of the devastated area will be able to make his way to safety. In New York most people would die wherever the blast found them, or not very far from there.

Jonathan Schell, *from* The Fate of the Earth. *Originating as a four-part series in* The New Yorker, The Fate of the Earth *was Schell's first of four works on nuclear weapons. "Usually, people wait for things to occur before trying to describe them," Schell writes elsewhere in the book, "but since we cannot afford under any circumstances to let a holocaust occur, we are forced in this one case to become the historians of the future—to chronicle and commit to memory an event that we have never experienced."*

1930: Vienna

ANIMAL INSTINCTS

Men are not gentle creatures who want to be loved, and who at the most can defend themselves if they are attacked; they are, on the contrary, creatures among whose instinctual endowments is to be reckoned a powerful share of aggressiveness. As a result, their neighbor is for them not only a potential helper or sexual object, but also someone who tempts them to satisfy their aggressiveness on him, to exploit his capacity for work without compensation, to use him sexually without his consent, to seize his possessions, to humiliate him, to cause him pain, to torture and

I am above the weakness of seeking to establish a sequence of cause and effect between the disaster and the atrocity.
—Edgar Allan Poe, 1843

to kill him. *Homo homini lupus* [Man is a wolf to man]. Who, in the face of all his experience of life and of history, will have the courage to dispute this assertion? As a rule this cruel aggressiveness waits for some provocation or puts itself at the service of some other purpose, whose goal might also have been reached by milder measures. In circumstances that are favorable to it, when the mental counterforces that ordinarily inhibit it are out of action, it also manifests itself spontaneously and reveals man as a savage beast to whom consideration toward his own kind is something alien. Anyone who calls to mind the atrocities committed during the racial migrations or the invasions of the Huns, or by the people known as Mongols under Genghis Khan and Tamerlane, or at the capture of Jerusalem by the pious Crusaders, or even, indeed, the horrors of the recent World War—anyone who calls these things to mind will have to bow humbly before the truth of this view.

The existence of this inclination to aggression, which we can detect in ourselves and justly assume to be present in others, is the fac-

tor that disturbs our relations with our neighbor and which forces civilization into such a high expenditure of energy. In consequence of this primary mutual hostility of human beings, civilized society is perpetually threatened with disintegration. The interest of work in common would not hold it together; instinctual passions are stronger than reasonable interests. Civilization has to use its utmost efforts in order to set limits to man's aggressive instincts and to hold the manifestations of them in check by psychical reaction-formations. Hence, therefore, the use of methods intended to incite people into identifications and aim-inhibited relationships of love, hence the restriction upon sexual life, and hence too the ideal's commandment to love one's neighbor as oneself—a commandment that is really justified by the fact that nothing else runs so strongly counter to the original nature of man. In spite of every effort, these endeavors of civilization have not so far achieved very much. It hopes to prevent the crudest excesses of brutal violence by itself assuming the right to use violence against criminals, but the law is not able to lay hold of the more cautious and refined manifestations of human aggressiveness. The time comes when each one of us has to give up as illusions the expectations that, in his youth, he pinned upon his fellow men, and when he may learn how much difficulty and pain has been added to his life by their ill will. At the same time, it would be unfair to reproach civilization with trying to eliminate strife and competition from human activity. These things are undoubtedly indispensable. But opposition is not necessarily enmity; it is merely misused and made an *occasion* for enmity.

Of all the slowly developed parts of analytic theory, the theory of the instincts is the one that has felt its way the most painfully forward. Starting from speculations on the beginning of life and from biological parallels, I drew the conclusion that, besides the instinct to preserve living substance and to join it into ever larger units, there must exist another, contrary instinct seeking to dissolve those units and to bring them back to their primeval, inorganic state.

Neville Chamberlain and Adolf Hitler shaking hands during Chamberlain's visit to Germany, September 30, 1938, the same day he declared the accord with Germany to be "peace for our time."

That is to say, as well as Eros there was an instinct of death. The phenomena of life could be explained from the concurrent or mutually opposing action of these two instincts. It was not easy, however, to demonstrate the activities of this supposed death instinct. The manifestations of Eros were conspicuous and noisy enough. It might be assumed that the death instinct operated silently within the organism toward its dissolution, but that, of course, was no proof. A more fruitful idea was that a portion of the instinct is diverted toward the external world and comes to light as an instinct of aggressiveness and destructiveness. In this way the instinct itself could be pressed into the service of Eros, in that the organism was destroying some other thing, whether animate or inanimate, instead of destroying its own self. Conversely, any restriction of this aggressiveness directed outward would be bound to increase the self-destruction, which is in any case proceeding.

The assumption of the existence of an instinct of death or destruction has met with resistance even in analytic circles. I remember my own defensive attitude when the idea of an instinct of destruction first emerged in psychoanalytic literature, and how long it took before I became receptive to it. That others should have shown, and still show, the same attitude of rejection surprises me less. For "little children do not like it" when there is talk of the inborn human inclination to "badness," to aggressiveness and destructiveness, and so to cruelty as well. God has made them in the image of his own perfection; nobody wants to be reminded how hard it is to reconcile the undeniable existence of evil.

1996: Paris

NOT BY CHANCE

The accident is an inverted miracle, a secular miracle, a revelation. When you invent the ship, you also invent the shipwreck; when you invent the plane, you invent the plane crash; and when you invent electricity, you invent electrocution. Every technology carries its own negativity, which is invented at the same time as technical progress. The development of technologies can only happen through the analysis and surpassing of these accidents. When the European railroads were introduced, the traffic was poorly regulated and accidents multiplied. The railroad engineers convened in Brussels in 1880 and invented the famous block system. The explosion of the *Challenger* space shuttle is a considerable event that reveals the original accident of the engine in the same way as the shipwreck of the first ocean liner.

Work on the accident is critical. Work on science can only advance through work on negativity. However, the dimension of the accident has changed, and we are faced with the emergence of an unprecedented accident. All technical objects brought about accidents that were specific, local, and situated in time and space. The *Titanic* leaked in one place, while the train derailed in another. As for us, we have created the possibility of an accident that is no longer particular but general, and this through the interactivity, the networks, and the globalization brought about by the communication revolution. So there is an accident brewing that would occur everywhere at the same time. This is in no way a pessimist's hypothesis, but a reality. In fact, interactivity is to society what radioactivity is to matter. Radioactivity is a constituent element of matter that can also destroy it by fission. Interactivity is of the same nature. It can bring about union of society, but it also has the power to dissolve it and disintegrate it on a world scale. We are faced with an original phenomenon: the emergence of the accident of accidents. It is a temporal phenomenon whose only reference is in the philosophy of time.

Paul Virilio, *from* Politics of the Very Worst. *Inspired by the 1979 Three Mile Island nuclear accident, French urbanist and philosopher Virilio proposed a Museum of Accidents. "If you build a plane for eight hundred passengers, one day you will have eight hundred dead," he explained in 2002, after creating a prototype of the museum in Paris. "The museum's purpose would not be to spread fear but to confront what is no longer a chance event."*

I adopt the standpoint, therefore, that the inclination to aggression is an original, self-subsisting instinctual disposition in man, and I return to my view that it constitutes the greatest impediment to civilization. At one point in the course of this inquiry I was led to the idea that civilization was a special process which mankind undergoes, and I am still under the influence of that idea. I may now add that civilization is a process in the service of Eros, whose purpose is to combine single human individuals, and after that families, then races, peoples and nations, into one great unity, the unity of mankind. Why this has to happen, we do not know; the work of Eros is precisely this. These collections of men are to be libidinally bound to one another. Necessity alone, the advantages of work in common, will not hold them together. But man's natural aggressive instinct, the hostility of each against all and of all against each, opposes this program of civilization. This aggressive instinct is the derivative and the main representative of the death instinct that we have found alongside of Eros and which shares world dominion with it. And now, I think, the meaning of the evolution of civilization is no longer obscure to us. It must present the struggle between Eros and Death, between the instinct of life and the instinct of destruction, as it works itself out in the human species. This struggle is what all life essentially consists of, and the evolution of civilization may therefore be simply described as the struggle for life of the human species. And it is this battle of the giants that our nursemaids try to appease with their lullaby about heaven.

Sigmund Freud, *from* Civilization and Its Discontents. *Freud once recalled that as a boy, owing to his classmates' anti-Semitism, his hero was a Carthaginian general: "Hannibal and Rome symbolized as a youth the antithesis between the tenaciousness of the Jews and the organization of the Catholic Church." The founder of psychoanalysis published his first major work,* The Interpretation of Dreams, *in 1899 and his last,* Moses and Monotheism, *in 1938—the same year Germany annexed Austria. The following year, Freud died at the age of eighty-three in London.*

1939: Warsaw

DIVIDED WE FALL

October 16

Life moves along by itself. There is no transportation, no water, no electricity. Everything creeps, and this has given foundation to flourishing rumors that the conquerors won't remain here. But there is one thing the conquerors do not ignore, that they return to incessantly, as though from the very outset they had come here for that purpose alone. A certain psychosis of hatred and loathing toward the "*Jude*" has infected them, and if they do anything with care and forethought, it is in the Jewish area.

October 18

Our lives grow gloomier from day to day. Racial laws have not yet been formally decreed, but actually our defeat is inevitable. The conqueror says bluntly that there is no hope for Jewish survival. There is room for the assumption that a beginning is being made now.

So far there has been free trade in the streets. This is a trade of pennies, whose practitioners are boys and girls, young men and women driven to this sort of business by poverty. It is destined to be forbidden. It too will be taken out of the hands of the Jews. Every public place shows hatred and loathing toward the Jews. Isolated incidents of blows and violence against Jews have grown too numerous to

Mother comforting her son after the Kashmir earthquake, Balakot, Pakistan, 2005. Photograph by Paula Bronstein.

count. Eyewitnesses tell horrifying stories, and they are not exaggerations.

The future of the schools for Jewish children is not yet known. In general the conquerors have no dealings with Jewish representatives. We are like grains of sand. There is no prior consultation regarding our own lives. They make decrees by themselves and there is no changing them. Reasons are not required. There is only one reason—to destroy, to kill, to eradicate.

May 2, 1940

In a spiritual state like the one in which I find myself at this time, it is difficult to hold a pen, to concentrate one's thoughts. But a strange idea has stuck in my head since the war broke out—that it is a duty I must perform. This idea is like a flame imprisoned in my bones, burning within me, screaming: Record! Perhaps I am the only one engaged in this work, and that strengthens and encourages me.

When the conqueror runs rampant, he makes no distinction between Jews and Poles, even though he knows the Jew has no thoughts of revolt. The Pole is beaten for whatever sin he commits; the Jew is beaten day and night at every opportunity, whether he has sinned or not. When the day of reckoning comes the tyrant lumps them both together, and there is no escaping his wrath.

October 8

Jewish Joke I: The Germans are beating the Jews because England doesn't want to make peace; the Poles are beating them because the same England did not prepare herself properly for battle and is being defeated.

Jewish Joke II: The Führer asks Hans Frank, "What evils and misfortunes have you brought upon the Jews of Poland?"

"I took away their livelihood; I robbed them of their rights; I established labor camps and we are making them work at hard labor there; I have stolen all their wealth and property." But the Führer is not satisfied with all these acts. So Frank adds: "Besides that, I have established *Judenrate* and Jewish Self-Aid Societies."

The Führer is satisfied and smiles at Frank. "You hit the target with the *Judenrate*, and Self-Aid will ruin them. They will disappear from the earth!"

October 10

Clouds are covering our skies. Racial segregation is becoming more apparent each day. Yesterday an order was published that the Jews must make way before every German, both soldiers and civil servants in uniform. Making way means that the Jews must step aside until the Germans leave the sidewalk. You must always keep your eyes open and guard yourself against daydreaming and conversation lest you fail to do the proper honor to a Nazi you encounter. Today we have already had our first victims, who were beaten because of the order. You go out trembling, full of panic lest you meet a Nazi.

All people whose ancestors did not stand before Mount Sinai are allowed to walk in the streets until eleven at night. For Jews outside the walls, the curfew is seven; inside the walls, nine. In the morning no Jew who lives outside the walls can be on the street before eight.

October 12, 1940/End of Yom Kippur, 5701

On the New Year we prayed illegally. The ban on communal worship was still in effect. In secret, in side rooms near the dark, closed synagogues we prayed to the God of Israel like Marranos in the fifteenth century.

At last the ghetto edict has gone into effect. For the time being it will be an open ghetto, but there is no doubt that in short order it will be closed. In Lodz the ghetto edict was not carried out all at once but rather step by step, and many signs indicate that it will be the same in Warsaw. After the ghetto plan was postponed two weeks ago, we were almost tranquil. But the enemy of Israel neither sleeps nor slumbers.

November 19

If it were said that the sun has darkened for us at noon it would not be merely a metaphor. We will molder and rot within the narrow streets

Strangers Come to Town

Invasive species wreaking havoc

Arrival time	Route	Invader	Consequence
Pliocene (about 3 million years ago)	North America to South America	The volcanic Isthmus of Panama forms between continents, allowing the southward migration of predator species, including **bears** and **cougars**.	Many outcompeted South American mammals go extinct, including species of **sabertooth cats**. Today more than half of the mammals in South America originally came from North America.
c. 2000 BC	Asia to Australia	**Dingoes** hitch to Australia in the boats of Southeast Asian seamen.	Dingo predation accelerates the death of all **Tasmanian devils** on mainland Australia, along with the extinctions of other mammals. By the 1880s dingo proliferation leads the government to build a 5,400-kilometer fence to prevent dingoes from eating their livestock.
c. 400 BC	India to the western Mediterranean (later to every continent but Antarctica)	Hidden away in holds, **ship rats (or black rats)** catch rides on military and grain-transport vessels.	Omnivorous predators, ship rats prey on a wide range of plants and animals in their adopted lands, including snails, spiders, cicadas, and the eggs and young of birds; their predation leads to the extinction of **many birds, small mammals, reptiles, invertebrates, and plants**.
c. 100	Danube River to rest of Roman Empire	Fans of **carp** cuisine, Romans spread fish farming throughout Roman territories.	As bottom feeders, carp stir up gunk other fish leave alone, sucking up debris and outcompeting **local fish and waterfowl**. A female carp can lay a million eggs in a season.
c. 1347	East Asia to Europe	**Fleas** carrying the plague catch an illicit ride into Europe in the fur of rodents stowing away on Italian merchant ships.	Plague outbreak kills **about one-third of Europe's population**.
c. 1600	Europe to North America	Earthworms such as **nightcrawlers** enter North American soil, likely by way of soil used as ship ballast by early European settlers.	Earthworms consume the natural detritus left on forest floors; their arrival disrupts North American ecosystems, destroying habitats of **many plants and animals**. Scientists have referred to the process as "global worming."
c. 1880	Britain to India	During colonial rule of India, the British governor initiates bounties for native cobras in Delhi in an effort to **reduce native cobra populations**.	People breed cobras to collect the bounty; when bounties end, breeders release the snakes, **increasing the cobra population**. This becomes known as the "cobra effect."
1890	Europe to New York City	Eugene Schieffelin releases sixty **European starlings** into Central Park in order to make the park resound with the song of birds mentioned in Shakespeare's plays.	U.S. starling population eventually reaches 200 million. The birds **destroy crops** and **compete for nest sites** with native hole nesters.
c. 2000	Southeast Asia to Everglades	**Burmese pythons**, brought to Florida as pets, escape or are released and quickly breed.	The pythons devour the local population of **rabbits, deer, and bobcats**; more than 2,000 are removed from the Everglades in a decade. Says one scientist, "Maybe next time we could prevent changes we don't want to happen."

and the crooked lanes in which tens of thousands of people wander idle and full of despair.

The matter of food supplies, in particular, has contributed to confusion. Since communication between us and the villages is cut off, our food will be given to us by the conquerors. This will amount to 90 percent starvation.

What good will ten decagrams of coarse bread a week do?

December 2
Life in the ghetto is becoming "normal." The chaos lasted no more than a week. When half a million people are locked in a small cage, faced

c. 800 BC: Britain

HEAVENLY COMPULSION

Gloucester: These late eclipses in the sun and moon portend no good to us. Though the wisdom of nature can reason it thus and thus, yet nature finds itself scourged by the sequent effects. Love cools, friendship falls off, brothers divide. In cities, mutinies; in countries, discord; in palaces, treason; and the bond cracked 'twixt son and father. This villain of mine comes under the prediction: there's son against father. The king falls from bias of nature, there's father against child. We have seen the best of our time. Machinations, hollowness, treachery, and all ruinous disorders follow us disquietly to our graves. Find out this villain, Edmond, it shall lose thee nothing. Do it carefully. And the noble and truehearted Kent banished; his offense, honesty. 'Tis strange.

[*Exit*]

Edmond: This is the excellent foppery of the world, that when we are sick in fortune, often the surfeits of our own behavior, we make guilty of our disasters the sun, the moon, and the stars; as if we were villains on necessity, fools by heavenly compulsion, knaves, thieves, and treachers by spherical predominance, drunkards, liars, and adulterers by an enforced obedience of planetary influence; and all that we are evil in, by a divine thrusting on. An admirable evasion of whoremaster man, to lay his goatish disposition on the charge of a star! My father compounded with my mother under the Dragon's tail, and my nativity was under Ursa Major, so that it follows, I am rough and lecherous. I should have been that I am had the maidenliest star in the firmament twinkled on my bastardizing.

[*Enter Edgar*]

Pat he comes like the catastrophe of the old comedy. My cue is villainous melancholy, with a sigh like Tom o' Bedlam. O these eclipses do portend these divisions. Fa, sol, la, me.

William Shakespeare, *from* King Lear. *First performed before King James I on St. Stephen's Day in 1606,* Lear *was revised after the Restoration by seventeenth-century Irish poet Nahum Tate to have a happy ending. The play's use of the word* disaster *came just a few years after it had entered English, carrying the astrological sense of an "ill-starred" event from* astrum, *Latin for "star" or "planet." "Nothing is solved in or by* King Lear," *wrote critic Harold Bloom, "and Lear loses his old gods without finding any new ones."*

with hunger, privation, epidemics, atrocities, naturally it causes a stir. Even the conquerors were confused. This is a unique political experiment. The intention was to starve and impoverish us in body and in spirit, to segregate us from the outside world; to undermine our very existence. A great project of this sort demands extraordinary exertions and cannot be brought into effect by words alone. But to our sorrow, it must be admitted that the tyrants succeeded.

January 4, 1942
The words of the poet have come true in all their dreadful meaning: "'Tis not a nation nor a sect but a herd." Gone is the spirit of Jewish brotherhood. The words *compassionate, modest, charitable* no longer apply to us. The ghetto beggars who stretch out their hands to us with the plea, "Jewish hearts, have pity," realized that the once tender hearts have become like rocks. Our tragedy is the senselessness of it all. Our suffering is inflicted on us because we are Jews, while the real meaning of Jewishness has disappeared from our lives.

Our oppressors herded us into the ghetto, hoping to subdue us into obedient animals. Instead, however, we are splitting and crumbling into hostile, quarrelsome groups. It is painful to admit that ever since we were driven into the ghetto our collective moral standard has declined sharply. Instead of uniting and bringing us closer, our suffering has led to strife and contention between brothers. The Nazis, possibly with malice aforethought, put us in the hands of the *Judenrat* so that we might be disgraced in the sight of all. It is as if they were saying, "Look at them! Do you call them a people? Is this your social morality? Are these your leaders?"

It is not at all uncommon on a cold winter morning to see the bodies of those who have died on the sidewalks of cold and starvation during the night. Many God-fearing, pious souls, who, if the day happens to be the Sabbath, are carrying the tallith under their arms, walk by the corpses and no one seems to be moved by the sight. Everyone hastens on his way praying silently that his will not be a similar fate. In the gutters, amid the refuse, one can see almost naked and

Battle between Roman and Germanic armies, detail of the Portonaccio sarcophagus, Rome, c. 180.

barefoot little children wailing pitifully. These are children who were orphaned when both parents died either in their wanderings or in the typhus epidemic. Yet there is no institution that will take them in and care for them and bring them up as human beings. Every morning you will see their little bodies frozen to death in the ghetto streets. It has become a customary sight. Self-preservation has hardened our hearts and made us indifferent to the suffering of others. Our moral standards are thoroughly corrupted. Disgraceful as it may sound, we must admit the bitter truth: everyone steals! Petty thievery, such as picking pockets or stealing a hat or an umbrella, is common. Because kosher meat is terribly expensive, people have relaxed their observance of the laws regarding the eating of kosher food. Not only atheists and derelicts are guilty of this, but synagogue sextons and pious men as well.

Nazism has forced Polish Jewry to degrade itself thus. Nazism has maimed the soul even more than the body!

Chaim Kaplan, *from* The Scroll of Agony. *Born in Belorussia in 1880, Kaplan came to Warsaw in the early 1900s and opened a Hebrew elementary school. He began keeping his war diary on the day of the Nazi's invasion of Poland on September 1, 1939; the last entry appeared on August 4, 1942, the month in which the Jews of the Warsaw Ghetto, including Kaplan, were deported to the Treblinka death camp. The notebooks were smuggled out of Warsaw to the nearby farm of a Polish man who preserved them through the war in a kerosene can.*

c. 95: Patmos

APOCALYPSE NOW

I looked, and behold, the temple of the tabernacle of the testimony in heaven was opened: and the seven angels came out of the temple, having the seven plagues, clothed in pure and white linen, and having their breasts girded with golden girdles. And one of the four beasts gave to the seven angels seven golden vials full of the wrath of God, who lives forever and ever. And the temple was filled with smoke from the glory of God, and from his power, and no man was able to enter into the temple, till the seven plagues of the seven angels were fulfilled.

And I heard a great voice out of the temple saying to the seven angels, "Go your ways, and pour out the vials of the wrath of God upon the earth." And the first went, and poured out his vial upon the earth, and there fell a noisome and grievous sore upon the men who had the mark of the beast, and upon them who worshiped his image.

And the second angel poured out his vial upon the sea, and it became as the blood of a dead man: and every living soul died in the sea.

And the third angel poured out his vial upon the rivers and fountains of waters, and they became blood. And I heard the angel of the waters say, "You are righteous, O Lord, who is and was and shall be, because you have judged thus. For they have shed the blood of saints and prophets, and you have given them blood to drink: for they are worthy." And I heard another out of the altar say, "Even so, Lord God Almighty, true and righteous are your judgments."

And the fourth angel poured out his vial upon the sun, and power was given to him to scorch men with fire. And men were scorched with great heat, and blasphemed the name of God, which has power over these plagues: and they repented not, to give him glory.

And the fifth angel poured out his vial upon the seat of the beast, and his kingdom was full of darkness, and they gnawed their tongues for pain, and blasphemed the God of heaven because of their pains and their sores, and repented not of their deeds.

And the sixth angel poured out his vial upon the great river Euphrates, and the water thereof was dried up, that the way of the kings of the east might be prepared. And I saw three unclean spirits like frogs come out of the mouth of the dragon, and out of the mouth of the beast, and out of the mouth of the false prophet. For they are the spirits of devils, working miracles, which go forth to the kings of the earth and of the whole world, to gather them to the battle of that great day of God Almighty. "Behold, I come as a thief. Blessed is he that watches, and keeps his garments, lest he walk naked, and they see his shame." And he gathered them together into a place called in the Hebrew tongue Armageddon.

And the seventh angel poured out his vial into the air, and there came a great voice out of the temple of heaven, from the throne, saying, "It is done." And there were voices, and thunders, and lightnings; and there was a great earthquake, such as was not since men were upon the earth, so mighty an earthquake, and so great. And the great city was divided into three parts, and the cities of the nations fell: and great Babylon came in remembrance before God, to give to her the cup of the wine of the fierceness of his wrath. And every island fled away, and the mountains were not found. And there fell upon men a great hail out of heaven, every stone about the weight of a talent, and men blasphemed God because of the plague of the hail: for the plague thereof was exceedingly great.

From the Book of Revelation. This final book of the New Testament was purportedly written by John of Patmos, a self-proclaimed "servant" of Jesus Christ. These verses offer the only biblical mention of Armageddon, *a word that derives from the Hebrew name of Mount Megiddo, where kings devoted to the Antichrist would receive the wrath of God. The term has come to refer to the final battles marking the end of the world. "We realize to our horror," wrote D.H. Lawrence, "that this is what we are up against today: not Jesus nor Paul, but John of Patmos."*

1939: Kansas City, MO

TORNADO WARNING

Each year on Mrs. Bridge's birthday she was distressed by the extravagance of her husband's gift. Invariably she protested to him, and meant it, but he was determined to give her costly presents and she could not dissuade him. Once he set his mind he was immovable. One year it had been the Lincoln, another year it was an ermine coat, another year it was a diamond necklace. She loved these things, to be sure, but she did not need them, and knew this quite well, and in spite of loving them she could not help being a little embarrassed by the opulence of her possessions. She was conscious of people on the street staring at her when, wrapped in ermine and driving the Lincoln, she started off to a party at the country club; she wanted to stop the car and explain to them that her husband was still at work in the office though it was nine in the evening, and that she had not asked for these expensive things but that he had given them to her for her birthday. But, of course, she could not stop to explain any more than she could stop people from staring.

This year, therefore, she was mildly surprised when her birthday arrived and all he said was that they were going to have dinner at the club. She supposed this was to be her gift. It was odd, considering the past, but she was not displeased; she was even a bit relieved.

Locust swarms from Saudi Arabia consuming crops in Dasht-e Arjan, Iran, 1952. In a unique cooperation, U.S. and Soviet pilots sprayed the region with pesticide and prevented a major catastrophe. Photograph by Erich Lessing.

And it came as an unforgettable shock when he remarked, slyly, pleased with himself, soon after they had been seated in the country-club dining room, that the two of them were leaving for Europe three weeks from Sunday. Mrs. Bridge at first thought he was joking. He was not. And she learned that all her friends had known about the trip for the past month, but not one of them had so much as hinted about the surprise in store for her. The tickets were already bought and he had reserved hotel accommodations in the countries they were to visit. They would be gone, he told her, for about six weeks.

"I feel giddy," said Mrs. Bridge. "I never dreamed of anything like this."

And when the waiter had taken their order Mr. Bridge proceeded to tell her of the cities they would visit, and as he talked she stopped listening because she could not help thinking of another evening when he had told her of all he planned to do. He had said he would take her to Europe one day; she remembered having smiled at him fondly; not really believing, not caring, happy enough to be with him anywhere. How long ago, she thought, how very long ago that was! It seemed like eight or ten years ago, but it was more than twenty, and on this day she was forty-eight years old. She grew a little sad at this, and while he talked on

and on—he was more excited than she—she gazed out the window at the gathering clouds. And the distant thunder seemed to be warning her that one day this world she knew and loved would be annihilated.

The clouds descended and the wind began to increase while they were eating. A few drops of rain spattered against the window. It was the season for tornadoes, and before much longer it had become evident that one was approaching. The club steward turned on the radio and listened to reports of the tornado's course; it was, he learned, bearing directly toward the country club at a speed of seventy miles an hour. The steward went from table to table explaining the situation and adding that if the storm continued to approach it would be necessary to take shelter in the basement.

"Thank you," said Mrs. Bridge. "Do you suppose there's much chance of it hitting us?"

The steward didn't know. The tornado was still quite a few miles west; the course of it might alter, or the funnel might degenerate before reaching Kansas City. "Well, you'll let us know," said Mrs. Bridge. The steward said he would keep them informed. Soon the trees on the terrace were bending from the wind, and the rain poured down. She saw a metal chair go skidding off the porch as though someone were pulling it away with a rope. A few of the diners

The Expulsion from Paradise, by Franz von Stuck, c. 1890.

had begun to leave the room, and the steward was coming around again.

"Goodness, this *is* a storm," said Mrs. Bridge. "Do you think we should go to the basement?"

Mr. Bridge replied that the storm was not going to strike the clubhouse and that he, for one, intended to finish his dinner.

"There goes the mayor," she said, looking around. The mayor and his wife often ate at the club and the Bridges were acquainted with them.

"Good evening," said the mayor as he passed by, preceded by his wife.

"Good evening," said Mrs. Bridge.

The rain was coming down so heavily it was no longer possible to see through the window. There was no lightning and very little thunder, only the rain and a sense of terrible oppression as though something were lurking nearby.

Mrs. Bridge placed her napkin on the table and said, "Well, it looks like we're in for it."

Her husband continued eating.

"Steward, have you any further information?" she asked as soon as he had finished speaking to a couple at the next table.

The steward said the tornado was still approaching and he thought it would be a good idea to go to the basement.

"Thank you," said Mrs. Bridge, and looked expectantly at her husband.

"I'm going to finish this steak," said he.

The steward did not know quite how to proceed; he knew it was his responsibility to get everyone to the basement, and if Mr. and Mrs. Bridge should be swept up and carried away he would be called upon by the club directors for an explanation. On the other hand he did not care to begin giving orders to Mr. Bridge, who, he knew, was not only short-tempered but very much aware of having been warned. He gazed earnestly at Mr. Bridge, who paid no attention to him, and at last, unable to decide whether he was more afraid of him or of the club directors, the steward hurried off to the radio in hopes that the decision would be taken out of his hands by the course of the storm.

The lights of the dining room looked extraordinarily bright because of the unnatural darkness outside. There was a curious stillness and the rain fell in waves. Mrs. Bridge, looking about, saw that except for her husband and herself everyone had left the dining room.

"Don't you think we should go?" she asked.

He was chewing and unable to answer at the moment. He swallowed, wiped his lips with his napkin, took a drink of water, and began to butter a piece of cornbread. Finding that he did not have enough butter he began to frown. He liked butter very much and at home he got all he wanted, but whenever they

To hide and feel guilty would be the beginning of defeat.   —*Milan Kundera, 1978*

ate out he kept asking for more. Mrs. Bridge, who was on a diet, had already given him the butter from her plate, but this was not enough. Both of them looked around. There was not a waiter in sight.

"Well, I'll steal some from the next table," said Mrs. Bridge. "I don't suppose anyone will mind." And she got up and walked over to get a piece of butter for her husband. Fortunately there was an untouched square of it on the table and so she leaned across, holding her beads with one hand so they would not dip into the abandoned dishes, and picked up the butter plate. It was a small china plate with the crest of the country club stamped in gold and she thought as she picked it up how attractive it was. Just then the lights flickered. Apparently the tornado had struck a power line somewhere. Mrs. Bridge turned to go back to the table. She noticed the club steward standing in the doorway. He was watching them. He was wringing his hands and standing on one foot. She smiled politely, feeling a little foolish because of the butter plate in her hand. He smiled briefly and resumed staring at Mr. Bridge.

From the distance came a hooting, coughing sound, like a railroad locomotive in a tunnel; a very weird and frightening sound it was.

c. 200: Rome

THE DEPARTED

When a house is on the verge of ruin the mice in it, and the martens also, forestall its collapse and emigrate. This, you know, is what they say happened at Helike, for when the people of Helike treated so impiously the Ionians who had come to them, and murdered them at their altar, then it was (in the words of Homer) that "the gods showed forth wonders among them." For five days before Helike disappeared all the mice and martens and snakes and centipedes and beetles and every other creature of that kind in the town left in a body by the road that leads to Keryneia. And the people of Helike seeing this happening were filled with amazement but were unable to guess the reason. But after the aforesaid creatures had departed, an earthquake occurred in the night; the town collapsed; an immense wave poured over it; and Helike disappeared, while ten Lacedaemonian vessels that happened to be at anchor close by were destroyed together with the city I speak of.

Aelian, *from* On the Nature of Animals. *A teacher of rhetoric, Aelian earned the nickname Meliglōttos, meaning "honey-tongued," based on his fluency with Greek. In addition to his seventeen-volume work on animals, Aelian published* Indictment of the Effeminate, *a posthumous attack on the emperor Marcus Aurelius Antoninus, and a collection of fictional letters about Attic country life. Elsewhere in* Animals, *he describes the tradition of tuna fishermen to pray to Poseidon, whom they called "Averter of Disaster," asking for neither swordfish nor dolphin to destroy their nets.*

"Well, that must be the tornado," she said, listening attentively, but Mr. Bridge, who was eating the cornbread with great gusto, did not reply. She spread her napkin in her lap again although she had finished eating; she spread it because when she was a child her parents had taught her it was impolite to place her napkin on the table until everyone had finished, and the manners she had been taught she had, in her turn, passed on to her own children.

As the tornado approached the country club Mrs. Bridge remained seated across the table from her husband. She listened to the curious grunting and snuffling of the storm; although she had never been in the path of a tornado before, she knew this must be it, this must be the sound it made—the hooting, sucking roar of the vacuum. Now that it was so close it reminded her of a pig rooting on the terrace.

It did not occur to Mrs. Bridge to leave her husband and run to the basement. She had been brought up to believe without question that when a woman married she was married for the rest of her life and was meant to remain with her husband wherever he was, and under all circumstances, unless he directed her otherwise. She wished he would not be so obstinate; she wished he would behave like everyone else, but she was not particularly frightened. For nearly a quarter of a century she had done as he told her, and what he had said would happen had indeed come to pass, and what he had said would not occur had not occurred. Why, then, should she not believe him now?

The lights of the country club went out and she thought the breath was being drawn from her lungs. Short streaks of lightning flickered intermittently, illuminating a terrible cloud just outside—rushing toward them like a kettle of black water—and she caught the unmistakable odor of electricity. In darkness and silence she waited, uncertain whether the munching noise was made by her husband or the storm.

In a little while the lights came on again and the diners, led by the mayor, came up from the basement.

"There!" said Mr. Bridge, looking about for something else to eat. "I told you, didn't I?"

The tornado, whether impressed by his intransigence or touched by her devotion, had drawn itself up into the sky and was never seen or heard of again.

Evan S. Connell, *from* Mrs. Bridge. *While in Rome on their vacation, Mr. and Mrs. Bridge learn of the Nazi's invasion of Poland and quickly return home. Evan S. Connell was born in Kansas City, Missouri, in 1924 and served in the U.S. Navy during World War II. He published* Mrs. Bridge, *his debut novel, in 1959, and its companion,* Mr. Bridge, *a decade later. After his 1984 book on Custer and Little Bighorn,* Son of the Morning Star, *became a bestseller, Connell moved to New Mexico, where he lived until his death in 2013.*

1847: Rutland, VT

WANT OF FORESIGHT

All the greater known causes on climate are constant, and therefore we should be authorized to conclude that the cycles of our seasons would be regular and invariable. The heavenly bodies whose movements occasion the alternation of spring and summer and autumn and winter revolve in almost unchanging orbits; the constituents of the atmosphere have been precisely determined and are everywhere and at all times substantially the same. We have certainly as yet little cause to hope that climatic influences can ever be subject, in any important degree, to voluntary human modification or control. But though man cannot at his pleasure command the rain and the sunshine, the wind and frost and snow, yet it is certain that climate itself has in many instances been gradually changed and ameliorated or deteriorated by human action. The draining of swamps and the clearing of forests perceptibly effect the evaporation from the earth and, of course, the mean quantity of moisture suspended in the air. The same causes modify the electrical condition of the atmosphere and the power of the surface to reflect, absorb, and radiate the rays of the sun, and consequently influence the distribution of light and heat, and the force and direction of the winds. Within narrow limits too, domestic fires and artificial structures create and diffuse increased warmth, to an extent that may effect vegetation. The mean temperature of London is a degree or two higher than that of the surrounding country, and Peter Simon Pallas believed that the climate of even so thinly a peopled country as Russia was sensibly modified by similar causes. But though, in general, climatic influences are beyond our reach, their pernicious tendencies may sometimes be neutralized or overcome.

Devastation following a cyclone, Orissa, India, 1999. Photograph by Raghu Rai.

I desire to draw your special attention to the introduction of a better economy in the management of our forestlands. The increasing value of timber and fuel ought to teach us that trees are no longer what they were in our fathers' time, an encumbrance. We have undoubtedly already a larger proportion of cleared land in Vermont than would be required, with proper culture, for the support of a much greater population than we now possess, and every additional acre both lessens our means for thorough husbandry by disproportionately extending its area and deprives succeeding generations of what, though

The industrial world destroys nature not because it doesn't love it but because it is not afraid of it.

—*Mary Ruefle, 2012*

comparatively worthless to us, would be of great value to them. The inconveniences resulting from a want of foresight in the economy of the forest are already severely felt in many parts of New England and even in some of the older towns in Vermont. Steep hillsides and rocky ledges are well suited to the permanent growth of wood, but when in the rage for improvement they are improvidently stripped of this protection, the action of sun and wind and rain soon deprives them of their thin coating of vegetable mold, and this, when exhausted, cannot be restored by ordinary husbandry. They remain therefore barren and unsightly blots, producing neither grain nor grass, and yielding no crop but a harvest of noxious weeds to infest with their scattered seeds the richer arable grounds below. But this is by no means the only evil resulting from the injudicious destruction of the woods. The vernal and autumnal rains, and the melting snows of winter, no longer intercepted and absorbed by the leaves or the open soil of the woods, but falling everywhere upon a comparatively hard and even surface, flow swiftly over the smooth ground, washing away the vegetable mold as they seek their natural outlets, fill every ravine with a torrent, and convert every river into an ocean. The

suddenness and violence of our freshets increases in proportion as the soil is cleared; bridges are washed away, meadows swept of their crops and fences, and covered with barren sand, or themselves abraded by the fury of the current, and there is reason to fear that the valleys of many of our streams will soon be converted from smiling meadows into broad wastes of shingle and gravel and pebbles, deserts in summer, and seas in autumn and spring. The changes, which these causes have wrought in the physical geography of Vermont within a single generation are too striking to have escaped the attention of any observing person, and every middle-aged man who revisits his birthplace after a few years of absence looks upon another landscape than that which formed the theater of his youthful toils and pleasures. The signs of artificial improvement are mingled with the tokens of improvident waste, and the bald and barren hills, the dry beds of the smaller streams, the ravines furrowed out by the torrents of spring and the diminished thread of interval that skirts the widened channel of the rivers seem sad substitutes for the pleasant groves and brooks and broad meadows of his ancient paternal domain. If the present value of timber and land will not justify the artificial replanting of grounds injudiciously cleared, at least nature ought to be allowed to reclothe them with a spontaneous growth of wood. In many European countries the economy of the forest is regulated by law; but here, where public opinion determines, or rather in practice constitutes law, we can only appeal to an enlightened self-interest to introduce the reforms, check the abuses, and preserve us from an increase of the evils I have mentioned.

George Marsh, *from an address to the Agricultural Society of Rutland County. As a U.S. congressman from Vermont, Marsh helped found the Smithsonian Institution and design the Washington Monument. In 1861 he became an ambassador to the newly created Kingdom of Italy. A lifelong conservationist, Marsh published* Man and Nature *in 1864; it was one of the earliest texts arguing that human action could have significant and lasting effect on the environment. "Of all organic beings," Marsh wrote, "man alone is to be regarded as essentially a destructive power."*

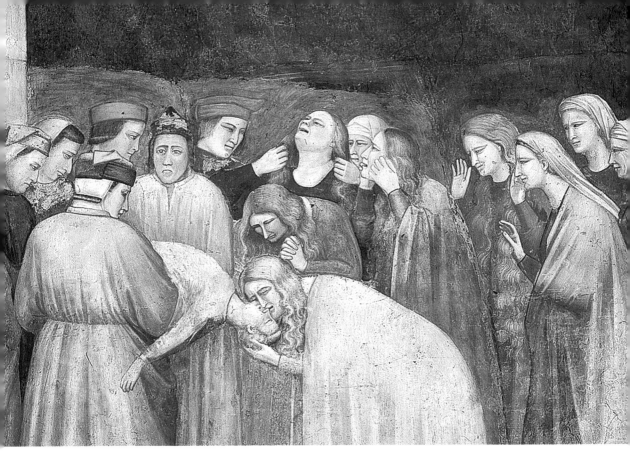

Boy killed by falling masonry, detail of a fresco from a series depicting the miracles of St. Francis of Assisi, School of Giotto, fourteenth century.

1986: Brigham City, UT

DISASTER MISMANAGEMENT

It's about noon at Thiokol space shuttle head-quarters. Several key engineers learned that temperatures around the *Challenger* shuttle launch pad in Cape Canaveral are unusually low, colder than they've ever been just before a launch. They meet hurriedly, urgently, in company hallways, and they all agreed that they've got to warn top management fast that the shuttle could be in serious trouble.

A handful of worried employees crowd around the desk of Vice President Robert Lund, and they lay out the evidence. If the temperatures in Florida don't get a lot warmer, they say, then the crucial seals that hold the rockets together might fail during takeoff.

"We all knew what the implication was without actually coming out and saying it," says one engineer. "We all knew if the seals failed, the shuttle would blow up."

Six P.M.: A bigger and more formal meeting in one of the company's main conference rooms. About a dozen engineers are there, along with four top managers, poring over charts and photographs of rocket seals and joints. They all agree that it's too risky for the shuttle to take off.

Eight P.M.: They call NASA officials over a special telephone conference network, and, one by one, four key Thiokol engineers lay out the troubling evidence.

Point number one: both NASA and company engineers have known for several years that when the shuttle starts to take off, tremendous forces warp the joints where sections of the solid rockets fit together, and some of those crucial seals don't work right.

Point number two: the colder the weather, the worse the seals work. In fact, they emphasize, when the shuttle took off in January 1985 in 53-degree temperatures, the coldest it has ever been until now, half of the seals in both solid rockets were damaged.

Point number three: Thiokol's own laboratory studies show that as temperatures drop below 50 degrees, the seals dramatically lose their ability to hold the rockets together. And tomorrow at Cape Canaveral, the engineers warn, it's going to be only around 30 degrees.

Thiokol executive Bob Lund wraps up the presentation to NASA with the company's official recommendation: "Do not launch the shuttle tomorrow."

The NASA officials listening on the telephone lines are shocked. "I am appalled," says George Hardy of NASA's Marshall Space Flight Center in Huntsville, Alabama. "I am appalled by your recommendation."

A grim specter has crept upon us almost unnoticed, and this imagined tragedy may easily become a stark reality we all shall know.
—Rachel Carson, 1962

Another top Marshall official, Larry Mulloy, argues with the Thiokol engineers. He challenges their figures. He says the company doesn't have firm enough proof that the seals will fail in cold weather. But Thiokol engineers vehemently disagree, at some points almost shouting with anger. They insist that NASA should postpone the launch until the weather climbs into the fifties.

And at that point, NASA's Mulloy exclaims, "My God, Thiokol, when do you want me to launch—next April?"

It's 8:30 P.M. now. Thiokol managers put NASA on hold on the telephone network and they ask their staff engineers one more time, "You're sure about all this?"

"Absolutely," the engineers say. And virtually no one in the conference room disagrees. But now Thiokol's general manager, Jerry Mason, speaks up. "Look," he says, "this has got to be a management decision."

So while a dozen engineers look on, fuming with anger, Mason asks the three other managers what they want to do. They each nod, okay, let's go ahead with the launch.

"Who knows why our managers overruled us?" one engineer will later reflect. "Our company's competing with several other corporations to get future shuttle contracts. I can only guess at the enormous pressures they were feeling."

8:45 P.M.: Thiokol general manager Mason takes NASA officials off hold and he tells them, "Okay, we'll approve the launch after all."

"Then sign the document right away," NASA's Mulloy tells them, "and send it to us by telefax."

Although one top Thiokol manager, who's been taking part in the conference call from the cape, refuses to sign the paper, the meeting breaks up. The engineers go home feeling downtrodden and defeated and terribly worried.

"I kept having fantasies that night," says one engineer, "that at the moment of ignition, the shuttle would blow up, instantly. See, we thought that if the seals failed, the shuttle would never get off the pad. There'd just be a big fireball and everything would vanish. I was so scared, I didn't even want to watch the launch."

But the next morning the engineer joins fifty other colleagues back at company headquarters in the same conference room where they'd argued the night before. They're all watching the countdown together on a large projection TV.

"When the shuttle lifted off the pad," he says, "I thought, 'Gee, it's going all right. It's a piece of cake.' And when we were one minute into the launch, a friend turned to me and he said, 'Oh God, we made it! We made it!' Then a few seconds later, the shuttle blew up. And we all knew exactly what happened."

Daniel Zwerdling, *a report on National Public Radio. Three weeks after the* Challenger *space shuttle exploded on January 28, 1986, killing all seven astronauts on board, Zwerdling and fellow NPR reporters broke the story that engineers at contractor Morton Thiokol had tried to warn NASA. Zwerdling's source, engineer Roger Boisjoly, had even written a memo six months earlier to his managers predicting "a catastrophe of the highest order." It was ignored. "I'm very angry that nobody listened," Boisjoly later told Zwerdling. "We were talking to the people who had the power to stop that launch."*

1756: Königsberg

NATURAL CAUSES

The sight of so many wretched people as the latest catastrophe caused among our fellow citizens ought to arouse our philanthropy and make us feel some of the misfortune that afflicted them with such cruelty. But we go against this very much if we always regard this sort of destiny as a punishment meted out, which afflicts the destroyed cities on account of their evil deeds, and if we regard these unfortunates as the target of God's vengeance over whom his justice pours out all its wrath. This kind of judgment is a culpable impertinence that arrogates to itself the ability to understand the intentions behind divine decisions and to interpret them according to its own opinions.

Man is so opinionated that he sees only himself as the object of God's activities, just as if the latter had only him to take account of in devising the appropriate measures for the ruling of the world. We know that the whole essence of nature is a worthy object of divine wisdom and its activities. We are a part of this and try to be all of it. The rules of perfection in nature at large are regarded as irrelevant, and everything is to be seen merely in relation to ourselves. All the things in the world that provide comfort and pleasure, people imagine to be there only for our sakes, and nature supposedly does not undertake any changes that might be any sort of cause for discomfort for mankind except to punish us, threaten us, or to wreak vengeance on us.

Nonetheless, we see that an infinite number of evildoers sleep in peace, the earthquakes have shattered certain countries since time immemorial with total indifference to the old and new inhabitants, that Christian Peru is shaken just as much as the heathen part, and that many cities have been spared this devastation from the beginning, cities that could not presume to be any less punishable than others that were destroyed.

Thus man is in the dark when he tries to guess the intentions that God envisages in the ruling of the world. We are, however, in no doubt when it is a question of applying these ways of providence in accordance with its purpose. Man is not born to build everlasting dwellings on this stage of vanity. Since his entire life has a far nobler aim, how well does this harmonize with all the destruction fit into this that allows us to see the transience of the world in even those things that seem to us the greatest and most important and to remind us that the goods of this world cannot provide any satisfaction for our desire for happiness.

I am in no way implying that man is subject to an unchanging fate of natural laws without respect to his particular virtues. That same supreme wisdom from which the course of nature derives the accuracy that requires no correction has subordinated lower purposes to higher ones, and in just those intentions in which the former has often made the most significant exceptions to the general rules of nature in order to attain those infinitely higher aims that far surpass all the resources of nature, in those intentions the leaders of the human race will also prescribe laws in their government of the world to regulate even the course of natural things. When a city or country perceives the disaster with which divine providence terrifies it or its neighbors, can there be any doubt as to the party it should support in order to prevent the threatened destruction, and will the signs still be ambiguous that make those comprehensible intentions to whose implementation all the paths of providence unanimously either invite or drive mankind?

Immanuel Kant, *from "On the Causes of Earthquakes on the Occasion of the Calamity that Befell the Western Countries of Europe Toward the End of Last Year." On November 1, 1755—All Saint's Day—an earthquake and tsunami hit Lisbon; seventy thousand people died. Churches were destroyed and many faithful killed, while brothels and sinners were spared. Kant's insistence on secular explanations defied the widespread theological interpretation of the day. The Enlightenment philosopher spent his entire life in Königsberg, never traveling more than sixty miles from his place of birth.*

c. 1180: Hekla

FIRE AND BRIMSTONE

In the north there is known to be a great island called Iceland belonging to the Christian faith. There is found a certain steep and enormous mountain taking up a large part of that country, beneath and in which the inhabitants believe the greatest inferno exists. This mountain, full of caverns and hollow and all burning and belching flame, stands in a perpetual blaze, which spreads over the mountain and wastes it outside and inside right down to its base and even beyond it. Assured

The fact that a cloud from a minor volcanic eruption in Iceland—a small disturbance in the complex mechanism of the earth—can bring aerial traffic to a standstill over an entire continent is a reminder of how, with all its tremendous activity of transforming nature, humankind remains just another living species on the planet.

—Slavoj Žižek, 2011

evidence proves that this same terrible fire lives and rages not only beneath the base of the mountain but also beneath the bottom of the sea. That famous fire kettle in Sicily, which is called the vent of Hell and to which, as has often been proved, the souls of the dying, condemned to burn, are daily dragged—men say that that is only like a little stove in comparison with this immense pit of Hell. Inside this terrifying chasm in the mountain is such a conflagration that pillars of flame rise up everywhere, manifold and huge, and reach right up to the clouds, and when they sink down again, others always rise up in their stead, as when the fierce burning of a raging fire stirs up the coals, shooting some up and swallowing others, so that that part of the heavens always appears to be ablaze. Moreover, in these fireballs there are seen to be rocks like mountain crags, which the savagery of the

fire has torn up from the belly of the abyss and flung with great force up into the air, but which afterward because of their weight sink down again into the chasm. Nor do I think it proper to pass over in silence the fact that this hellfire sometimes, albeit rarely, exceeds its bounds. In our time it has been seen that it erupted so furiously that it destroyed most of the surrounding land. It burned not only towns and all buildings but also plants and trees down to the roots and even the ground itself with its very bones. And, marvelous to relate, mountains of stone, even mountains of metal, were melted utterly like wax in this fire—they ran over the earth and covered it, so that the valleys were filled with the mire and hill land was leveled with the plain. The molten rocks, having run out over the earth in all directions, were thus dispersed when the fire abated, and then the surface of the earth appeared as if it were of marble and like a street paved with stone, and what was previously land inhabitable and fertile was reduced to desert. When in its insatiable greed this most cruel fire had destroyed this land and all that was in it, then it yielded a still more terrible marvel for it invaded the sea on the shore. And when it reached the deep sea, it began to burn and consume the water with unheard-of fury right down to the depths. In addition to this, it carried with it in its course huge fragments of mountains and hills, overthrown by other devouring fire, so that as the waters withdrew, their place was filled with land, and mountains were carried into the heart of the sea. And when they had completely filled the sea both far and wide and made the depths of ocean level with the shore, the sea became dry land, so that where there had previously been water there was now firm ground for twelve miles, and perhaps it is there still. Moreover, in this conflagration was destroyed a famous and populous city, and an excellent port, which it had on an arm of the sea, was also destroyed, as it is established, when the sea dried up. It is also to be understood that this perpetual fire is known to be not only under

The Kent Fire (detail), by Théodore Gudin, 1828.

the base of the mountain, as we have touched upon earlier, but also under the bottom of the sea. For fire is often seen to spout up in fury from the depths of the ocean, high over the waves, burning fish and all living things in the sea, igniting and consuming ships and sailors unless they speedily save themselves by flight. What is more marvelous than these marvels, or what can be conceived more terrible? Who is now so perverse and incredulous that he will not believe that eternal fire exists to make souls suffer, when with his own eyes he sees that fire of which we now speak burn in such fearful fashion not only the ground and marbly rocks, but also the invincible water that is accustomed to extinguish other fire

with such ease? But those who will not believe in the punishments of eternal fire prepared for the devil and his angels, nor hear of them, they will afterward be themselves cast among those torments that they disdain to avoid while there is yet time.

Herbert of Clairvaux, *from his* Book of Miracles. *Chaplain in the monastery at Clairvaux and later archbishop of Torres in Sardinia, Herbert was the author of three surviving manuscripts containing accounts of religious visions and miracles, though only* Book of Miracles *has been preserved intact. Believed in the medieval period to be the entrance to hell, Hekla erupted more than twenty times between 1104 and 2000, with eruptions sometimes lasting more than a year. An earlier medieval chronicle claimed the volcano to be the prison of Judas Iscariot.*

1978: Turin

WORDS OF CAUTION

Since the anguish of each belongs to us all
We're still living yours, scrawny little girl
Clinging convulsively to your mother
As if you wanted to get back inside her
When the sky went black that afternoon.
To no avail, because the sky, turned poison,
Infiltrated the shut windows of your quiet
House with its thick walls to find you
Happy before in your song and timid laughter.
The centuries have passed, the ash has turned to stone,
Locking in these gentle limbs forever.
So you stay with us, contorted plaster cast,
Endless agony, horrific witness
To how our proud seed matters to the gods.
But there's nothing left for us of your faraway sister,
The girl from Holland walled up in four walls
Who wrote about her childhood without a tomorrow:
Her quiet ashes have been spread by the wind,
Her brief life held inside a crumpled notebook.
Nothing's left of the Hiroshima schoolgirl,
Shadow transfixed on the wall by the light of a thousand suns,
Victim sacrificed on the altar of fear.
Masters of the earth, lords of new poisons,
Sad secret guardians of definitive thunder,
The afflictions heaven offers us are sufficient.
Stop and consider before you push the button.

Primo Levi, *"The Girl of Pompeii." Arrested for his involvement with
Italian partisans during World War II, Levi was sent to Auschwitz,
where he worked in a synthetic-rubber factory that used prisoners
for slave labor. Soviet troops liberated the camp eleven months after
Levi's arrival, and he made his way home to Turin by foot and by
train. He published* If This Is a Man *in 1947 and* The Periodic
Table *in 1975. "If I hadn't had the experience of Auschwitz," Levi
said, "I probably would not have written anything."*

Two-headed *wanyugo* helmet mask, Côte d'Ivoire, nineteenth or early twentieth century. The mask's wooden warthog tusks represent the disorder in Senufo society resulting from supernatural and human malevolence.

c. 65: Rome

SUPERFLUOUS TORMENT

There are more things, Lucilius, likely to frighten us than there are to crush us; we suffer more often in imagination than in reality. I am not speaking with you in the Stoic strain but in my milder style. For it is our Stoic fashion to speak of all those things that provoke cries and groans as unimportant and beneath notice. But you and I must drop such great-sounding words, although heaven knows they are true enough. What I advise you to do is not to be unhappy before the crisis comes, since it may be that the dangers before which you paled as if they were threatening you will never come upon you; they certainly have not yet come. Accordingly, some things torment us more than they ought; some torment us before they ought; and some torment us when they ought not to torment us at all. We are in the habit of exaggerating, imagining, or anticipating sorrow.

Let us then look carefully into the matter. It is likely that some troubles will befall us, but it is not a present fact. How often has the unexpected happened! How often has the expected never come to pass! And even though it is ordained to be, what does it avail to run out to meet your suffering? You will suffer soon enough when it arrives, so look forward meanwhile to better things. What shall you gain by doing this? Time. There will be many happenings meanwhile that will serve to postpone, end, or pass on to another person the trials that are near or even in your very presence. A fire has opened the way to flight. Men have been let down softly by a catastrophe. Sometimes the sword has been checked even at the victim's throat. Men have survived their own executioners. Even bad fortune is fickle. Perhaps it will come, perhaps not. In the meantime it is not. So look forward to better things.

The mind at times fashions for itself false shapes of evil when there are no signs that point to any evil. It twists into the worst construction some word of doubtful meaning. Or it fancies some person's grudge to be more serious than it really is, considering not how angry the enemy is, but to what lengths he may go if he is angry. But life is not worth living, and there is no limit to our sorrows if we indulge our fears to the greatest possible extent. In this matter let prudence help you, and contemn fear with a resolute spirit even when it is in plain sight. If you cannot do this, counter one weakness with another and temper your fear with hope. There is nothing so certain among these objects of fear that it is not more certain still that things we dread sink into nothing and that things we hope for mock us.

Seneca, *from* Moral Letters to Lucilius. *After being exiled to Corsica by Claudius in 41, Seneca was recalled to Rome in 49 and made the tutor of Nero, whom he later served as a political adviser. His essayistic epistles to Lucilius, a fellow member of Nero's imperial staff, detail much of Seneca's Stoic philosophy. In 65 Nero demanded that he commit suicide for purported involvement in a conspiracy. Seneca slit his veins, dictated a dissertation, drank hemlock, and died in a vapor bath.*

Voices in Time

SURVIVAL

2003: Fort Irwin, CA

TOM BISSELL BRACES FOR IMPACT

NASA's Deep Space Network antennas at the Goldstone Deep Space Communications Complex are spread out along twenty-six miles on the grounds of Fort Irwin, a U.S. Army training center in the desert wastes between Los Angeles and Las Vegas. I am traveling to the complex, which is fenced off from the surrounding military base, with Steve Ostro, a radar astronomer who works out of NASA's Jet Propulsion Laboratory, in Pasadena, California. Ostro is a handsome, southern-California-fit man in his early fifties. His resemblance to a more dashing version of Russell Johnson's Professor from *Gilligan's Island* is spoiled very slightly by his glasses, which although not unflattering are as thick as bulletproof glass.

For the last several years Ostro has been coming to Goldstone to map by radar our solar system's larger known asteroids. Goldstone's centerpiece antenna is the DSS-14. Inside the lab housed in the antenna's pedestal I meet Lance Benner, John Giorgini, and Ray Jurgens, JPL scientists adept in the different areas of astronomy and planetary science that allow the team to apply an astonishing interpretive breadth to the antenna's radar readings. Jurgens, the oldest of the men, seems to be providing a good deal of support merely by standing on the lab's fringes and quietly observing. All of them are distracted, as the antenna's transmit-receive cycle is about to begin. I stand to the side, staring at a few taped-up

Miners' Wives, by Ben Shahn, c. 1948.

computer-generated images of Goldstone-mapped asteroids.

The lab's equipment appears, to me, strangely antiquated. Somehow our technology improves but gets no closer to the touch-screen sleekness of cinematic futurism. Little red and white lights blink on the hulking computers' faces alongside small screens active with greenish waveforms. A spray of cables hangs from seemingly every panel. Jurgens, who has worked at Goldstone since the 1970s, walks over and explains that much of this equipment is twenty years old. Later inquiries as to how adequately NASA funds Goldstone's radar astronomy work—it is about one ten-thousandth of NASA's overall budget—will result in meaningful silences.

This world is a comedy to those that think, a tragedy to those that feel.
—Horace Walpole, 1776

Ostro escorts me to another computer at the room's far end, the real-time sawtooth display of which will soon show us the electromagnetic Doppler frequency the antenna is receiving back from the asteroid. This information will be used, Ostro explains, to calculate the asteroid's orbit uncertainty. "We go through this process where we have a projected orbit. We see how good the prediction was, and then we make a better orbit and a new prediction of uncertainty. There's always uncertainty, and that's one of the really interesting domains of this whole problem. What is the uncertainty, and how do we reduce it? That's why we're here."

I am here, I remind him, to find out about the chances of one of these asteroids colliding with Earth. But this is where the uncertainty comes in, he tells me. Every asteroid travels along a path we can determine using orbital trajectories, but within that trajectory there exists an error ellipse in which we cannot be sure where the asteroid will be. This ellipse can be many hundreds of thousands of miles in width, which makes reducing the uncertainty of an object that passes near Earth that much more

important. Asteroid 1997 XF11, the asteroid we will be observing today, has a curious history of uncertainty. Five years ago, 1997 XF11 was predicted to have a small but nonzero chance of hitting Earth in 2028. Whether this was due to hasty "back of the envelope" calculations or a real uncertainty in its error ellipse is still debated. What is known is that the media frenzy was so immediate ("Killer Asteroids!") that NASA created a Near-Earth Objects Office to handle future impact threats. It was later determined that 1997 XF11 had no chance of hitting Earth, and before the day ends we will know everything else there is to know about this defanged rock.

"A lot of the confusion about this topic," Ostro goes on, "ultimately comes down to miscommunication. All of this is unfamiliar and intrinsically arcane and inaccessible and beyond the experience of humanity." I ask Ostro if he personally worries about the day they discover an asteroid that has a high probability of hitting Earth. He is silent for such a long time that I ask again. "Let me rephrase your question," he says. "Is there a God?" After some uncomfortable laughter on my part, Ostro tells me about 1950 DA, the only large asteroid currently known that has a nonzero chance of colliding with Earth before the next millennium. If it does strike, it will impact the North Atlantic just off the U.S. coast in March 2880. "It's a little bit of a stretch to say it might hit Earth—the probability is one in three hundred—but it's the most dangerous object we know. Now, do we care about that? Should anybody care at all about the fact that an asteroid might hit Earth nearly a millennium from now?"

I imagine standing in a room with three hundred people, then being told that one of us will be taken outside and shot. I tell Ostro that I think I can care about that.

"What if I had said, 'Well, we found an object that has a pretty good chance of hitting Earth in 500,000 years.' Would that concern you? Should we care about that?"

I admit that I have a hard time gathering the emotional momentum that allows my concern to travel ahead a half million years.

Cape Coral #1, Lee County, Florida, USA, 2012, by Edward Burtynsky.

Ostro nods. "What it comes down to is that this is a very new kind of topic, and it's hard to get one's bearings thinking about it, much less for society to decide whether to worry and spend money on it. And if so, how much, and how?"

The lab's small, encaged red light begins to flash in alert: the antenna is finally transmitting its half-million-watt, pencil-thin beam of energy seven million miles into deep space. Its round-trip time back to Goldstone will take a little under eighty seconds. As we wait, I find myself thinking of Whitman's "When I Heard the Learn'd Astronomer." In the poem Walt grows so "tired and sick" of an astronomer's "charts and diagrams" that he goes out "in the mystical moist night-air, and from time to time,/ Look'd up in perfect silence at the stars." I wonder what poem he might have written had he known that some of those stars had the

potential to end poetry, and everything else, for all time.

In its journey around the sun, Earth passes through the orbits of twenty million asteroids. Many of these Earth-crossers are called near-Earth asteroids. NEAs much smaller than 100 meters wide are basically undetectable but for a fluke of stargazing luck; unfortunately, an object of only, say, 90 meters possesses the collisional capability of roughly 30 megatons of explosive energy, a figure that is dreadful but globally manageable. NEAs larger than 100 meters are thought to number 100,000, a fraction of which have been located; in the event of an impact these could effect serious global climate change. Around 20,000 NEAs are large enough, individually, to annul a country the size of the Czech Republic. The number of NEAs bigger than one kilometer in diameter is currently thought to be around 1,000. At astronomers' current rate of

1946: Paris

SCARE STORY

They asked me what I thought of the atomic bomb. I said I had not been able to take any interest in it.

I like to read detective and mystery stories. I never get enough of them but whenever one of them is or was about death rays and atomic bombs I never could read them. What is the use, if they are really as destructive as all that there is nothing left and if there is nothing there nobody to be interested and nothing to be interested about. If they are not as destructive as all that then they are just a little more or less destructive than other things and that means that in spite of all destruction there are always lots left on this earth to be interested or to be willing and the thing that destroys is just one of the things that concerns the people inventing it or the people starting it off, but really nobody else can do anything about it so you have to just live along like always, so you see the atomic bomb is not at all interesting, not any more interesting than any other machine, and machines are only interesting in being invented or in what they do, so why be interested. I never could take any interest in the atomic bomb, I just couldn't any more than in everybody's secret weapon. That it has to be secret makes it dull and meaningless. Sure it will destroy a lot and kill a lot, but it's the living that are interesting not the way of killing them, because if there were not a lot left living how could there be any interest in destruction. Alright, that is the way I feel about it. And really way down that is the way everybody feels about it. They think they are interested about the atomic bomb but they really are not not any more than I am. Really not. They may be a little scared, I am not so scared, there is so much to be scared of so what is the use of bothering to be scared, and if you are not scared the atomic bomb is not interesting.

Everybody gets so much information all day long that they lose their common sense. They listen so much that they forget to be natural. This is a nice story.

Gertrude Stein, *"Reflection on the Atomic Bomb." Raised in Oakland, Stein moved to Paris in 1903. Her fractured writing style was influenced by cubist painting. "Look here," she said in a 1934 radio interview, "being intelligible is not what it seems." In 1947, the year after her death, the* Yale Poetry Review *posthumously published this piece, which one newspaper announced with the headline:* GERTRUDE STEIN SAID ATOM BOMB DULL, MEANINGLESS.

detection—roughly one a day—a survey of the entire population of one-kilometer NEAs will be complete within the next decade.

This one-kilometer threshold is important, for asteroids above it are known as "civilization-enders." They would do so first by the kinetic energy of their impact, striking with a velocity hitherto unknown in human history. The typical civilization-ender would be traveling roughly 20 kilometers a second, or 45,000 miles per hour—for visualization's sake, this is more than fifty times faster than your average bullet—producing an impact fireball several miles wide that, very briefly, would be as hot as the surface of the sun. If the asteroid hit land, a haze of dust and asteroidal sulfates would enshroud the entire stratosphere. This, combined with the soot from the worldwide forest fire the impact's thermal radiation would more or less instantaneously trigger, would plunge Earth into a cosmic winter lasting anywhere from three months to six years. Global agriculture would be terminated, and horrific greenhousing of the climate and mass starvation would quickly ensue, to say nothing of the likely event of world war—over the best caves, say. In the event of a ten-kilometer impact, everything within the ocean's photic zone, including food-chain-vital phytoplankton, would die, but this would hardly matter, as the deadly atmospheric production of nitrogen oxides, which would fall as acid rain, would for the next decade poison every viable body of water on Earth. Chances are, however, that the impact would be a water strike, as 72 percent of meteorite landings are thought to have been. This scenario is little better. A one-kilometer impact would, in seconds, evaporate as many as 700 cubic kilometers of water, shooting a tower of steam several miles high and thousands of degrees hot into the atmosphere, once again blotting out incoming solar radiation and triggering cosmic winter. The meteorite itself would most likely plunge straight to the ocean floor, opening up a crater five kilometers deep, its blast wave cracking open Earth's crust to uncertain seismic effect. The resultant tsunami, radiating outward in every direction from the point of impact, would begin as a wall of water as high as the ocean is deep. If a coastal dweller were to look up and see this wave coming he or she would be killed seconds later, as it would be traveling as fast as a 747.

Nearly half of the asteroids believed capable of destroying one quarter of humanity currently remain uninventoried. Not until 1998 did the U.S. Congress direct NASA to identify, by 2008, 90 percent of all asteroids and comets greater than one kilometer in diameter with orbits approaching Earth. Unfortunately, the government agency—of any government, anywhere—that would react to and be expected to deal with the likelihood of an asteroid impact does not currently exist. The impact threat is what Ostro calls "low probability and high consequence," and bureaucracies scatter like roaches from the kitchen-bright possibility of severe consequences. We need only to consider the disgraceful games of administrative duck-duck-goose played in the aftermath of comparatively smaller disasters, such as the terrorist attacks of September 2001, to recognize the federal unwillingness to counter its own congenital laxity.

Reading about asteroid impacts will undoubtedly cause many people distress. I feel bad about that, and I would like to say that although these threats are terrifying all is not lost. Concerned, dedicated people are working on the asteroid-impact threat, and one need not be a

A Deluge, by Leonardo da Vinci, c. 1517.

deluded idealist to believe that they may succeed. Hope, after all, takes as its foundation not likelihood but possibility. There is, however, another threat to ourselves and our civilization, one that cannot be stopped or avoided. You readers who find yourselves already traumatized, let me entreat you here, please, to stop reading.

Comets differ from asteroids in several ways. Consensus holds that they are "dirty snowballs" made up of ice and carbon-bearing rock. Before the comet Hyakutake was found in 1996, only five previous comets had been detected, by radar. Traveling like frozen freight

On great emergencies,
The law must be remodeled or amended.
*   —Lord Byron, 1821*

trains along the loneliest edges of the solar system, comets occasionally enter the inner solar system, the neighborhood of Earth, at twenty-six miles a second, leaving behind them a long tail of dust and gas crystals that can stretch back as far as sixty million miles. Replacement dust accumulates on cometary surfaces; when the dust layer becomes thick enough, comets gain an excellent shield against solar heating. An icy skein builds and they get bigger. One comet-like object, Quaoar, recently found floating out around Pluto, is eight hundred miles across. As comets approach the sun, however, their frozen gases expand and form makeshift jets that can alter their course. This makes predicting accurate orbits of newly discovered comets nearly impossible. But discovering them is also challenging. They are too fast, not typically seen until they pass near the sun, and in any event their gas- and dust-obscured passage across the universe's dark, starry backfield is often difficult to discern.

We know of two types of comets. The closest to Earth, called short-period comets, are found just beyond Neptune in the Kuiper Belt. Long-period comets make up what is known as the Oort cloud—an envelope of as many as a trillion comets that travel around the sun far beyond Pluto. Almost all long-period comets have

orbital periods of 100,000 years or more, making it all but certain that there are literally millions of comets with periodic near-Earth passes we know nothing about. We could have as little as three months' warning when a comet on a collision course with Earth appears in the sky. Most are too big to stop with nuclear weapons, which does not much matter, as their meddled-with, chaotic trajectories make intercepting them fantasy.

Scientists are divided on whether the K-T mass extinction sixty-five million years ago was caused by a comet or an asteroid. The severity of the event—miles of evaporated ocean; the very high chance that a hundred trillion tons of molten rock were thrown into space, frozen, and then pulled back down to the surface of Earth in the form of more impacting meteorites; an ozone layer so shredded that any creature peeking out of its cave even a year after the impact would have found its skin on fire in the ultraviolet spring; the sheer number of extinctions—points to a comet. It is empirically inarguable that every few dozen million years a mass extinction is visited upon Earth. Various arguments place these mass extinctions, the extent and agencies of which are still debated, at intervals ranging from twenty-six million to thirty million years. A theory called the "Shiva Hypothesis," named after the Hindu god of destruction, holds that mass extinctions occur in startling simultaneity with the movement of our solar system through the galactic plane, a passage that is thought to perturb millions of Oort-cloud comets into our path. Comets, and the mass extinctions they cause, might very well be the piston that drives Earth's biological processes. If the Shiva Hypothesis is correct, we are all just marking time until the next comet arrives.

From "A Comet's Tale." "Life is a huge blackboard filled with a million marks of chalk," Tom Bissell writes elsewhere in this essay, which first appeared in Harper's Magazine. "Every thirty million years that chalkboard is forcefully wiped clean, leaving only a few small smudges in the corners, whereupon life begins again." Bissell is the author of nine books, including Apostle: Travels Among the Tombs of the Twelve.

125 BC: North Africa

INVASIVE SPECIES

Scarcely had Africa quieted down from the ravages of war when a horrible and unusual destruction came upon it. For when great numbers of locusts had gathered over all Africa and had not only destroyed all hope of crops, but had consumed all plants with parts of their roots, and the foliage of trees with their tender branches, and had even gnawed the bitter bark and dry wood, being swept away by a sudden wind and driven into masses and carried through the air for a long time, they were finally plunged into the African Sea. When, as the waters forced large masses of these a long distance and drove them far and wide along a wide expanse of the shore, the decaying and putrefying masses gave forth a foul and noxious odor beyond belief, from which followed so great a pestilence of all living beings alike that the putrefying bodies of birds, cattle, and wild beasts everywhere destroyed by the contaminated air increased the destruction of the pestilence. Moreover, as I relate these things, I shudder with my whole body at the great destruction of human beings that took place. Indeed in Numidia, where at that time Micipsa was king, it is handed down that 800,000 men perished, and along the maritime coast that lies especially close to Carthage and Utica more than 200,000, and at the city of Utica itself 30,000 soldiers who had been stationed there for the protection of all Africa were destroyed and wiped out. This calamity was so sudden and so violent that at Utica at that time, in one day through one gate, more than 1,500 bodies of the youth are said to have been carried out for burial. Nevertheless, by the amity and grace of the omnipotent God, I should say, by whose mercy and in whose trust I speak these words: although even in our time locusts have sprung up on occasions in different places, and for the most part with tolerable damage, yet never in Christian times has so great a force of inextricable evil taken place that the calamity of the locusts, which could not have been endured when alive, did more harm when dead, and while they lived all was destined to perish, and when they were destroyed all on the point of death would have preferred that the locusts had not perished.

> **Orosius**, *from* Seven Books of History Against the Pagans. *Paulus Orosius left his home in Portugal and arrived in 414 in Hippo, where he studied with St. Augustine, who asked him to write a history of calamity as proof that recent disasters (including the fall of Rome) had not been caused by Christianity. Writing that the pagans "either forget or do not know the past," Orosius set about chronicling "ravages of disease or sorrows of famine or horrors of earthquakes or of unusual floods or dreadful outbreaks of fire or cruel strokes of lightning."*

Displaced, by Manuel Cunjamá, 2000.

Human remains from a mass grave discovered in a desert on the outskirts of Musayyib, Iraq, 2003. The victims were executed by Saddam Hussein's regime following the 1991 Shia uprising. Photograph by Marco Di Lauro.

1945: Hiroshima

SKY SPLIT OPEN

On the morning of the sixth, I happened to be near Mukainada, walking toward Hiroshima.

It was a fine morning, windless and sultry, typical for the area around Hiroshima. The midsummer morning sunlight filled the sky to the point of overflowing. The brilliance of the light glinting off the mist in the blue sky was almost painful. The air-raid alert had been lifted about thirty minutes or an hour before and I was walking absentmindedly along the dusty paved road. I came to the east side of Shin'ozu Bridge. I stopped there for a minute, and just as I looked toward the sea and noticed the way the waves were sparkling, I saw, or rather felt, an enormous bluish white flash of light, as when a photographer lights a dish of magnesium. Off to my right the sky split open over the city of Hiroshima. I instinctively flung myself face down onto the ground.

I lay there without moving. Then I raised my head and looked up over the city. To the west, in the sky that had been blue a minute before, I saw a mass of white clouds—or was it smoke? Whichever it was, it had taken shape in an instant. Then a halo of sparkling lights, a little bit like the ring that forms around the moon as a sign of rain, appeared near the cloud mass and expanded like a rainbow. The outer edges of the white cloud mass rolled down and curled inward toward the center while the entire shape ballooned out to the sides.

Immediately another mountain of clouds, accompanied by a huge column of red flame like lava from a volcano that had erupted in midair, formed under the first cloud mass. I don't know how to describe it. A massive cloud column defying all description appeared, boiling violently and seething upward. It was so big it blotted out much of the blue sky. Then the top of it began to spill down, like the breakup of some vast thundercloud, and the whole thing started to seep out and spread to the sides. The first cloud mass set down a foot like a huge waterspout, suddenly growing into the form of a monstrous mushroom. The two immense masses of clouds, one above the other, then rapidly formed into a single vast column of vapor, reaching all the way to the ground. Its shape was constantly changing and its colors were kaleidoscopic. Here and there it glittered with some small explosion.

I thought it must be a manifestation of the *shumisen* cosmos that is supposed to exist at an astronomical distance from the earth, the one the ancient Buddhists of India talked about. But the drawings of *shumisen*, as I recalled them to mind, paled into insignificance. I tried to visualize the cloud pillar seen by Moses that is mentioned in the Old Testament, but I couldn't. The unsophisticated concepts and fantasies dreamed up by the ancients were useless to describe this horrible pageant of clouds and lights staged in the firmament.

For a moment I was in a trance, struck dumb. But the reality of the war that was in progress soon jolted me back to awareness. I tried to remember what little I had previously read or heard about bombs and other weapons. It couldn't have been flares at this time of day, I said to myself. I was sure it was neither incendiaries nor conventional bombs. In any case, I didn't see any aircraft. What was that flash of light? Those clouds? Maybe it was some kind of flame projection, or a death ray?

At the thought of a "death ray," my body tensed as if electricity had suddenly surged through it. Though I had heard the phrase before, I had no idea what it actually meant. I was filled with dread.

I glanced at my watch. It was just past 8:15 A.M. Just then there was a dull but tremendous roar as a crushing blast of air pressure assailed me.

I kept still, stretched out flat on the ground. At the moment of the roar and the blast I had heard tremendous ripping, slamming, and crashing sounds as houses and buildings were torn apart. I also thought I had heard screams. But these may simply have drifted into my memory later, or been products of my imagination.

However, I definitely did hear people crying afterward, "What's that?" "What happened?" And I saw people rushing from their houses out into the streets. I got up and looked around. I didn't see any houses in ruins then, nor any fires. I only saw figures running into the street. From where I stood at the foot of Shin'ozu Bridge,

I can't go on, I'll go on.
—*Samuel Beckett, 1953*

a wide road led right toward the city of Hiroshima. There were only a few houses nearby, at either end of the bridge. So it was easy for me to see people scattering like ants from a hill that had been kicked aside.

My thoughts were racing as a half-buried memory rose to mind: a roaring sound and a huge blast; a flash of light and ballooning clouds. An ammunition-depot explosion!

That's it! I'd forgotten how many years before they had occurred, but I recalled cases of depots exploding in Hirakata in Osaka Prefecture and in Uji in Kyoto Prefecture.

I learned later that I was not the only one who came up with a mistaken explanation. There were a lot of proponents of the "death ray" theory. A naval officer told some people that the explosion had been caused by an "aerial mine." I heard that theories about an ammunition-depot explosion, a gas-tank explosion, or a fuel-storage-depot fire were popular not only among laymen but also with a considerable number of so-called experts. It seems I was in good company.

Toyofumi Ogura, *from* Letters from the End of the World. *"Think of this book as a grave," reads the epigraph to Ogura's account of the Hiroshima bombing, written as letters to his wife, who died of radiation poisoning two weeks after the attack. "Not just one cold stone on the earth over you/but countless paper graves." Ogura, a professor of history at Hiroshima University, published the work in 1948. "I felt at the time," he wrote later, "that firsthand accounts should be published as soon as possible, before people's memories could become clouded with the passage of time."*

1342: Calicut

NO PORT IN THE STORM

We continued our journey to town of Calicut, which is one of the chief ports in Malabar. It is visited by men from China, Jawah, Ceylon, the Maldives, al-Yaman, and Fars, and in it gather merchants from all quarters. Its harbor is one of the largest in the world. We entered it in great pomp, the like of which I have never seen in those lands, but it was a joy that was to be followed by distress. We stopped in the port, in which there were at the time thirteen Chinese vessels, and disembarked. Every one of us was lodged in a house, and we stayed there three months as the guests of the infidel sultan, awaiting the season of the voyage to China.

Afflictions sent by Providence melt the constancy of the noble minded but confirm the obduracy of the vile. The same furnace that hardens clay liquefies gold.
—*Charles Caleb Colton, c. 1820*

On the sea of China traveling is done in Chinese ships only. The Chinese vessels are of three kinds: large ships called junks, middle sized ones called *zaws*, and small ones called *kakams*. When the time came for the voyage to China, the sultan of Calicut, who is called al-Samari, equipped for us one of the thirteen junks. The factor on the junk was called Sulaiman of Safad. I had made his acquaintance previously and I said to him, "I want a set of rooms to myself because of my slave girls, for it is my habit never to travel without them." He replied, "The merchants from China have hired them for the outward and return journey. My son-in-law has rooms that I can give you, but they have no lavatory; perhaps you may be able to exchange them for others." So I ordered my companions to take on board all my effects, and the male and female slaves embarked on the junk. This was on a Thursday, and I stayed

on shore in order to attend the Friday prayers and join them afterward. My companions, Sumbul and Zahir al-Din, also went on board with a present for the sultan. Early on Friday morning a slave boy I had named Hilal came to me and said that the rooms we had taken on the junk were small and unsuitable. When I spoke of this to the captain he said, "It cannot be helped, but if you like to transfer to the kakam there are rooms on it at your choice." I agreed to this and gave orders accordingly to my companions, who transferred the slave girls and effects to the kakam and were settled in it before the hour of the Friday prayer.

Now it is usual for this sea to become stormy every day in the late afternoon, and no one can embark then. The junks had already set sail, and none of them were left but the one that contained the sultan's present, another junk whose owners had decided to pass the winter up the coast at Fandarayna, and the kakam referred to. We spent Friday night on the seashore, we unable to embark on the kakam, and those on board unable to disembark and join us. I had nothing left but a carpet to spread out. On Saturday morning the junk and kakam were both at a distance from the port, and the junk whose owners were making for Fandarayna was driven ashore and broken into pieces. Some of those who were on board died and some escaped. In it there was a slave girl who belonged to one of the merchants, and a favorite of his. He offered to give ten dinars in gold to anyone who would rescue her, for she had clung to a spar in the stern of the junk. A sailor from Hormuz undertook to do it, and brought her ashore but would not take the dinars, saying, "I did this only for the sake of God."

That night the sea struck the junk that carried the sultan's present, and all on board died. In the morning we went to the scene of the disaster. I saw Zahir al-Din with his head smashed and his brains scattered, and Sumbul had a nail driven through one of his temples and coming out at the other, and having prayed over them we buried them. I saw the infidel, the sultan of Calicut, wearing a large white

The Destruction of the Temple of Jerusalem, by Francesco Hayez, 1867.

cloth around his waist, folded over from his navel down to his knee, and with it a small turban on his head, barefoot, with the parasol carried by a slave over his head and a fire lit in front of him on the beach; his police officers were beating the people to prevent them from plundering what the sea cast up. In all the lands of Malabar, except in this one land alone, it is the custom that whenever a ship is wrecked all that is taken from it belongs to the treasury. At Calicut, however, it is retained by its owners, and for that reason Calicut has become a flourishing and much frequented city. When those on the kakam saw what had happened to the junk they spread their sails and went off, with all my goods and slave boys and slave girls on board, leaving me alone on the beach with but one slave whom I had enfranchised. When he saw what had befallen me he deserted me, and I had nothing left with me at all except ten dinars and the carpet I had used to spread out.

Ibn Battuta, *from his* Travels. *Born in 1304 in North Africa, Ibn Battuta left home at twenty-one to make a pilgrimage to Mecca; he ended up traveling for three decades, covering 75,000 miles and visiting lands now comprising more than forty countries. His* Travels, *published after his return, gained a wide and fervent readership. One Moroccan prince who read it a half millenium later annotated a passage about certain Indian women's "knowledge of erotic movements"; his note said, "O God, give me a taste of this delight!" Battuta died in—according to one account—"some town or other."*

1912: Atlantic Ocean

HAROLD BRIDE ABOARD THE TITANIC

To begin at the beginning, I joined the *Titanic* at Belfast. I was born at Nunhead, England, twenty-two years ago and joined the Marconi wireless telegraph forces last July. I first worked on the *Hoverford* and then on the *Lusitania*.

I didn't have much to do aboard the *Titanic* except to relieve the first wireless officer, Phillips, from midnight until some time in the morning, when he should be through sleeping. On the night of the accident I was not sending but was asleep. I was due to be up and relieve Phillips earlier than usual. And that reminds me—if it hadn't been for a lucky thing we never could have sent any call for help.

The lucky thing was that the wireless broke down early enough for us to fix it before the accident. We noticed something wrong on Sunday, and Phillips and I worked seven hours to find it. We found a "secretary" burned out, at last, and repaired it just a few hours before the iceberg was struck.

Phillips said to me as he took the night shift, "You turn in, boy, and get some sleep, and go up as soon as you can and give me a chance. I'm all done for with this work of making repairs."

There were three rooms in the wireless cabin. One was a sleeping room, one a dynamo room, and one an operating room. I took off my clothes and went to sleep in bed. Then I was conscious of waking up and hearing Phillips sending to Cape Race. I read what he was sending. It was traffic matter.

I remembered how tired he was, and I got out of bed without my clothes on to relieve him. I didn't even feel the shock. I hardly knew it had happened after the captain had come to us. There was no jolt whatever.

Rope Out, Regan, North Dakota, by Mitch Dobrowner, 2014. Archival pigment print.

I was standing by Phillips telling him to go to bed when the captain put his head in the cabin.

"We've struck an iceberg," the captain said, "and I'm having an inspection made to tell what it has done for us. You had better get ready to send out a call for assistance. But don't send it until I tell you."

The captain went away and in ten minutes, I should estimate the time, he came back. We could hear a terrible confusion outside, but there was not the least thing to indicate that there was any trouble. The wireless was working perfectly.

"Send the call for assistance," ordered the captain, barely putting his head in the door.

"What call should I send?" Phillips asked.

"The regulation international call for help. Just that."

Then the captain was gone. Phillips began to send "CQD." He flashed away at it, and we joked while he did so. All of us made light of the disaster.

We joked that way while he flashed signals for about five minutes. Then the captain came back.

"What are you sending?" he asked.

"CQD," Phillips replied.

The humor of the situation appealed to me. I cut in with a little remark that made us all laugh, including the captain.

"Send 'SOS,'" I said. "It's the new call, and it may be your last chance to send it."

Phillips with a laugh changed the signal to "SOS." The captain told us we had been struck amidships, or just back of amidships. It was ten minutes, Phillips told me, after he had noticed the iceberg that the slight jolt that was the collision's only signal to us occurred. We thought we were a good distance away.

We said lots of funny thing to each other in the next few minutes. We picked up first the steamship *Frankfurt*. We gave her our position and said we had struck an iceberg and needed assistance. The *Frankfurt* operator went away to tell his captain.

He came back and we told him we were sinking by the head. By that time we could observe a distinct list forward.

The *Carpathia* answered our signal. We told her our position and said we were sinking by the head.

I heard Phillips giving the *Carpathia* fuller directions. Phillips told me to put on my clothes. Until that moment I forgot that I was not dressed.

I went to my cabin. I brought an overcoat to Phillips. It was very cold. I slipped the overcoat upon him while he worked.

Every few minutes Phillips would send me to the captain with little messages. They were merely telling how the *Carpathia* was coming our way and gave her speed.

When any calamity is suffered, the first thing to be remembered is how much has been escaped.
—Samuel Johnson, 1770

I noticed as I came back from one trip that they were putting off women and children in lifeboats. I noticed that the list forward was increasing.

Phillips told me the wireless was growing weaker. The captain came and told us our engine rooms were taking water and that the dynamos might not last much longer.

I went out on deck and looked around. The water was pretty close up to the boat deck. There was a great scramble aft, and how poor Phillips worked through it I don't know.

He was a brave man. I learned to love him that night, and I suddenly felt for him a great reverence to see him standing there sticking to his work while everybody else was raging about.

I thought it was about time to look about and see if there was anything detached that would float. I remembered that every member of the crew had a special lifebelt, and ought to know where it was. I remembered mine was under my bunk. I went and got it. Then I thought how cold the water was.

I remembered I had some boots and I put these on, and an extra jacket and I put that on. I saw Phillips standing out there still sending away, giving the *Carpathia* details of just how we were doing.

Aftershocks

In April 1815 Indonesia's Mount Tambora erupted in the largest volcanic event in recorded history. The explosion produced a global volcanic winter; 1816 became known as the "year without a summer." The pall cast over the world inspired artistic advances, scientific discoveries, and new religious beliefs.

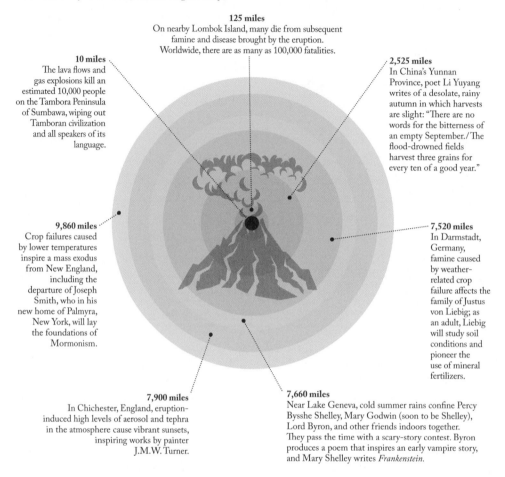

125 miles
On nearby Lombok Island, many die from subsequent famine and disease brought by the eruption. Worldwide, there are as many as 100,000 fatalities.

10 miles
The lava flows and gas explosions kill an estimated 10,000 people on the Tambora Peninsula of Sumbawa, wiping out Tamboran civilization and all speakers of its language.

2,525 miles
In China's Yunnan Province, poet Li Yuyang writes of a desolate, rainy autumn in which harvests are slight: "There are no words for the bitterness of an empty September. / The flood-drowned fields harvest three grains for every ten of a good year."

9,860 miles
Crop failures caused by lower temperatures inspire a mass exodus from New England, including the departure of Joseph Smith, who in his new home of Palmyra, New York, will lay the foundations of Mormonism.

7,520 miles
In Darmstadt, Germany, famine caused by weather-related crop failure affects the family of Justus von Liebig; as an adult, Liebig will study soil conditions and pioneer the use of mineral fertilizers.

7,900 miles
In Chichester, England, eruption-induced high levels of aerosol and tephra in the atmosphere cause vibrant sunsets, inspiring works by painter J.M.W. Turner.

7,660 miles
Near Lake Geneva, cold summer rains confine Percy Bysshe Shelley, Mary Godwin (soon to be Shelley), Lord Byron, and other friends indoors together. They pass the time with a scary-story contest. Byron produces a poem that inspires an early vampire story, and Mary Shelley writes *Frankenstein*.

I saw a collapsible boat near a funnel and went over to it. Twelve men were trying to boost it down to the boat deck. They were having an awful time. It was the last boat left. I looked at it longingly a few minutes. Then I gave them a hand, and over she went. They all started to scramble in on the boat deck, and I walked back to Phillips. I said the last raft had gone.

Then came the captain's voice: "Men, you have done your full duty. You can do no more. Abandon your cabin. Now it's every man for himself. You look out for yourselves. I release you. That's the way of it at this kind of time. Every man for himself."

I looked out. The boat deck was awash. Phillips clung on sending and sending. He clung on for about ten minutes or maybe fifteen minutes after the captain had released him. The water was then coming into our cabin.

While he worked something happened I hate to tell about. I was back in my room getting Phillips' money for him, and as I looked out the door I saw a stoker, or somebody from below decks, leaning over Phillips from behind. He was too busy to notice what the man was doing. The man was slipping the lifebelt off Phillips' back.

He was a big man, too. I don't know what it was I got hold of. I remembered in a flash the way Phillips had clung on—how I had to fix that lifebelt in place because he was too busy to do it.

I knew that man from below decks had his own lifebelt and should have known where to get it.

I suddenly felt a passion not to let that man die a decent sailor's death. I wished he might have stretched rope or walked a plank. I did my duty. I hope I finished him. I don't know. We left him on the cabin floor of the wireless room and he was not moving.

From aft came the tunes of the band. It was a ragtime tune; I don't know what. Phillips ran aft, and that was the last I ever saw of him alive.

I went to the place I had seen the collapsible boat on the boat deck, and to my surprise I saw the boat and the men still trying to push it off. I guess there wasn't a sailor in the crowd. They couldn't do it. I went up to them and was just lending a hand when a large wave came awash of the deck.

The big wave carried the boat off. I had hold of an oarlock and I went off with it. The next I knew I was in the boat.

But that was not all. I was in the boat and the boat was upside down and I was under it. And I remember realizing I was wet through, and that whatever happened I must not breathe, for I was underwater.

I knew I had to fight for it, and I did. How I got out from under the boat I do not know, but I felt a breath of air at last.

There were men all around me—hundreds of them. The sea was dotted with them, all depending on their lifebelts. I felt I simply had to get away from the ship. She was a beautiful sight then. Smoke and sparks were rushing out of her funnel. There must have been an explosion, but we had heard none. We only saw the big stream of sparks. The ship was gradually turning on her nose—just like a duck does that goes down for a dive. I had only one thing on my mind—to get away from the suction. The band was still playing. I guess all of the band went down.

They were playing "Autumn" then. I swam with all my might. I suppose I was 150 feet away when the *Titanic*, on her nose, with her after-quarter sticking straight up in the air, began to settle—slowly.

When at last the waves washed over her rudder there wasn't the least bit of suction I could feel. She must have kept going just so slowly as she had been.

I felt, after a little while, like sinking. I was very cold. I saw a boat of some kind near me and put all my strength into an effort to swim to it. It was hard work. I was all done when a hand reached out from the boat and pulled me aboard. It was our same collapsible. The same crowd was on it.

Pride and excess bring disaster for man.
　　　　　　　　　　　　　　—Xunzi, c. 250 BC

There was just room for me to roll on the edge. I lay there, not caring what happened. Somebody sat on my legs. They were wedged in between slats, and were being wrenched. I had not the heart left to ask the man to move. It was a terrible sight all around—men swimming and sinking.

I lay where I was, letting the man wrench my feet out of shape. Others came near. Nobody gave them a hand. The bottom-up boat already had more men than it would hold, and it was sinking.

At first the larger waves splashed over my clothing. Then they began to splash over my head, and I had to breathe when I could.

As we floated around on our capsized boat, and I kept straining my eyes for a ship's lights, somebody said, "Don't the rest of you think we ought to pray?" The man who made the suggestion asked of what religion the others were. Each man called out his religion. One was a Catholic, one a Methodist, one a Presbyterian.

It was decided the most appropriate prayer for all was the Lord's Prayer. We spoke it over in chorus with the man who first suggested that we pray as the leader.

Some splendid people saved us. They had a right-side-up boat, and it was full to its capacity. Yet they came to us and loaded us all into it.

1971: Nigeria

CASUISTRY

And because somebody
fired a gun
at somebody else
at Sarajevo
   but more because
   of a man named Darwin
   who said his daddy
   was an ape
   and proved it in a book;
therefore did the nations
fight amongst themselves
to see who was fittest to survive
and killed a few million people
among whom were Africans
conscripted to serve;
   bloodied, that is, to prove a point
   concerning civilization's
   monkey-mongering ways.

Ifeanyi Menkiti, *"Veteran's Day." Born in Onitsha, Nigeria, Menkiti came to the U.S. in 1961 to attend Pomona College and later earned a doctorate in philosophy from Harvard, where he studied under political philosopher John Rawls. He published his first volume of poetry in 1971 and two years later became a professor of philosophy at Wellesley College. "There are a lot of problems in the world," Menkiti told a reporter in 2011. "To think that philosophy and literature don't have anything to do with fixing them is wrongheaded."*

I saw some lights off in the distance and knew a steamship was coming to our aid.

I didn't care what happened. I just lay and gasped when I could and felt the pain in my feet. At last the *Carpathia* was alongside, and the people were being taken up a rope ladder. Our boat drew near, and one by one the men were taken off of it.

One man was dead. I passed him and went to the ladder, although my feet pained terribly. The dead man was Phillips. He had died on the raft from exposure and cold, I guess. He had been all in from work before the wreck came. He stood his ground until the crisis had passed, and then he had collapsed, I guess.

But I hardly thought that then. I didn't think much of anything. I tried the rope ladder. My feet pained terribly, but I got to the top and

felt hands reaching out to me. The next I knew a woman was leaning over me in a cabin, and I felt her hand waving back my hair and rubbing my face.

I felt somebody at my feet, and felt the warmth of a jolt of liquor. Somebody got me under the arms. Then I was bustled down below to the hospital. That was early in the day I guess. I lay in the hospital until near night, and they told me the *Carpathia's* wireless man was getting "queer" and would I help.

After that I never was out of the wireless room, so I don't know what happened among the passengers. I saw nothing of Mrs. Astor or any of them. I just worked wireless. The splutter never died down. I knew it soothed the hurt and felt like a tie to the world of friends and home.

How could I then take news queries? Sometimes I let a newspaper ask a question and got a long string of stuff asking for full particulars about everything. Whenever I started to take such a message I thought of the poor people waiting for their messages to go—hoping for answers to them.

I shut off the inquiries and sent my personal messages. And I feel I did the right thing.

There were maybe one hundred left. I would like to send them all, because I could rest easier if I knew all those messages had gone to the friends waiting for them.

The way the band kept playing was a noble thing. I heard them first while still we were working wireless, when there was a ragtime tune for us, and the last I saw of the band, when I was floating out in the sea with my lifebelt on, they were still on deck playing "Autumn." How they ever did it I cannot imagine.

From an account in the New York Times. *Bride received a thousand dollars from the* Times *for his story, told in the presence of his boss, wireless telegraph inventor Guglielmo Marconi. (Marconi was already in New York, having forgone free passage on the* Titanic *and taken the* Lusitana *three days earlier.) The SOS signal had been officially adopted by an international convention in 1906, but Marconi company operators still preferred the older, conventional distress signal of CQD, the company's own standard.*

580: Auvergne

CHAIN REACTION

In the fifth year of King Childebert's reign great floods devastated parts of Auvergne. The rain continued for twelve days and the Limagne was under such a depth of water that all sowing had to cease. The Loire River, the Allier River, and the mountain streams that run into the latter were so swollen that they rose higher above the flood level than ever before. Many cattle were drowned, the crops were ruined, and buildings inundated. The Rhône, at the spot where it meets the Saône, overflowed its banks and brought heavy loss to the inhabitants, undermining parts of the city walls of Lyons. When the rains stopped the trees came out in leaf once more, although by now it was September. In Touraine this same year, one morning before the day had dawned, a bright light was seen to traverse the sky and then disappear in the east. A sound as of trees crashing to the ground was heard throughout the whole region, but it can hardly have been a tree for it was audible over fifty miles and more. In this same year again the city of Bordeaux was sadly shaken by an earthquake. The city walls were in great danger of collapsing. The entire populace was filled with the fear of death, for they imagined that they would be swallowed up with their city unless they fled. Many of them escaped to neighboring townships. This terrible disaster followed them to the places where they had sought refuge and extended even into Spain, but there it was less serious. Huge rocks came cascading down from the mountain peaks of the Pyrenees, crushing in their wake the local inhabitants and their cattle. Villages around Bordeaux were burned by a fire sent from heaven; it took so swift a hold that homesteads and threshing floors with the grain still spread out on them were reduced to ashes.

Suicide bombing attack on former prime minister Benazir Bhutto, Rawalpindi, Pakistan, 2007. Photograph by John Moore.

There was no other apparent cause of this fire, and it must have come from God. The city of Orleans blazed with a great conflagration. Even the richer citizens lost their all, and if anyone managed to salvage anything from the flames it was immediately snatched away by the thieves who crowded around. Somewhere near Chartres blood poured forth when a loaf of bread was broken in two. At the same time the city of Bourges was scourged by a hailstorm.

A most serious epidemic followed these prodigies. While the kings were quarreling with each other again and once more making preparations for civil war, dysentery spread throughout the whole of Gaul. Those who caught it had a high temperature, with vomiting and severe pains in the small of the back; their heads ached and so did their necks. The matter they vomited up was yellow or even green. Many people maintained that some secret poison must be the cause of this. The country folk imagined that they had boils inside their bodies, and actually this is not as silly as it sounds, for as soon as cupping glasses were applied to their shoulders or legs great tumors formed, and when these burst and discharged their pus they were cured. Many recovered their health by drinking herbs that are known to be antidotes to poisons. The epidemic began in the month of August. It attacked young children first of all and to them it was fatal; and so we lost our little ones, who were so dear to us and sweet, whom we had cherished in our bosoms and dandled in our arms, whom we had fed and nurtured with such loving care. As I write I wipe away my tears and I repeat once more the words of Job the blessed: "The Lord gave, and the Lord hath taken away; as it hath pleased the Lord, so is it come to pass. Blessed be the name of the Lord, world without end."

> **Gregory of Tours**, *from* The History of the Franks. *Born in Auvergne around 538, Gregory was at various times a monk, writer, builder, ambassador, and politician as well as the bishop of Tours from 573 until his death in 594. His compositional style was criticized by fellow historians as artless, but he claimed he was trying to offer pure truth: "I apologize if I offend the art of grammar," Gregory wrote, "but I only desire to hold steadfast."*

The Horrors of War, by Peter Paul Rubens, c. 1638.

1572: Paris

FOR WHOM THE BELLS TOLL

Afterward, when the Seine flowed with corpses and thousands were dead, there were some who said that if only the assassin had not bungled his job in the first place all of the subsequent trouble might have been avoided.

But at the crucial instant, as the admiral entered the rue des Fossés-Saint-Germain late on a bright summer's morning on his usual route from the Louvre, he had bent down to adjust an ill-fitting shoe, or perhaps to consult more closely a letter he was reading, or perhaps just to spit; and the arquebus balls that struck him merely carried away a right index finger and plowed a furrow in his left forearm up to the elbow.

A party of the admiral's men ran to the house from which the shots had come and broke down the front door; they rushed in just in time to hear, through a back door that stood swinging open, the sound of clattering hoofs as the would-be assassin made good his escape on a horse that, subsequent investigation would reveal, had been left saddled and bridled in the cloister of Saint-Germain-l'Auxerrois just to the rear. The still-smoking arquebus lay on a bed in a chamber on the ground floor.

In view of the bewilderingly contradictory royal statements that would emanate from the palace in the ensuing days—righteous indignation one day, bloodthirsty approval the next—the initial reaction of his Most Christian Majesty Charles IX to the news that Gaspard de Coligny, seigneur de Châtillon, admiral of France, adviser to the king, had been shot in broad daylight not a hundred paces from the Palace of the Louvre at least had the virtue of petulant frankness. The twenty-two-year-old king cursed, smashed his tennis racket, screamed, "What, nothing but trouble?" and went off to sulk.

The royal surgeon, having snipped off the mangled end of Coligny's severed finger and painfully extracted the copper ball from his arm, declared his patient out of danger.

A medical diagnosis: not a political one.

Later in the day the king swore he would see justice and went on to say that "this wicked act stems from the enmity between Coligny's house and that of the Duke of Guise," nothing more. That the admiral was the military hero of the Protestants in the late, terrible civil wars of religion, that the Guises were the most powerful and vehement Catholic party, was not to be considered.

All very fine and magnificent, but the subjects had their own ideas. Throughout that sweltering August, Paris—Catholic, ruined, hungry, poor—had filled with strutting Huguenot noblemen, many openly carrying arms, many wearing the austere, dark, somber clothing of Calvinist believers, in its own way

When arms speak, the laws are silent.
—*Cicero, 52 BC*

just as ostentatious and maddening as if they had flaunted their wealth and newly recovered status with a brilliant display of silk, lace, and jewels. Their coming was to seal a final act of religious reconciliation, the wedding of their Protestant prince of Navarre with the Catholic king's sister. Instead it had brought every fanatic out of the woodwork. "God will not suffer this execrable coupling!" Franciscan preachers screamed, prophesying torrents of blood, urging the mob to grasp salvation by slaughtering the heretics.

The four days of official festivities following the wedding had been a succession of more subtle and courtly taunts. The king's brother Henry, the twenty-year-old Duke of Anjou—"Monsieur," he was always called—arranged a series of elaborate pageants and tournaments that somehow always ended in the humiliation of the Huguenot lords. At the Petit-Bourbon the king and his noble guests enacted the Mystery of the Three Worlds; the Protestants found themselves held "prisoner" by Tartarus and his devils for an hour while their ladies, cast as nymphs in Paradise, danced and held hands with the angels.

The admiral was shot late on the morning of Friday, August 22, at the end of the week of wedding festivities. An order went out from the palace forbidding citizens to take up arms. A royal guard of fifty French and Swiss arquebusiers was commanded to protect the wounded admiral against any further outrages.

But as night closed over Paris, with the shadows came whispers of other, stealthy preparations. The district captains of the town militia were to have a man in every house armed, with a white scarf tied to his left arm and a torch at the ready, prepared to assemble when the tocsin sounded. The gates of the city were shut, the keys secured. The boats across the Seine were quietly gathered, artillery moved into place before the Hôtel de Ville, the seat of the Paris city

Once you hear the details of a victory it is hard to distinguish it from a defeat.
—Jean-Paul Sartre, 1951

government. It was at four in the morning when the unexpected sound of the ringing bells of the church of Saint-Germain-l'Auxerrois, halfway between the Louvre and the rue de Béthisy, broke the still of the ominous night.

By dawn the clash of other bells, punctuated now by gunfire and the unmistakable bruit of a city in full riot, could be heard coming from across the river.

Shortly before four o'clock in the morning armed men had suddenly pounded on the door of Coligny's house, demanding to be admitted in the name of the king. They instantly stabbed one of the admiral's gentlemen who had been guarding the door from the inside, cleared the stairway with a volley of arquebus fire, then rushed the stair and finished off the admiral with a pike thrust through his body.

The Duke de Guise, who had come to make sure the job was done right this time, shouted up from the street below to throw the body out the window. He briefly surveyed the lifeless form of his dead adversary lying on the street in front of him, then kicked it in the face. One of his men cut off the head to take back to the Louvre. And then the crowd of hundreds of street urchins

that had instantly gathered to cheer the proceedings set upon what was left, hacking off the hands and genitals and dragging the remainder on a macabre tour through the city that would continue for the next three days.

Troops of Guise's men and the king's guard then fanned out through the surrounding streets to hunt down other Protestant lords who lodged nearby. The ringing of the bells of Saint-Germain-l'Auxerrois had been the signal for a simultaneous massacre of the king's guests at the Louvre to begin. Swiss guards went from room to room, methodically seizing the Huguenots, disarming them, and pushing them into the inner courtyard of the palace, where they were run through with pikes and added to a growing pile of corpses.

Some of the victims were taken to the Seine bridges and thrown into the river. Others plunged in themselves as a last resort to escape the mob, only to be set upon by particularly determined pursuers in boats, who pushed them under until they drowned.

The following day the king took part in a great jubilee and procession proclaimed by the Catholic Church to celebrate the extermination of the Huguenots. The king and his court proceeded to the gibbet at Montfaucon, where, by order of the Parlement, what was left of the admiral's corpse had at last been reclaimed from the mob and hung up by the feet, as a traitor. Some members of the king's royal party were offended by the smell of the four-day-old remains, but the king, according to his personal historiographer, quoted the Roman emperor who had on a similar occasion declared, "The smell of a dead enemy is sweet and delightful."

Stephen Budiansky, *from* Her Majesty's Spymaster. *Budiansky studied applied mathematics and chemistry and worked at the American Chemical Society before in 1986 becoming a journalist and editor at* U.S. News & World Report, *where he worked for twelve years. Praising work at a newsweekly, Budiansky told an interviewer, "You get to become the world's greatest expert on something new each week—and then you never have to do it again."*

1916: Combles

ERNST JÜNGER ON THE WESTERN FRONT

After breakfast I took a little look around Combles. In the course of a very few days, heavy artillery had transformed a peaceable town in the hinterland to the image of dread. Whole houses had been flattened or ripped apart by shells, so that the rooms and their furnishings were left hanging over the chaos like theater flats. The smell of corpses oozed from some buildings, because the first abrupt assault had taken the inhabitants by surprise, and buried many of them in the ruins before they could leave their dwellings. On one doorstep lay a little girl, stretched out in a lake of crimson.

All that was left of the streets were narrow footpaths that went snaking through huge mounds of beams and masonry. Fruit and vegetables were moldering away in the ravaged gardens.

After lunch, which we put together in the kitchen from an oversupply of iron rations, and which was concluded, of course, by a potent cup of coffee, I went and stretched out in an armchair upstairs. From letters that were lying around I saw that the house had belonged to a brewer by the name of Lesage. There were open cupboards and wardrobes in the room, an upset washstand, a sewing machine, and a pram. On the walls hung smashed paintings and mirrors. On the floor were drifts, sometimes several feet deep, of drawers pulled out of chests, linen, corsets, books, newspapers, nightstands, broken glass, bottles, musical scores, chair legs, skirts, coats, lamps, curtains, shutters, doors off their hinges, lace, photographs, oil paintings, albums, smashed chests, ladies' hats, flowerpots, and wallpaper, all tangled together.

Through the splintered shutters, the view was of a square furrowed by bombs, under the boughs of a ragged linden. This confusion of impressions was further darkened by the incessant

Celestial fire destroying the army of Satan, miniature from a thirteenth-century edition of the Book of Revelation.

c. 620: Medina

FIRE IN THE HOLE

The Disaster! What is the Disaster?
Would that you knew what the Disaster is!
On that day men shall become like scattered
    moths and the mountains like tufts of
    carded wool.
Then he whose good deeds weigh heavy in
    the scales shall dwell in bliss; but he
    whose deeds are light, the Abyss shall be
    his home.
Would that you knew what this is like!
It is a scorching fire.

From the Qur'an. Islam holds that between 610 and 632 the archangel Gabriel began revealing the message of Allah to the Prophet Muhammad; these revelations were later compiled into the written text of the Qur'an. According to Islamic lore, the scorching fire of the Abyss is the lowest of seven layers of hell; less-severe sections above include Hellfire, Raging Fire, and Fierceflame. The seventeenth-century cleric al-Majlisi believed that the flames of hell surround the earth, in a manner similar to flames around a kettle.

artillery fire that was raging around the town. From time to time, the gigantic impact of a fifteen-inch shell drowned out all other noise. Clouds of shards washed through Combles, splattering against the branches of the trees, or striking the few intact roofs, sending the slates slithering down.

In the course of the afternoon, the bombing swelled to such a pitch that all that was left was the feeling of a kind of oceanic roar, in which individual sounds were completely subordinated. From seven o'clock, the square and the houses on it were subjected to fifteen-inch-shell bombardment at thirty-second intervals. There were many that did not go off, whose short, dull thumps shook the house to its foundations. Throughout, we sat in our basement, on silk-upholstered armchairs around a table, with our heads in our hands, counting the seconds between explosions. The witticisms dried up, and finally the boldest of us had nothing to say. At eight o'clock the house next door came down after taking two direct hits; its collapse occasioned a huge cloud of dust.

From nine till ten, the shelling acquired a demented fury. The earth shook, the sky seemed like a boiling cauldron. Hundreds of heavy batteries were crashing away at and around Combles, innumerable shells crisscrossed hissing and howling over our heads. All was swathed in thick smoke, which was in the ominous underlighting of colored flares. Because of racking pains in our heads and ears, communication was possible only by odd, shouted words. The ability to think logically and the feeling of gravity both seemed to have been removed. We had the sensation of the ineluctable and the unconditionally necessary, as if we were facing an elemental force. An NCO in Platoon No. 3 went into a frenzy.

At ten o'clock this infernal carnival gradually seemed to calm itself, and settled into a sedate drumfire, in which, admittedly, one still was not able to make out an individual shot.

At eleven o'clock a runner arrived with orders to take the men out on to the church square. We joined up with the other two platoons in marching order. A fourth platoon, under Lieutenant Sievers, had dropped out because they were to take provisions up to the front. They now ringed us as we assembled in this perilous location, and loaded us with bread, tobacco, and canned meat. Sievers insisted I take a pan of butter, shook hands, and wished us luck.

Then we marched off in Indian file. Everyone was under strict orders absolutely to stay in touch with the man in front. No sooner were we out of the village, than our guide realized he'd gone wrong. We were forced, under heavy shrapnel fire, to retrace our steps. Then, mostly at a jog, we crossed open country, following a white ribbon laid out to guide us, though it was shot in pieces. We were forced to stop periodically, often in the very worst places, when our guide lost his way. To keep the unit together, we were not allowed to lie down or take cover.

Even so, the first and third platoon had suddenly vanished. On, on! In one violently bombarded defile, the sections backed up. Take cover! A horribly penetrating smell told us that this passage had already taken a good many lives. After running for our lives, we managed to reach

Pain Is Universal but So Is Hope (white), by Liset Castillo, 2007. Flex print on anodized aluminum, 71 x 92 inches.

a second defile that concealed the dugout of the front-line commanding officer, then we lost our way again, and in a painful crush of excited men, had to turn back once more. At the most five yards from Vogel and me, a middle-sized shell struck the bank behind us with a dull thump, and hurled mighty clods of earth over us, as we thought our last moment had come. Finally, our guide found the path again—a strangely constellated group of corpses serving as landmark. One of the dead lay there as if crucified on the chalk slope. It was impossible to imagine a more appropriate landmark.

On, on! Men collapsed while running, we had to threaten them to use the last energy from their exhausted bodies. Wounded men went down left and right in craters—we disregarded their cries for help. We went on,

eyes implacably on the man in front, through a knee-high trench formed from a chain of enormous craters, one dead man after another. At moments, we felt our feet settling on soft, yielding corpses, whose form we couldn't make out on account of the darkness. The wounded man collapsing on the path suffered the same fate; he too was trampled underfoot by the boots of those hurrying ever onward.

And always the sweetish smell! Even little Schmidt, my orderly, who had accompanied me on perilous reconnaissance, was beginning to reel. I snatched his rifle out of his hands, which even in his extremity, the good lad tried to resist.

At last we reached the front line, which was occupied by men huddled together in little holes. Their dull voices trembled with joy when they learned that we were come to relieve them. A Bavarian sergeant handed over the sector and his flare pistol to me with a few words.

My platoon's sector was on the right flank of the regiment's position, and consisted of a defile hammered by constant shelling into little more than a dip, running through open country from a couple of hundred paces to the left of Guillemont, to a little less than that to the right of the Bois de Trônes. Some five hundred paces separated us from the troops to our right, the Seventy-Sixth Infantry. The shelling here was so heavy that nothing could survive.

There is fatigue so great that the body cries, even in its sleep. There are times of complete frustration; there are daily small deaths.
—Martha Graham, c. 1953

Suddenly the Bavarian sergeant had disappeared, and I stood all alone, with my flare pistol in my hand, in the midst of that eerie cratered landscape, masked now by patches of creeping fog. Behind me I heard a stifled, unpleasant sound; with a degree of calm that astonished me, I registered that it came from a bloated disintegrating corpse.

Since I had no idea as to the enemy's possible whereabouts, I went back to my men and told them to be ready for the worst. All of us stayed awake; I spent the night with Paulicke and my two orderlies in a foxhole no bigger than a cubic yard.

When morning paled, the strange surroundings gradually revealed themselves to our disbelieving eyes.

The defile proved to be little more than a series of enormous craters full of pieces of uniform, weapons, and dead bodies; the country around, so far as the eye could see, had been completely plowed by heavy shells. Not a single blade of grass showed itself. The churned-up field was gruesome. In among the living defenders lay the dead. When we dug foxholes, we realized that they were stacked in layers. One company after another, pressed together

in the drumfire, had been mown down, then the bodies had been buried under showers of earth sent up by shells, and then the relief company had taken their predecessors' place. And now it was our turn.

The defile and the land behind was strewn with German dead, the field ahead with British. Arms and legs and heads stuck out of the slopes; in front of our holes were severed limbs and bodies, some of which had had coats or tarpaulins thrown over them, to save us the sight of the disfigured faces. In spite of the heat, no one thought of covering the bodies with earth.

The village of Guillemont seemed to have disappeared without trace; just a whitish stain on the cratered field indicated where one of the limestone houses had been pulverized. In front of us lay the station, crumpled like a child's toy; further to the rear the woods of Delville, ripped to splinters.

No sooner had day broken than a low-flying RAF plane whirled toward us and, vulturelike, began drawing its circles overhead, while we fled into our holes and huddled together. The sharp eye of the observer must have noticed something anyway, because before long the plane began to emit a series of low, long-drawn-out siren tones, coming at short intervals. They put one in mind of the cries of a fabulous creature, hanging pitilessly over the desert.

A little later, and the battery seemed to have taken the signals. One heavy, low-arcing shell after the other came barging along with incredible force. We sat helplessly in our refuges, lighting a cigar and then throwing it away again, prepared at any moment to find ourselves buried.

From Storm of Steel. *Jünger's diaristic World War I novel was first published in 1920 in a run of two thousand copies, with his family's gardener designated as the publisher. After gaining fame with several other books on war written for a local military press, Jünger revised* Storm of Steel *as many as seven times. In 1924 it grew more violent and nationalistic, in 1934 more meditative and included a dedication "for the fallen." A captain during World War II, Jünger spent most of it as part of the occupying force in Paris. He died in 1998, a month before turning 103.*

Sheltered Lives

Bunkers protect against a dangerous world

Stone brochs
Northern Scotland, c. 100 BC–c. 100

Houses
Small communities of ancient Scottish tribes

Protecting against
Rival tribes

Defensive measures
Underground chambers, towers rising up 12 or 13 meters, windowless stonework walls

Amenities
Living quarters inside walls, interior courtyard, cooking tank, cistern

Derinkuyu underground city
Cappadocia, Turkey, c. 600

Houses
Up to 20,000

Protecting against
Muslim Arabs during Arab–Byzantine Wars; later against Ottoman persecution

Defensive measures
All eleven levels are independently capable of being sealed by rolling stone doors

Amenities
Wine and oil presses, refectories, shops, cruciform church, 15,000 air shafts

Luxury Survival Condos
Kansas, 2014

Houses
70 people for more than five years

Protecting against
Promo materials cite "present worldwide economic conditions, historical disaster evidence, and the obvious signs of global climate changes"

Defensive measures
Built into missile silos; "military-grade security"; dome structure to withstand winds up to 500 mph

Amenities
Hydroponic food production; shooting range, gym, pool, spa, bar; advertisements promise "ultra modern" furnishings; pets allowed with proper shots

Fallout shelter
Advertised fabrication by Koven, a New Jersey–based steel manufacturer, 1952

Houses
American nuclear family of six

Protecting against
Atomic warfare and radiation

Defensive measures
Submarine-style airlock

Amenities
Bunks and hammocks; food and water storage; air filter; Koven guarantees "ample headroom"

Dixia Cheng underground city
Beijing, 1969–1979

Houses
Entirety of Beijing's 6 million citizens (according to government claims)

Protecting against
Attacks from Soviet Union; now occupied by those unable to afford high Beijing rents

Defensive measures
Entrances hidden in Beijing shops

Amenities
Movie theater, roller-skating rink, restaurants, grain and oil warehouses, mushroom farm

Refuge chamber
Touraine, France, c. 1100

Houses
Family of 5 to 6 elites

Protecting against
Warfare between counts of Anjou and Blois during territory dispute

Defensive measures
Entrance hidden under floor of small building; assailants are slowed by sharp hallway turns

Amenities
Niches for oil lamps, benches carved into limestone; well

Cité Souterraine
Naours, France, c. 300

Houses
Up to 3,000 people

Protecting against
Marauding armies, possibly also used by early Christians to escape persecution; also as refuge during Hundred Years' War, Burgundian Wars, Thirty Years' War, WWI, and WWII

Defensive measures
Smoke from cooking fires surreptitiously routes to surface via cottages

Amenities
Stalls for livestock, 300 rooms (including chapels), bakery

c. 100: India

ACT OF GOD

Arjuna:
I see the gods
in your body, O God,
and hordes
of varied creatures:
Brahma, the cosmic creator,
on his lotus throne,
all the seers
and celestial serpents.

I see no beginning
or middle or end to you;
only boundless strength
in your endless arms,
the moon and sun in your eyes,
your mouths of consuming flames,
your own brilliance
scorching this universe.

Erimo Cape, 1976, from the series *Solitude of Ravens,* by Fukase Masahisa, 1976.

You alone
fill the space
between heaven and earth
and all the directions;
seeing this awesome,
terrible form of yours,
Great Soul,
the three worlds
tremble.

Vishnu, seeing you brush
the clouds with flames
of countless colors,
your mouths agape,
your huge eyes blazing,
my inner self quakes
and I find no resolve
or tranquility.

Rushing through
your fangs
into grim
mouths,
some are dangling
from heads
crushed
between your teeth.

As roiling
river waters
stream headlong
toward the sea,
so do human
heroes enter
into your blazing
mouths.

As moths
in the frenzy
of destruction
fly into a blazing flame;
worlds
in the frenzy
of destruction
enter your mouths.

You lick at the worlds
around you,
devouring them

with flaming mouths;
and your terrible fires
scorch the entire universe,
filling it, Vishnu,
with violent rays.

Tell me—
who are you
in this terrible form?
Homage to you, Best of Gods!
Be gracious! I want to know you
as you are in your beginning.
I do not comprehend
the course of your ways.

Lord Krishna:
I am time grown old,
creating world destruction,
set in motion
to annihilate the worlds;
even without you,
all these warriors
arrayed in hostile ranks
will cease to exist.

Therefore, arise
and win glory!
Conquer your foes
and fulfill your kingship!
They are already
killed by me.
Be just my instrument,
the archer at my side!

From the Bhagavadgita. *Written as a dialogue between Prince Arjuna and Lord Krishna, the Sanskrit poem forms one part of the Hindu war epic the* Mahabharata. *When Arjuna expresses to a disguised Krishna his reluctance to kill family members in a factional struggle, the god reveals his true cosmic nature and argues that Arjuna should embrace devotion to act without desire. While watching the first atomic bomb explode, J. Robert Oppenheimer recalled the words of Vishnu from the poem: "Now I am become Death, the destroyer of worlds."*

Toxic clouds and ash spewing from Mount Tokachi, Hokkaido, Japan. Photograph by Hiroshi Hamaya.

1995: Portugal

BLIND LEADING THE BLIND

The old man with the black eyepatch told what he knew, what he had seen with his own eyes when he could still see, what he had overheard during the few days that elapsed between the start of the epidemic and his own blindness.

In the first twenty-four hours, he said, if the rumor going around was true, there were hundreds of cases, all alike, all showing the same symptoms, all instantaneous, the disconcerting absence of lesions, the resplendent whiteness of their field of vision, no pain either before or after. On the second day there was talk of some reduction in the number of new cases, it went from hundreds to dozens and this led the government to announce at once that it was reasonable to suppose the situation would soon be under control. The government therefore ruled out the originally formulated hypothesis that the country was being swept by an epidemic without precedent, provoked by some morbid as yet unidentified agent that took effect instantaneously and was marked by a complete absence of any previous signs of incubation or latency. Instead, they said, that in accordance with the latest scientific opinion and the consequent and updated administrative interpretation, they were dealing with an accidental and unfortunate temporary concurrence of circumstances, also as yet unverified, in whose pathogenic development it was possible, the government's communiqué emphasized, starting from the analysis of the available data, to detect the proximity of a clear curve of resolution and signs that it was on the wane. A television commentator came up with an apt metaphor when he compared the epidemic, or whatever it might be, to an arrow shot into the air, which upon reaching its highest point, pauses for a moment as if suspended, and then begins to trace its obligatory descending curve, which, God willing, and with this invocation the commentator returned to the triviality of human discourse and to the

Drawing from *Stereoscope*, by William Kentridge, 1998–99.

so-called epidemic, gravity tending to increase the speed of it, until this terrible nightmare tormenting us finally disappears, these were words that appeared constantly in the media, and always concluded by formulating the pious wish that the unfortunate people who had become blind might soon recover their sight, promising them meanwhile, the solidarity of society as a whole, both official and private. In some remote past, similar arguments and metaphors had been translated by the intrepid optimism of the common people into sayings such as, Nothing lasts forever, be it good or bad, the excellent maxims of one who has had time to learn from the ups and downs of life and fortune, and which, transported into the land of the blind, should be read as follows, Yesterday we could see, today we can't, tomorrow we shall see again, with a slight interrogatory note on the third and final line of the phrase, as if prudence, at the last moment,

had decided, just in case, to add a touch of a doubt to the hopeful conclusion.

Sadly, the futility of such hopes soon became manifest, the government's expectations and the predictions of the scientific community simply sank without trace.

Blindness was spreading, not like a sudden tide flooding everything and carrying all before it, but like an insidious infiltration of a thousand and one turbulent rivulets which, having slowly drenched the earth, suddenly submerge it completely. Faced with this social catastrophe, already on the point of taking the bit between their teeth, the authorities hastily organized medical conferences, especially those bringing together ophthalmologists and neurologists. Because of the time it would inevitably take to organize, a congress that some had called for was never convened, but in compensation there were colloquia, seminars, round-table discussions, some open to the public, others held behind closed doors. The overall effect of the patent futility of the debates and the occurrence of certain cases of sudden blindness during the sessions, with the speaker calling out, I'm blind, I'm blind, prompted almost all the newspapers, the radio, and television to lose interest in such initiatives, apart from the discreet and, in every sense, laudable behavior of certain organs of communication that, living off sensational stories of every kind, off the fortunes and misfortunes of others, were not prepared to miss an opportunity to report live, with all the drama the situation warranted, the sudden blindness, for example, of a professor of ophthalmology.

The proof of the progressive deterioration of morale in general was provided by the government itself, its strategy changing twice within the space of some six days. To begin with, the government was confident that it was possible to circumscribe the disease by confining the blind and the contaminated within specific areas. Then the inexorable rise in the number of cases of blindness led some influential members of the government, fearful that the official initiative would not suffice for the task in hand, and that it might result in heavy political costs, to defend the idea that it was up to families to keep their blind indoors, never allowing them to go out on the street, so as not to worsen the already difficult traffic situation or to offend the sensibility of persons who still had their eyesight and who, indifferent to more or less reassuring opinions, believed that the white disease was spreading by visual contact, like the evil eye. Indeed, it was not appropriate to expect any other reaction from someone who, preoccupied with his thoughts, be they sad, indifferent, or happy, if such thoughts still exist, suddenly saw the change in expression of a person heading in his direction, his face revealing all the signs of total horror, and then that inevitable cry, I'm blind, I'm blind. No one's nerves could withstand it. The worst thing is that whole families, especially the smaller ones, rapidly became families of blind people, leaving no one who could guide and look after them, nor protect sighted neighbors from them, and it was

clear that these blind people, however caring a father, mother, or child they might be, could not take care of each other, otherwise they would meet the same fate as the blind people in the painting, walking together, falling together, and dying together.

Faced with this situation, the government had no alternative but to go rapidly into reverse gear, broadening the criteria it had established about the places and spaces that could be requisitioned, resulting in the immediate and improvised utilization of abandoned factories, disused churches, sports pavilions, and empty warehouses. At the beginning, the very beginning, several charitable organizations were still

Calamities are of two kinds: misfortune to ourselves, and good fortune to others.
—Ambrose Bierce, 1906

offering volunteers to assist the blind, to make their beds, clean out the lavatories, wash their clothes, prepare their food, the minimum of care without which life soon becomes unbearable, even for those who can see. These dear people went blind immediately but at least the generosity of their gesture would go down in history. Did any of them come here, asked the old man with the black eyepatch, No, replied the doctor's wife, no one has come, Perhaps it was a rumor, And what about the city and the traffic, asked the first blind man, remembering his own car and that of the taxi driver who had driven him to the surgery and had helped him to dig the grave, Traffic is in a state of chaos, replied the old man with the black eyepatch, and gave details of specific cases and accidents. When, for the first time, a bus driver was suddenly struck by blindness as he was driving his vehicle on a public road, despite the casualties and injuries resulting from the disaster, people did not pay much attention for the same reason, that is to say, out of force of habit, and the director of public relations of the transport company felt able to declare, without further ado, that the disaster had been caused by human error, regrettable no doubt, but, all things

c. 2200 bc: Akkad

END TIMES

Enlil, the roaring storm god that subjugates the entire land, the rising deluge that cannot be confronted, was considering what should be destroyed in return for the wrecking of his beloved temple. He lifted his gaze toward the Gubin Mountains, and made all the inhabitants of the broad mountain ranges descend, the Gutians, an unbridled people with human intelligence but canine instincts and monkeys' features. Like small birds they swooped on the ground in great flocks. Because of Enlil they stretched their arms out across the plain like a net for animals. Nothing escaped their clutches, no one left their grasp. Messengers no longer traveled the highways, the courier's boat no longer passed along the rivers. The Gutians drove the goats of Enlil out of their folds and compelled their herdsmen to follow them. Prisoners manned the watch. Brigands occupied the highways. The doors of the city gates of the land lay dislodged in mud. As if it had been before the time when cities were built, the arable tracts yielded no grain, the inundated tracts yielded no fish, the irrigated orchards yielded no syrup or wine, the thick clouds did not rain, the *masgurum* plant did not grow.

In those days one shekel's worth of oil was only half a liter, one shekel's worth of grain was only half a liter—these sold at such prices in the markets of the cities! Those who lay down on the roof died on the roof; those who lay down in the house were not buried. People were flailing at themselves from hunger. Dogs were packed together in the silent streets; if two men walked there they would be devoured by them, and if three men walked there they would be devoured by them. Noses were punched, heads were smashed, noses were piled up, heads were sown like seeds. Honest people were confounded with traitors, heroes lay dead on top of heroes, the blood of traitors ran upon the blood of honest men.

From "The Curse of Akkad." The descriptions of devastated landscape in this lamentation about the fall of Akkadian civilization were long thought to be based in myth—until 1978, when archaeologist Harvey Weiss uncovered the lost city of Tell Leilan. A layer of barren soil corresponding to the years 2200 bc to 1900 bc revealed the city had been completely abandoned around the time of Akkad's fall; there had been a drought so severe that even the earthworms had died out. It was, according to Weiss, an example of climate change.

considered, as unforeseeable as a heart attack in the case of someone who had never suffered from a heart complaint. Our employees, explained the director, as well as the mechanical and electrical parts of our buses, are periodically subjected to rigorous checks, as can be seen, showing a direct and clear relation of cause and effect, in the extremely low percentage of accidents in which, generally speaking, our company's vehicles have been involved. This labored explanation appeared in the newspapers, but people had more on their minds than worrying about a simple bus accident, after all, it would have been no worse if its brakes had failed. Moreover, two days later, this was precisely the cause of another accident, but the world being what it is, where the truth often has to masquerade as falsehood to achieve its ends, the rumor went around that the driver had gone blind. There was no way of convincing the public of what had in fact happened, and the outcome was soon evident, from one moment to the next people stopped using buses, they said they would rather go blind themselves than die because others had gone blind. A third accident, soon afterward and for the same reason, involving a vehicle that was carrying no passengers, gave rise to comment such as the following, couched in a knowingly popular tone, That could have been me. Nor could they imagine, those who spoke like this, how right they were. When two pilots both went blind at once, a commercial plane crashed and burst into flames the moment it hit the ground, killing all the passengers and crew, notwithstanding that in this case the mechanical and electrical equipment were in perfect working order, as the black box, the only survivor, would later reveal. A tragedy of these dimensions was not the same as an ordinary bus accident, the result being that those who still had any illusions soon lost them, from then on engine noises were no longer heard and no wheel, large or small, fast or slow, was ever to turn again. Those people who were previously in the habit of complaining about the ever-increasing traffic problems, pedestrians who, at first sight, appeared not to know where they were going because the cars, stationary or moving, were constantly impeding

The goddess Durga slaying the buffalo demon Mahishasura, Nepal, fourteenth century.

their progress, drivers who having gone around the block countless times before finally finding a place to park their car, became pedestrians and started protesting for the same reasons, after having first voiced their own complaints, all of them must now be content, except for the obvious fact that, since there was no one left who dared to drive a vehicle, not even to get from A to B, the cars, trucks, motorbikes, even the bicycles, were scattered chaotically throughout the entire city, abandoned wherever fear had gained the upper hand over any sense of propriety, as evidenced by the grotesque sight of a tow-away vehicle with a car suspended from the front axle, probably the first man to turn blind had been the truck driver. The situation was bad for everyone, but for those stricken with blindness it was catastrophic, since, according to the current expression, they could not see where they were putting their feet. It was pitiful to watch them bumping into the abandoned cars, one after the other, bruising

their shins, some fell, pleading, Is there anyone who can help me to my feet, but there were also those who, naturally brutish or made so by despair, cursed and fought off any helping hand that came to their assistance, Leave me alone, your turn will come soon enough, then the compassionate person would take fright and make a quick escape, disappear into that dense white mist, suddenly conscious of the risk to which their kindness had exposed them, perhaps to go blind only a few steps further on.

José Saramago, *from* Blindness. *Born José de Sousa in 1922 to peasants in Portugal, Saramago was given his surname by his town's registrar; the name—a reference to a wild herbaceous plant often eaten by the town's poor—was one by which Saramago's paternal family had been known. He worked as a mechanic and civil servant before publishing his first novel,* Land of Sin, *at twenty-four; his second didn't appear for another thirty years. "Either we are blind," Saramago said about* Blindness *in 1997, the year before he won the Nobel Prize in Literature, "or we are mad."*

1348: England

PESTILENCE

In this year and the following one there was a general mortality of men throughout the whole world. It first began in India, then in Tharsis, then it came to the Saracens, and finally to the Christians and Jews, so that in the space of one year, from Easter to Easter, as the rumor spread in the Roman curia, there had died, as if by sudden death, in those remote regions eight thousand legions, besides the Christians. The king of Tharsis, seeing such a sudden and unheard-of slaughter of his people, began a journey to Avignon with a great multitude of his nobles, to propose to the pope that he would become a Christian and be baptized by him, thinking that he might thus mitigate the vengeance of God upon his people because of their wicked unbelief. Then, when he had journeyed for twenty days, he heard that the pestilence had struck among the Christians, just as among other peoples. So, turning in his tracks, he traveled no farther but hastened to return home. The Christians, pursuing these people from behind, slew about seven thousand of them.

At this same time the pestilence became prevalent in England, beginning in the autumn in certain places. It spread throughout the land, ending in the same season of the following year. At the same time many cities in Corinth and Achaea were overturned, and the earth swallowed them. Castles and fortresses were broken, laid low, and swallowed up. Mountains in Cyprus were leveled into one, so that the flow of the rivers was impeded, and many cities were submerged and villages destroyed.

During this same year there was a great mortality of sheep everywhere in the kingdom. In one place and in one pasture more than five thousand sheep died and became so putrefied that neither beast nor bird wanted to touch them. And the price of everything was cheap, because of the fear of death; there were very few who took any care for their wealth, or for anything else. For a man could buy a horse for half a mark, which before was worth forty shillings, a large, fat ox for four shillings, a cow for twelve pence, a heifer for sixpence, a large, fat sheep for four pence, a sheep for threepence, a lamb for two pence, a fat pig for five pence, a stone of wool for nine pence. And the sheep and cattle wandered about through the fields and among the crops, and there was no one to go after them or to collect them. They perished in countless numbers everywhere, in secluded ditches and hedges, for lack of watching, since there was such a lack of serfs and servants that no one knew what he should do.

The Scots, hearing of the cruel pestilence in England, suspected that this had come upon the English by the avenging hand of God, and when they wished to swear an oath, they swore this one, as the vulgar rumor reached the ears of the English: "Be the foul deth of Engelond." And so the Scots, believing that the horrible vengeance of God had fallen on the English, came together in the forest of Selkirk to plan an invasion of the whole kingdom of England. But savage mortality supervened, and the sudden and frightful cruelty of death struck the Scots. In a short time about five thousand died; the rest, indeed, both sick and well, prepared to return home, but the English, pursuing them, caught up with them and slew a great many of them.

After the aforesaid pestilence, many buildings both large and small in all cities, towns, and villages had collapsed and had completely fallen to the ground in the absence of inhabitants. Likewise, many small villages and hamlets were completely deserted; there was not one house left in them, but all those who had lived in them were dead. It is likely that many such hamlets will never again be inhabited.

Henry Knighton, *from his* Chronicles. *The Black Death ravaged Europe from 1347 to 1351. Earlier scholars believed it originated in China, spreading to Europe when a Kipchak army besieged a Genoese trading post in Crimea by catapulting plague-infested corpses into the town. In 2011 archaeologist Barney Sloane concluded that rats, also long blamed for spreading plague, were unlikely carriers. "We ought to be finding great heaps of dead rats,"* he noted about his excavations of medieval waterfront sites, "but they just aren't there."*

1978: Burlington, VT

THE BEAUTY IN THE SORROW

So many poems about the deaths of animals.
Wilbur's toad, Kinnell's porcupine, Eberhart's squirrel,
and that poem by someone—Hecht? Merrill?—
about cremating a woodchuck. But mostly
I remember the outrageous number of them,
as if *every* poet, I too, had written at least
one animal elegy; with the result that today
when I came to a good enough poem by Edwin Brock
about finding a dead fox at the edge of the sea
I could not respond; as if permanent shock
had deadened me. And then after a moment
I began to give way to sorrow (watching myself
sorrowlessly the while), not merely because
part of my being had been violated and annulled,
but because all these many poems over the years
have been necessary—suitable and correct. This
has been the time of the finishing off of the animals.
They are going away—their fur and their wild eyes,
their voices. Deer leap and leap in front
of the screaming snowmobiles until they leap
out of existence. Hawks circle once or twice
above their shattered nests and then they climb
to the stars. I have lived with them fifty years,
we have lived with them fifty million years,
and now they are going, almost gone. I don't know
if the animals are capable of reproach.
But clearly they do not bother to say goodbye.

Hayden Carruth, *"Essay." The editor of* Poetry *magazine from 1949 to 1950, Carruth lived much of his life in what his friends called "voluntary poverty." Following hospitalization for alcoholism and mental illness, in 1953 Carruth moved to northern Vermont and worked as a farm laborer. "I had always been aware that the universe is sad; everything in it, animate or inanimate, the wild creatures, the stones, the stars," he wrote. "I knew that the only rest from my anxiety—for I had been trembling even in infancy—lay in acknowledging and absorbing this sadness."*

c. 1220: Khwarezm

THE WEIGHT OF HISTORY

For several years I continued to avoid mention of the Tartar invasion as it horrified me and I was unwilling to recount it. I was taking one step toward it and then another back. Who is there who would find it easy to write the obituary of Islam and the Muslims? For whom would it be a trifling matter to give an account of this? Oh, would that my mother had not given me birth! Oh, would that I had died before it occurred and been a thing forgotten, quite forgotten! However, a group of friends urged me to record it, although I was hesitant. I saw then that to leave

It's the end of the world every day, for someone.
—Margaret Atwood, 2000

it undone was of no benefit, but we state that to do it involves recounting the most terrible disaster and the greatest misfortune, one the like of which the passage of days and nights cannot reproduce. It comprised all mankind but particularly affected the Muslims. If anyone were to say that since God (glory and power be his) created Adam until this present time mankind has not had a comparable affliction, he would be speaking the truth. History books do not contain anything similar or anything that comes close to it.

One of the greatest disasters they mention is what Nebuchadnezzar II did to the Israelites, slaughtering them and destroying Jerusalem. What is Jerusalem in relation to the lands that these cursed ones destroyed, where each city is many times larger than Jerusalem? And what are the Israelites compared with those they killed? Among those they killed the inhabitants of a single city are more numerous than were the Israelites. Perhaps humanity will not see such a calamity, apart from Gog and Magog, until the world comes to an end and this life ceases to be.

As for the Antichrist, he will spare those who follow him and destroy those who oppose him, but these did not spare anyone. On the contrary, they slew women, men, and children. They split open the bellies of pregnant women and killed the fetuses. To God do we belong and to him do we return. There is no power nor strength except in God.

This is the calamity whose sparks flew far and wide and whose damage was all-embracing. It spread through the lands like a cloud driven on by the wind, for a people emerged from the confines of China and made for the cities of Transoxania, such as Samarkand, Bukhara, and others. A group of them then crossed into Khorasan and thoroughly dealt with it, conquering, destroying, slaughtering, and plundering. Then they passed on to Rayy and Hamadan, the uplands, and cities up to the boundary of Iraq. Subsequently they attacked Azerbaijan and Arran, which they ruined and most of whose people they killed. Only the rare fugitive survived. All this was in less than a year. Nothing like this had ever been heard of.

When they had finished with Azerbaijan and Arran, they proceeded to Darband, Shirvan, and took the cities there. Only the citadel, where their king was, remained safe. From there they crossed into the lands of the Alan and the Lakz and the various peoples of that region. They dealt them widespread slaughter, plunder, and destruction. Then they attacked the land of the Kipchaks, some of the most numerous of the Turks, and killed all who resisted them. The rest fled to the woods and the mountaintops, abandoning their lands, which these Tartars seized. They achieved this in the quickest possible time and only lingered according to the daily amount they could travel, nothing more.

Nothing like this has ever been heard of before. Alexander, who is agreed by historians to have conquered the world, did not conquer it with this rapidity. He only conquered it in about ten years and did not kill anyone. He merely accepted the allegiance of people. In about a year these men conquered most of the known earth, its fairest part and the most civilized and populated, and of its inhabitants the most equitable in manners and conduct. In the lands they did not reach there was

Family members arriving at the Wangjialing mine after a flooded shaft trapped 153 miners, Shanxi Province, China, 2010.

nobody who was not in fearful expectation of them, watching for their arrival.

The Tartars do not need a supply of provisions and foodstuffs, for their sheep, cattle, horses, and other pack animals accompany them, and they consume their flesh and nothing else. The animals they ride dig the earth with their hooves and eat the roots of plants, knowing nothing of barley. Thus when they make a camp, they require nothing from without.

Indeed, these Tartars had done something unheard of in ancient or modern times. A people emerges from the borders of China, and before a year passes some of them reach the lands of Armenia in this direction and go beyond Iraq in the direction of Hamadan. By God, there is no doubt that anyone who comes after us, when a long time has passed, and sees the record of this event will refuse to accept it and think it most unlikely, although the truth is in his hands. When he deems it unlikely, let him consider that we and all who write history in these times have made our record at the time when everybody living knew of this disaster, both the learned and

the ignorant, all equal in their understanding of it because of its notoriety. May God provide for the Muslims and Islam someone to preserve and guard them, for they have been forced to meet a terrible enemy and reduced, as for Muslim princes, to those whose aspirations do not go beyond their bellies and their private parts. Since the coming of the Prophet until this present time the Muslims have not suffered such hardship and misery as afflict them now.

This enemy, the infidel Tartars, trampled over the lands of Transoxania, and seized and ruined them. That is an extensive enough territory for you!

Ibn al-Athir, *from* The Complete History. *The middle child of a family of Arab scholars—his older brother published a dictionary that clarified obscure terms spoken by the Prophet Muhammad; his younger brother was a noted literary critic who worked for Sultan Saladin—Ibn al-Athir was a historian whose* Complete History *tells the story of the world from its pre-Muhammadan beginnings to the year 1231. "Some would call him the only real Arab historian of the period," wrote twentieth-century Arabist Francesco Gabrieli.*

1995: Tokyo

UNDERGROUND DOOMSDAY

I wake up at 6:30, eat a simple breakfast, and leave the house at around 7:05. I get the Toyoko Line to Nakameguro, which takes thirty minutes. It's not too crowded, though I almost never find a seat. If an express comes along I'll always change. I'm a man in a hurry.

If I do get a seat, I read. Though I haven't done much reading since the gas attack. I like history books. At the time I was reading *Zero Fighter*. Long ago I used to dream of flying, and I still take an interest in airplanes. I was page-turning straight through on the Toyoko Line, a fascinating read. Which is why I didn't notice we'd reached Nakameguro.

We line up in rows of three on the Hibiya Line platform. I usually line up around the third car from the front, but I was so preoccupied with my book I ended up farther back, about the sixth car down.

As soon as the door opened I turned right and got a seat. But then a woman came along and squeezed herself in, the fourth person in a seat meant for three, so that things were a little tight. "Well," I thought, "better get my book out now. People get the wrong idea if you start fumbling around later." I pulled out the book and carried on reading. I only had ten or twenty pages left and I wanted to finish it before I reached my station. But at Hiroo I looked up to see this man sitting directly to my left wearing a leather coat. I was still wrapped up in my book, but around Hiroo it really began to get on my nerves. Leather coats often smell funny, don't they? A disinfectant or nail-polish-remover kind of smell. "This guy stinks," I thought, and I stared him right in the eye. He just stared back at me with this "You-got-a-problem, mister?" look.

But it really did stink, so I went on staring, only he doesn't seem to be looking at me. He's looking past me to something on my right. I turned around to look and saw something about the size of a notebook lying at the feet of the second person on my right. It's like a plastic pack. In the news, they said it was wrapped in newspaper, but what I saw was plastic, and something spilling out of it.

Photograph purporting to show the iceberg that sank the *Titanic*, taken by Hope Chapin on the morning of April 15, 1912, from the deck of the *Carpathia* while *Titanic* survivors were being rescued.

"Ah, so that's what's making the place smell," I thought, but I still just sat there. By that point the third person to my right had gone. It must have been around Hiroo or Roppongi I noticed that.

Soon everyone was saying, "Open the windows—it stinks." So they all open the windows. I remember thinking, "It's so cold, can't you just put up with the smell?" Then an old lady sat down next to me. It was all wet under her feet, so she stood up and moved to a seat opposite, walking straight through the pool of sarin.

There's nobody left at the back of the car. Everyone's moved to the front, saying, "It stinks! It stinks!" This was around the time we'd reached Roppongi. By then my head was spinning. I heard the announcement, "Next stop, Roppongi," and I thought to myself, "I really must be anemic today." The symptoms were pretty much the same: a little nauseous, can't see so well, breaking out in a sweat.

Still, I didn't connect it at all with the smell. I was utterly convinced it was anemia. Lots of my relatives are doctors, so I'm familiar with the smell of medicinal alcohol or cresol. I thought maybe some medical person had dropped a bag of something and it had leaked out. "But why can't someone pick it up?" I thought. I'm a little angry by now. Honestly, our morals have declined so far of late. If I'd been a bit more sound of body, I would have picked it up myself and tossed it out onto the platform.

But then after Roppongi, where the train slows, I knew something was wrong. My anemia was so bad I decided to get off at Kamiyacho and rest for a while, maybe let two or three trains go by. But when I tried to stand I couldn't get up. My legs had gone. I grabbed the handstrap and sort of dangled from it.

I moved from strap to strap until I reached the pole near the door. Finally I stepped off the train, my hand out ready to catch myself at the far wall of the Kamiyacho platform. I remember thinking, "If I don't make it to that wall and crouch down, I'm gonna fall and hit my head." Then I blanked out.

Actually, I hadn't left the train. I'd grabbed the stainless steel pole and just slid down to the floor. What I thought was a wall was in fact the floor of the car, which felt chilly to my right hand. They ran a photo of me in the tabloids, so I could see later what happened.

They videoed me too. I was seen on television, lying like that on the car floor. I was flat out for at least half an hour. Nice and spread out. Then the station attendants carried me away. You can see it in the videos.

I came to in Toho University Omori Hospital, but I don't know when that was. Maybe that afternoon of March 20, when I had a moment of consciousness, then fell unconscious again.

When I finally came around for good, I was told I was well enough to move to the general hospital wing. It was March 23, though I was utterly convinced it was March 21, the day after the gas attack. I had no awareness at all. But then, no awareness is paradise. True nothingness.

I didn't have any near-death experience or anything like that. Only, I swear I heard a faint roar of voices coming from far off on the wind, like kids cheering at a baseball game, something like that, but hushed and indistinct, cut off now and then by the wind.

Actually, around that time one of my daughters was pregnant—in her fourth month, was it? I'd been anxious about it. It would be my first grandchild. Well, apparently my sister-in-law came in and said to me, "What if you never see your grandchild's face?" Until then I'd shown absolutely no reaction to anything anyone had said, but this I heard and suddenly regained consciousness. My daughter had been at my side, saying, "Dad hold on! Don't die!" and all I had heard was a vague murmur. But "What if you never see your grandchild's face?"—those were the only words that reached me. My grandson was born in September, and thanks to him I came back to life.

I didn't regain consciousness for three days, and after that my memory didn't quite connect. Something somebody told me only half an hour before would go clean out of my head. That seems to be characteristic of sarin poisoning. The company president came to visit me several times, but I don't remember him being there, or what we talked about. I hope I didn't slight him. They say he dropped by ten times and I don't remember a thing.

It was only around the eighth day that my memory began to kick in again. It was about that long, too, before I could eat real food. I had no physical symptoms: no eye pain, no headaches, no other pains, no itching. I didn't notice that my vision was odd.

I probably shouldn't say this, but all the nurses were beautiful! I even said so to my wife: "Nurse So-and-so is *so* beautiful. They say beautiful women are cold, but she's so kind." For some time after I came around, I was convinced everyone in the world had turned beautiful on me.

I found nights at the hospital frightening, though. Lying in bed, I'd brush up against the bed frame and I'd feel like a cold, damp hand was about to drag me into the darkness. There was always someone around during the daytime so it was all right, but at night when I'd be trying to sleep, my hand or foot would touch the frame, and that cold hand would pull me under. The more conscious I became, the better my memories linked up and these frights got worse. I didn't recognize them as hallucinations; I was sure there was a dead person in the ward whispering, "Come with me! This way, this way…" It was scary, but I couldn't mention it to anyone. Ordinarily I'm the boss around the house, so I couldn't admit to being scared.

I knew I had to get out of that hospital as soon as possible. If I couldn't finish the hospital food, I'd get my wife to bag up what I had left and throw it out, to make it look as though I'd recovered. In that way, I was able to force the issue and get released in eleven days. I was supposed to have stayed in for at least fifteen days.

But back at home it was the same thing. Whenever I stepped onto a tatami mat, whenever I touched anything cold, those fears resurfaced. Even when I took a bath by myself. I couldn't do it alone, I was too scared. My wife had to scrub my back. "Stay with me until I get out," I told her. "I don't want to be the last to leave."

Some of the victims are afraid to take the subway, even now. I was scared at first, too. The company thought I'd be reluctant to use the subway and told me to take the bullet train instead. They even offered to buy me a commuter pass, but I turned it down. I didn't want to be coddled, and I didn't want to run away, either. I went back to work on May 10, and from that very first day I took the exact same 7:15 Hibiya Line train that had been targeted in the gas attack. I even made sure I sat in the same car—the same seat. Once the train passed Kamiyacho, I looked over my shoulder and said to myself, "That's where it happened." At that moment I felt a bit queasy, but having gotten it over and done with, my spirits lifted. That wiped the slate clean of any anxieties.

Those who died from inhaling sarin probably had no idea they were going to die. The last few minutes they were unconscious, after all. There was no time to see their wives, their children. No one could have foreseen something like this was going to happen—there has to be a better way to put it—what I want to say is: What on earth were those people sacrificed for?

I want anyone who could do such a thing given the maximum punishment. I say this on behalf of the people who died. I can say this because I came back to life—but what did they possibly have to gain from killing them? It wasn't this; it wasn't that; I don't know a thing about it; my disciples did it—all that is just crap. Killing people as if they were ants, all for purely selfish, egotistical reasons, or even just on a whim: it's unforgivable. I pray that those who were sacrificed may rest in peace.

Haruki Murakami, *from* Underground. *On March 20, 1995, the Aum Shinrikyo doomsday cult released sarin gas—estimated to be twenty-six times more deadly than cyanide—in the Tokyo subway system, killing thirteen and injuring one thousand. Inspired by the oral histories of Studs Terkel and Bob Greene, Murakami spent a year interviewing victims, including Hiroshige Sugazaki, who spent three days in a coma. "The Japanese media," wrote Murakami, "has bombarded us with so many in-depth profiles of the Aum cult perpetrators—the 'attackers'—forming such a slick, seductive narrative that the average citizen— the 'victim'—was almost an afterthought."*

Gustav Klimt's The Kiss (Freedom Graffiti), from the series *Syrian Museum*, by Tammam Azzam, 2013. Archival print on cotton paper, 44 X 44 inches, edition of 25.

27: Rome

DEATH IN THE ROUND

A sudden disaster that now occurred was as destructive as a major war. It began and ended in a moment. An ex-slave called Atilius started building an amphitheater at Fidenae for a gladiatorial show. But he neither rested its foundations on solid ground nor fastened the wooden superstructure securely. He had undertaken the project not because of great wealth or municipal ambition but for sordid profits. Lovers of such displays, starved of amusements under Tiberius,

flocked in—men and women of all ages. Their numbers, swollen by the town's proximity, intensified the tragedy. The packed structure collapsed, subsiding both inward and outward and precipitating or overwhelming a huge crowd of spectators and bystanders.

Those killed at the outset of the catastrophe at least escaped torture, as far as their violent deaths permitted. More pitiable were those, mangled but not yet dead, who knew their wives and children lay there too. In daytime they could see them, and at night they heard their screams and moans. The news attracted crowds, lamenting kinsmen, brothers,

Funeral Honors Rendered to Titian After His Death at Venice During the Plague of 1576 (detail), by Alexandre Hesse, 1833.

and fathers. Even those whose friends and relations had gone away on other business were alarmed, for while the casualties remained unidentified, uncertainty gave free range for anxieties. When the ruins began to be cleared, people rushed to embrace and kiss the corpses—and even quarreled over them, when features were unrecognizable but similarities of physique or age had caused wrong identifications.

Fifty thousand people were mutilated or crushed to death in the disaster. The senate decreed that in the future no one with a capital of less than 400,000 sesterces should exhibit a gladiatorial show, and no amphitheater should be constructed except on ground of proved solidity. Atilius was banished. Immediately after the catastrophe leading Romans threw open their homes, providing medical attention and supplies all around. In those days Rome, for all its miseries, recalled the practice of our ancestors, who after great battles had lavished gifts and attentions on the wounded.

This calamity had not been forgotten when Rome suffered an exceptionally destructive fire, which gutted the Caelian Hill. This was a fatal year, people said. Fastening on a scapegoat for chance happenings (as the public does), they detected an evil omen in the emperor's decision to leave Rome. Tiberius disarmed criticism by distributing money in proportion to losses incurred. This earned him votes of thanks in the senate by eminent members and, as the news got around, a feeling of gratitude among the general public, because the donations were made without respecting persons or favoring relatives' petitions; sometimes the beneficiaries were unknown victims applying in response to the emperor's invitation. It was proposed that the Caelian should in future be called the Augustan Hill, since while flames roared on all sides the one thing unharmed was a statue of Tiberius in the house of a senator named Junius.

Tacitus, *from his* Annals. *Tacitus married the daughter of Consul Agricola in 77 and gained a praetorship in 88. One of the greatest prose stylists of Latin literature, his reputation as a historian is based primarily on the* Histories, *written c. 107, and the* Annals, *written c. 120; it is believed he died shortly after completing the latter. Of Tacitus' timeless understanding of human nature, Montaigne wrote, "You would often think it is us whom he is describing and criticizing."*

1666: London

It pleased God, contrary to all expectation, that about four or five of the clock in the afternoon the wind fell, and as in an instant the fire decreased, having burned all on the Thames side to the new buildings of the Inner Temple next to Whitefriars. And it ceased in all other parts of the town near the same time, so that the greatest care then was to keep good guards to watch the fire that was upon the ground, that it might not break out again. And this was the better performed, because they who had yet their houses standing had not the courage to sleep, but watched with much less distraction, though the same distemper still remained in the utmost extent "that all this had fallen out by the conspiracy of the French and Dutch with the papists." And all gaols were filled with those who were every hour apprehended upon that jealousy, or rather upon some evidence that they were guilty of the crime. And the people were so sottish that they believed that all the French in the town, which no doubt were a very great number, were drawn into a body to prosecute those by the sword who were preserved from the fire. And the inhabitants of a whole street have ran in a great tumult one way upon the rumor that the French were marching at the other end of it, so terrified men were with their own apprehensions.

When the night, though far from being a quiet one, had somewhat lessened the consternation, the first care the king took was that the country might speedily supply markets in all places, that they who had saved themselves from burning might not be in danger of starving. And if there had not been extraordinary care and diligence used, many would have perished that way. The vast destruction of corn and all other sorts of provisions in those parts where the fire had prevailed had not only left all that people destitute of all that was to be eat or drunk, but the bakers and brewers, which inhabited the other parts which were unhurt, had forsaken their houses and carried away all that was portable, insomuch as many days passed before they were enough in their wits and in their houses to fall to their occupations. And those parts of the town which God had spared and preserved were many hours without anything to eat, as well as they who were in the fields. And yet it can hardly be conceived how great a supply of all kinds was brought from all places within four and twenty hours. And which was more miraculous, in four days, in all the fields about the town, which had seemed covered with those whose habitations were burned, and with the goods which they had saved, there was scarce a man to be seen. All

> *Man endures earthquakes, epidemics, the horrors of disease, and all sorts of emotional torment, but the most agonizing tragedy was, is, and will be the tragedy of the bedroom.*
> —Leo Tolstoy, c. 1900

found shelter in so short a time, either in those parts which remained of the city and in the suburbs or in the neighbor villages; all kind of people expressing a marvelous charity toward those who appeared to be undone.

The king was not more troubled at any particular than at the imagination which possessed the hearts of so many, that all this mischief had fallen out by a real and formed conspiracy, which, albeit he saw no color to believe, he found very many intelligent men, and even some of his own council, who did really believe it. Whereupon he appointed the privy council to sit both morning and evening to examine all evidence of that kind that should be brought before them. Many witnesses who were produced as if their testimony would remove all doubts made such senseless relations of what they had been told, without knowing the condition of the persons who told them or where to find them, that it was a hard matter to forbear smiling at their evidence. Some Frenchmen's houses had been searched in which had been found many of those shells for squibs and other fireworks frequently used in nights of

Madding Crowds

Fatality counts of mass stampedes

6 Florence (1379)
The beheading of two aristocrats draws a huge crowd. One woman's cry causes a stampede to clear the area; many lose their shoes and hats, others their lives.

21 Chicago (2003)
Security guards use pepper spray to break up a fight at the E2 nightclub; several guests report hearing someone say, "I'll bet it's bin Laden." Patrons panic and are crushed at the bottom of a stairway.

73 Calumet, MI (1913)
At a Christmas Eve party for striking miners at the Italian Hall, someone yells "Fire!" and causes a stampede down the stairs. Later research suggests the panic was started by opponents of the miners' union.

80 Agra Polo Grounds (c. 1575)
A rush ensues as Mughal emperor Akbar attempts to distribute one golden coin to each of 100,000 poor men assembled on the polo grounds. Full moneybags recovered from the site afterward show that wealthy citizens had also come to collect.

115 Birmingham, AL (1902)
After a speech by Booker T. Washington to the National Convention of Negro Baptists, a cry of "Quiet!" misheard as "Fire!" spurs a rush for the door. "Investigation shows," reads a *New York Times* report, "that no white people were killed."

1,389 Khodynka (1896)
Five hundred thousand people gather for the coronation of Tsar Nicholas II, where promised gifts include sausage, pretzels, gingerbread, and beer. A deadly stampede begins when rumor spreads that the beer has run out.

2,411 Mecca (2015)
Two groups of Muslims on their hajj pilgrimage, both attempting to take part in a ritual representing Abraham's stoning of the devil, meet at an intersection in the Mina tent city. Pathways have not been properly allocated, and the massive crush leads to the deadliest hajj disaster in history.

20,000 Jerusalem (c. 50)
A Roman soldier stationed at the Jewish temple during a celebration of Passover insults the crowd by exposing himself. After the crowd demands justice, the Roman procurator orders in more troops and a deadly stampede ensues.

joy and triumph. The men were well known, and had lived many years there by that trade, and had no other. Yet these men were looked upon as in the number of the conspirators and remained still in prison till their neighbors solicited for their liberty. And it cannot be enough wondered at that in this general rage of the people no mischief was done to the strangers, that no one of them was assassinated outright, though many were sorely beaten and bruised.

The value or estimate of what that devouring fire consumed, over and above the houses, could never be computed in any degree. For besides that the first night, which in a moment swept away the vast wealth of Thames Street, there was not anything that could be preserved in respect of the suddenness and amazement, all people being in their beds till the fire was in their houses, and so could save nothing but themselves. Nor did many believe that the fire was near them, or that they had reason to remove their goods, till it was upon them and rendered it impossible. Then it fell out at a season in the year, the beginning of September, when very many of the substantial citizens and other wealthy men were in the country, whereof many had not left a servant in their houses, thinking themselves upon all ordinary accidents more secure in the goodness and kindness of their neighbors than they could be in the fidelity of a servant. And whatsoever was in such houses was entirely consumed by the fire or lost as to the owners. And of this class of absent men, there was scarce one to whom those lodgings appertained who was in town, so that whatsoever was there, their money, books, and papers, besides the evidences of many men's estates deposited in their hands, were all burned or lost to a very great value. But of particular men's losses could never be made any computation.

It was an incredible damage that was and might rationally be computed to be sustained by one small company, the company of stationers, in books, paper, and the other lesser commodities which are vendible in that corporation, which amounted to no less than

200,000 pounds. All those who dwelled near St. Paul's carried their goods, books, paper, and the like into the large vaults which were under the church before the fire came thither; which vaults, though all the church above the ground was afterward burned, with all the houses round about, still stood firm and supported the foundation and preserved all that was within them. The impatience of those who had lost their houses and whatsoever they had else in the fire made them very desirous to see what they had saved, upon which all their hopes were founded to repair the rest.

It was the fourth day after the fire ceased to flame, though it still burned in the ruins, from whence there was still an intolerable heat, when the booksellers came to behold all their wealth, which to that moment was safe. But the doors were no sooner opened and the air from without fanned the strong heat within, but first the driest and most combustible matters broke into a flame, which consumed all of what kind soever that till then had been unhurt there.

If so vast a damage as 200,000 pounds befell that little company of stationers in books and paper and the like, what shall we conceive was lost in cloth, in silks of all kinds, in linen, and those richer manufactures? Not to speak of money, plate, and jewels, whereof some were recovered out of the ruins of those houses which the owners took care to watch, as containing somewhat that was worth the looking for, and in which deluge there were men ready enough to fish.

> **Edward Hyde, earl of Clarendon**, *from his* Life. *Hyde became lord chancellor to Charles II after the Restoration, but was dismissed from his chancellorship in August 1667. Three months later he was forced to flee to France. He wrote his* Life *and completed his* History of the Rebellion *while in exile. A month after his death in Rouen in 1674, he was buried in Westminster Abbey. "Clarendon," said journalist and critic Murray Kempton, "was always on the losing side, but he was a towering spirit."*

Refugee camp, Democratic Republic of Congo, 2008. Photograph by Jim Goldberg.

1907: Madrid

BREAKING NEWS

This just in—the earth quakes!
4-stars brew war at The Hague.
The Royals are running scared.
Something stinks around the world.
There is no more balm in Gilead.
Wicked times for Marquis de Sade—
the last man out of Zeboim.
Terror tides in the Gulf Stream.
Paris whipped for pleasure.
Comet coming closer.
All that I have prophesied
will come true, says Malachi.
Devil finds faith in churchyard.
Nun gives birth to child. (Had you heard?)
Barcelona is a tomb—
ready to blow like a bomb.
In China pigtails are cut.
Henry de Rothschild: poet.
In Madrid the cape is passé.
Pope says eunuchs gone today.
Parliament's latest bill—
child prostitution is legal.
What was white is now dead.
What is black is still ahead.
Where do we go to find grace?
Try the Antichrist's grand estate.
The first words spoken between
faggots and lesbians.
Nearly home, our wandering Jew?
My God, what else is new?

Rubén Darío, *"Wire Service."* The leader of the Spanish American literary movement Modernismo, Darío was born in Metapa, Nicaragua, in 1867. Beginning in 1898 he became a correspondent for the Buenos Aires newspaper La Nación, *traveling extensively throughout Europe. According to Octavio Paz, "his constant travels and his generous activity on behalf of others made him the point of connection for the many scattered poets and groups on two continents. He not only inspired and captained the battle; he was also its observer and critic."*

1936: Prague

CHIEF SALAMANDER SPEAKING

Three days after the Louisiana earthquake a new geological disaster was reported, this time from China. With a massive thunderous earth tremor the coast in Kiangsu Province had burst open north of Nanking, about halfway between the Yangtze estuary and the ancient bed of the Huang Ho. The sea had rushed into the breach and linked up with the big lakes Pan-jün and Hung-tse Hu between the cities of Hwaingan and Fugjang. It seemed that as a result of the earthquake the Yangtze had shifted its riverbed below Nanking, flowing instead toward Lake Tai and onto Hangchow. No estimate, even approximate, could yet be made of the loss of life. Hundreds of thousands were fleeing into the northern and southern provinces. Japanese warships had been ordered to make for the stricken coast.

Although the scale of the earthquake in Kiangsu greatly exceeded the disaster in Loui-siana it received little attention on the whole: the world was accustomed to catastrophes in China and, so it seemed, the odd million lives did not matter greatly there. Besides, it was scientifically obvious that this was a mere tectonic earthquake, associated with a deep ocean trench near the Ryukyu and Philippine archipelagos. Three days later, however, European seismographs registered renewed tremors with an epicenter somewhere near the Cape Verde Islands. More detailed reports stated that a severe earthquake had hit the Senegambian coast south of Saint-Louis. A deep subsidence had occurred between the towns of Lampoul and Mboro; this was flooded by the sea, which penetrated as far as Merinaghene and the Dimar wadis. According to eyewitness accounts a column of fire and steam had burst from the ground, accompanied by a frightful rumble, flinging sand and stones over a wide radius; after that the sea was heard rushing into the opened rift. Loss of life was not heavy.

This third earthquake caused something akin to panic. IS VOLCANIC ACTIVITY REVIVING

"Monumental Chaos," by Mitchell Krog, 2011.
Simultaneous lightning strikes at the Voortrekker Monument near Pretoria, South Africa.

The Temptation of Saint Anthony, by the workshop of Herri met de Bles, c. 1550.

ON EARTH? the newspapers asked. EARTH'S CRUST BEGINNING TO CRACK reported the evening papers. The experts suggested that the "Senegambian rift" might have been caused by the eruption of a volcanic vein associated with the Pico volcano on Fogo Island in the Cape Verde archipelago; that volcano had last erupted in 1847 and had since been regarded as extinct. The West African earthquake, therefore, had nothing in common with the seismic phenomena in Louisiana or Kiangsu, which had evidently been of a tectonic character. People, however, did not seem to care greatly whether it was as a result of tectonic or volcanic causes that the earth was cracking. The fact was that churches everywhere were crowded with people who had come to pray. In some parts even the churches had to be kept open at night.

About one o'clock in the morning—that was on November 20—radio hams throughout most of Europe observed heavy interference on their receivers, just as if some new, unusually powerful transmitter had gone into operation. They found it on a wavelength of 203; there was a rushing noise as though from machinery or the waves of the sea. From that protracted, unending hum suddenly came a terrible croaking voice (they all described it in similar terms: hollow, quacking, as if artificial, and simultaneously, enormously magnified by a loudspeaker), and that froglike voice shouted excitedly: "Hello, hello, hello! The chief salamander speaking. Hello, the chief salamander speaking. Stop all broadcasting, you men! Stop your broadcasting! Hello, the chief salamander speaking!" Then another strangely hollow voice asked: "Ready?" "Ready." Next came a click as if a circuit was being switched, and again another unnaturally squawky voice called: "Attention! Attention! Attention!" "Hello!" "Now!"

And now a croaky, weary, but nevertheless commanding voice broke the nocturnal silence: "Hello, you humans! Louisiana calling. Kiangsu calling. Senegambia calling. We regret the loss of human lives. We do not wish to inflict unnecessary losses on you. We only want you to evacuate the seashores in the places we shall notify you of from time to time. If you conform, you will avoid regrettable accidents. Next time we shall give you at least a fortnight's advance warning of the areas where we will enlarge our sea. So far we merely have been conducting technical experiments. Your high explosives have worked well. Thank you.

"Hello, you people! No need for alarm. We have no hostile intentions toward you. We only need more water, more coasts, more shallows to live in. There are too many of us. There's no longer enough room for us on your coasts. That's why we have to dismantle your continents. We shall turn them all into bays and islands. In this way the overall length of the world's shorelines can be increased by a factor of five. We shall construct new shallows. We cannot live in the deep ocean. We shall need your continents as infill material. We have nothing against you, but there are too many of us. For the time being you can move inland. You can move up into the mountains. The mountains will be demolished last.

"You wanted us. You spread us all over the globe. Now you've got us. We want to be on good terms with you. You will supply us with steel for our drills and picks. You will supply us with high explosives. You will supply us with torpedoes. You will work for us. Without you we cannot remove the old continents. Hello, you people. On behalf of the newts of all the world the chief salamander offers you cooperation. You will work with us on the demolition of your world. We thank you."

The weary, croaky voice fell silent and a protracted hum was heard as of machinery or the sea. "Hello, hello, you people," the squawky voice spoke up again; "and now you'll hear a program of light music from your gramophone records. We start with 'The March of the Tritons' from the film spectacular *Poseidon*."

The newspapers, of course, described this nocturnal broadcast as a "crude joke in poor taste" by some pirate transmitter. Nevertheless, millions of people sat by their radio receivers the following night, waiting to hear whether that frightening, fanatic, squawky voice would speak again. It came on the air at exactly one o'clock to the accompaniment of a loud splashing and rushing noise. "Good evening, you people," it squeaked cheerfully. "To start with we shall play for you a recording of the Salamander Dance from your operetta *Galathea*." When the penetrating and shameless music was over the same frightful yet somehow joyful, squawky voice returned. "Hello, you people! A moment ago the British gunboat *Erebus*, which tried to destroy our transmitter station on the Atlantic Ocean, was sunk by a torpedo. The crew were drowned. Hello, we are calling the British government: stand by your loudspeakers. The ship *Amenhotep*, home port Port Said, refused to hand over to us at our port of Makallah the high explosives we had ordered. She claimed to have received orders to stop all further shipments of explosives. The ship, of course, was sunk. We advise the British government to revoke that

When an author has nearly finished his story and finds a whole bookload of hale, hearty characters left upon his hands, these little thunderstrokes of disease or disaster simplify matters wonderfully.
—Henry Mills Hurd, 1870

order by tomorrow morning; otherwise the ships *Winnipeg*, *Manitoba*, *Ontario*, and *Quebec*, all of them en route from Canada to Liverpool with cargoes of grain, will be sunk. Hello, we are calling the French government: stand by your loudspeakers. Recall the cruisers now sailing toward Senegambia. We still need to widen the newly formed inlet there. The chief salamander has instructed me to convey to both governments his unshakable wish to establish with them the most friendly relations. This is the end of the news. We shall now broadcast a recording of your song 'Salamandria, valse érotique.'"

The following afternoon the ships *Winnipeg*, *Manitoba*, *Ontario*, and *Quebec* were sunk southwest of Mizen Head. A wave of horror swept over the world. In the evening the BBC announced that His Majesty's Government had issued an order prohibiting the supply to the newts of any kind of foodstuffs, chemicals, equipment, weapons, or metals. At one o'clock at night an excited voice squawked on the radio: "Hello, hello, hello, the chief salamander speaking! Hello, the chief salamander is about to speak!" And then

1424: Hanyang

LET THEM EAT GRAIN

We consider the harm of the Buddhists to be prevalent still. Since the Han period the reverence for Buddha has been increasingly fervent, yet neither happiness nor profit has been gained. This is recorded in the historical books, which Your Majesty has certainly perused thoroughly. Must you therefore wait for your ministers to tell you?

We think that of all the heterodox teachings, Buddhism is the worst. The Buddhists live alone with their barbaric customs, apart from the common productive population, yet they cause the people to be destitute and to steal. What is worse than their crimes? Beasts and birds that damage grain are certainly chased away because they harm the people. Yet even though beasts and birds eat the people's food, they are nevertheless useful to the people. The Buddhists, however, sit around and eat, and there has not yet been a visible profit. No rain falls now—it is a year of drought. The public granaries are empty, and as to the livelihood of our people, neither life nor death is guaranteed. And yet the food these Buddhists eat is the same in good years as well as bad. One sees only the people starving, never a monk. One sees only the people dying of starvation, never a monk. They are reckless in daily deceiving and betraying the people. We are indeed concerned about it, and in the past many superior men earnestly pointed out their harm.

Yun Hoe, *from the* Annals of King Sejong. *In 1420 Chosŏn monarch Sejong founded a scholarly institution called the Hall of the Worthies, one of whose tasks was inventing the Korean alphabet. Buddhism had been a state religion since the sixth century, but by the time of Sejong, neo-Confucianism had taken over as the animating religion for politics. Hall scholar Yun Hoe was among those who believed Buddhism to be the "law of barbarians" and, hoping to lessen its influence on government, urged the destruction of pagodas and the burning of sutras.*

came that weary, croaky, angry voice: "Hello, you people! Hello, you people! Hello, you people! Do you think we shall allow ourselves to be starved out? Stop your nonsense at once! Any action you take will rebound on you! In the name of all newts everywhere I am addressing Great Britain. From now on we are imposing a total blockade of the British Isles with the exception of the Irish Free State. I am closing the English Channel. I am closing the Suez Canal. I am closing the Strait of Gibraltar to all shipping. All British ports are closed. All British ships in whatever sea they may be will be torpedoed. Hello, I am addressing Germany. I am increasing my order for high explosives tenfold. To be delivered immediately to the Skagerrak main depot. Hello, I am addressing France. Speed up deliveries of the ordered torpedoes to submarine forts C-3, BFF, and Ouest-5. Hello, you people! I am warning you. If you restrict deliveries of foodstuffs to us I shall commandeer them myself from your ships. I am warning you again." The weary voice sank to a husky, scarcely comprehensible croak. "Hello, hello, I am addressing Italy. Prepare to evacuate the region Venice-Padua-Udine. This is my final warning, you people. We've had enough of your nonsense." There followed a lengthy pause, with a background rushing as of a black and cold sea. Then the cheerful, squawky voice was back again: "And now, again from one of your recordings, we shall play that latest success, 'The Triton Trot.'"

It was an odd sort of war, if indeed it can be called a war since there was no newt state nor any recognized newt government against which war might be formally declared. The first country that found itself in a state of war with the salamanders was Great Britain. During the very first hours the newts sank virtually all her ships anchored in ports anywhere; there was no way of offering resistance. Only vessels on the high seas were relatively safe for the moment, especially if they were cruising over the deeper ocean areas; thus that section of the British navy was saved which broke through the blockade of Malta and concentrated above the Ionian Deep. But even these units were soon tracked down by small newt submarines and sunk one by one. Within the first six weeks Britain lost four-fifths of all her tonnage.

Not for the first time in history did John Bull reveal his famous tenacity. His Majesty's Government did not negotiate with the newts nor did it revoke its embargo on supplies. "A British gentleman," the prime minister declared, speaking for the whole nation, "will protect animals, but he does not negotiate with them." Within a few weeks there was a shortage of food in the British Isles. Only children received a small slice of bread and a few spoonfuls of tea or milk daily; the British people bore it all with exemplary fortitude, even though they sank so low as to eat all their racehorses. The Prince of Wales with his own hands plowed the first furrow on the links of the Royal Golf Club for carrots to be raised for the London orphanages. The tennis courts at Wimbledon were planted with potatoes, the racecourse at Ascot was sown to wheat. "We shall make any sacrifices, even the heaviest," the leader of the Conservative Party assured Parliament, "but we will not surrender British honor."

As the navy had been eliminated from the start, military operations against the newts were conducted on land and from the air. The land forces fired their guns and machine guns into the water, without, however, seeming to inflict any significant losses on the salamanders. Aerial bombardment of the sea was a little more successful. The newts retaliated by shelling the British ports with their underwater guns, reducing them to heaps of rubble. They also shelled London from the Thames estuary, whereupon army command made an attempt to poison the salamanders with bacteria, crude oil, and caustic substances poured into the Thames and into certain bays of the sea. To this the newts replied by releasing a screen of poison gas over 120 kilometers of British coastline. It was only a demonstration but it sufficed: for the first time in history the British government was obliged to request

Buddhist monk Nichizo and a companion encountering an eight-headed beast in hell, handscroll from the *Illustrated Legends of the Kitano Tenjin Shrine*, Japan, late thirteenth century.

other powers to intervene, referring to the prohibition of gas warfare.

The following night the croaky, angry, and heavy voice of the chief salamander again came on the air: "Hello, you people! Britain had better stop her nonsense! If you poison our water, we will poison your air. We are only using your own weapons. We are no barbarians. We don't want to make war on humans. We don't want anything except our right to live. We are offering you peace. You will supply us with your manufactures and you will sell us your continents. We are willing to pay a fair price for

There's nothing like a jolly good disaster to get people to start doing something.
—*Charles, Prince of Wales, 2014*

them. We are offering you nothing but peace. We are offering you gold for your lands. Hello, I am addressing Great Britain. Notify me of your price for the southern part of Lincolnshire along the Wash. You have three days to consider it. For that period I am suspending all hostilities except the blockade."

A few weeks subsequently a world conference of states met in Vaduz. It was held in Vaduz because there was no danger from the newts in the High Alps and also because the majority of wealthy and socially important people from coastal regions had already settled there. The conference, as was universally conceded, got down very briskly to the resolution of all topical international issues. In the first place, all countries (except Switzerland, Abyssinia, Afghanistan, Bolivia, and other landlocked states) refused as a matter of principle to recognize the newts as a sovereign belligerent power, mainly because if they did so their own salamanders might regard themselves as members of such a newt state. It could not be ruled out that a newt state, if recognized, might attempt to exercise sovereignty over all waters and coasts inhabited by newts. For that reason it was both legally and practically impossible to declare war on the salamanders or to bring any

international pressure to bear on them; each state was entitled only to take action against *its own* newts; it was, in fact, a purely domestic matter. For that reason there could be no question of any collective diplomatic or military action against the newts. The only international aid that could be given to states attacked by the salamanders was the granting of foreign loans for their successful defense.

Britain thereupon submitted a proposal that all states should at least undertake not to supply weapons or explosives to the newts. After mature deliberation the proposal was turned down, mainly because such an undertaking was already contained in the London Convention but also, secondly, because a country could not be prevented from supplying to its own newts technical equipment "solely for their own requirements" and arms for the defense of their own coasts; thirdly, because maritime countries were "naturally interested in maintaining good relations with the denizens of the sea" and therefore considered it desirable "to refrain at this moment from any measures that the newts might regard as discriminatory." Nevertheless, all states were prepared to vouchsafe that they would supply weapons and high explosives also to the states attacked by the newts.

In confidential discussion a Columbian proposal was adopted to the effect that at least unofficial talks should be initiated with the newts. The chief salamander would be invited to send his plenipotentiaries to the conference. The British representative strongly objected to this, refusing to sit at the same table as the newts; in the end, however, he agreed to absent himself by taking a trip to the Engadin for reasons of health.

Karel Čapek, *from* War with the Newts. *Born in a village in northeast Bohemia in 1890, Čapek became known as an author of science fiction—his play R.U.R. introduced the word robot—while also enjoying a long career in journalism. When he died on Christmas Day in 1938, two months after the Munich Agreement granted the annexation of portions of the Czechoslovak Republic to Nazi Germany, he was number three on the Gestapo's arrest list of Czech nationals.*

Circulation Desk, by Lori Nix, 2012. Archival pigment print, 30 x 40 inches.

2015: Syria

ONWARD TO ARMAGEDDON

The Islamic State uses terror tactics against its enemies similar to how the Mongols and the Crusaders and colonialists used terror to defeat the Muslims when the Muslims were a rich civilization.

Abu Bakr Naji was a jihad theorist in the mid-2000s. He proposed that mujahideen should use *tawahhush* to defeat their enemies. *Tawahhush* in Arabic comes from the word *wahsh*, "to be like a wolf or beast," which only cares about its own wolf family while being harsh against all other animals. This seclusion allows the wolf family to be strong because it does not care what outsiders say or think about it. Abu Bakr Naji explains that all savage nations like the Mongols, the old and the new Crusaders did not care what the world said about them. They broke all civilized laws and continued to choose their path of war until they crumbled superpowers, and in the end they were victorious and they became the kings. Uncivilized nations have always defeated civilized nations because uncivilized people have less rules to follow. They have less to lose and more to win. So Abu Bakr Naji says that the Sahaba (companions of Prophet Muhammad) who were men of the desert were able to defeat the Persian (Iranian) and Roman (European) superpowers through constant war and attrition. If the mujahideen continue in the path of jihad while ignoring the media criticism against them, they will continue to be victorious. Allah says about the victorious group: "They fight in the cause of Allah, and they do not fear the blame of the blamers. That is the favor of Allah, which he gives to whoever he wants."

"West Memphis, Arkansas. After the Flood," by Eugene Richards.

Unlike the majority of Muslims, who hate the negative attention Islam gets in the media, the mujahideen feel happy that their enemies say scary things about them (such as a beheading or terror attack). Why? Because the scary media attention puts fear into the heart of the enemies fighting the mujahideen. There are many cases when Iraqi troops flee even before a battle begins after hearing about a beheading video, and more American soldiers committed suicide in Iraq than those killed in battle. Many Russian troops today say they are scared and do not want to enter Syria to fight a battle that has nothing to do with them. Why would they want to be beheaded for nothing?

We are living in the prophetic end time "deceptive years" wherein Muslims look evil even though we are fighting the tyrant New World Order. Muslims cannot do much about this negative perception because it is the way of God's prophets to be harsh when the Muslims are weak (so their enemy does not feel too confident against a weaker enemy), and to be gentle with the people when we are strong. Study the life of Prophet Muhammad (peace be on him) and you will see this pattern. You will see how the order to behead the enemy (Qur'an 8:67) is after the battle of Badr when Muslims were weak, and the mercy of freeing the people of Mecca is after the conquest of Mecca when the Muslims were strong.

So do not feel saddened by the bad media attention Islam and mujahideen get. Your job is to continue the jihad, convey the truth, and in the end people will see the truth, and the sincere from the people will become guided after seeing through the deception.

From "Black Flags from the Islamic State." "All these prophecies of the end times you have already read," elsewhere reads this manifesto, released by the Islamic State in November 2015, "now they are becoming a reality." Another manifesto, recovered in July 2015, called for "the final battle" between the Muslim caliphate and the New World Order. "Accept the fact that this caliphate will survive and prosper until it takes over the entire world and beheads every last person that rebels against Allah," reads the document. "This is the bitter truth, swallow it."

1453: Constantinople

OTTOMAN ANTICHRIST

The Romans and the emperor Constantine XI did not know what had happened because the entry of the Turks took place at a distance; indeed, their paramount concern was the enemy before them. The fierce Turkish warriors outnumbered the Romans twenty to one. The Romans, moreover, were not as experienced in warfare as the ordinary Turks. Their attention and concern, therefore, were focused on the Turkish ground attack. Then suddenly arrows fell from above, slaughtering many Romans. When they looked up and saw the Turks, they fled behind the walls. When the tyrant's troops witnessed the rout of the Romans, they shouted with one voice and pursued them inside, trampling upon the wretches and slaughtering them.

The emperor, despairing and hopeless, stood with sword and shield in hand and poignantly cried out, "Is there no one among the Christians who will take my head from me?" He was abandoned and alone. Then one of the Turks wounded him by striking him flush, and he, in turn, gave the Turk a blow. A second Turk delivered a mortal blow from behind and the emperor fell to the earth. They slew him as a common soldier and left him, because they did not know he was the emperor.

Only three Turks perished and all the rest made their way inside. It was the first hour of the day, and the sun had not yet risen. As they entered the city and spread out from the Gate of Charisius to the palace, they slew those who resisted and those who fled. Breaking into the home of the protostrator [the emperor's chief horseman], they broke open the coffers full of treasures amassed long ago. In so doing they aroused the noblewomen from their sleep. It was the twenty-ninth day of May, and the morning sleep of the youths and maidens was sweet indeed; they slept unafraid and carefree as they had done yesterday and the day before.

Then a great horde of mounted infidels charged down the street leading to the Great Church [Hagia Sophia]. The actions of both Turks and Romans made quite a spectacle! In the early dawn, as the Turks poured into the city and the citizens took flight, some of the fleeing Romans managed to reach their homes and rescue their children and wives. As they moved, bloodstained, across the Forum of the Bull and passed the Forum of Constantine, their wives asked, "What is to become of us?" When they heard the fearful cry, "The Turks are slaughtering Romans within the city's walls," they did not believe it at first. They cursed and reviled the ill-omened messenger instead. But behind him came a second, and then a third, and all were covered with blood, and they knew that the cup of the Lord's wrath had touched their lips. Monks and nuns, therefore, and men and women, carrying their infants in their arms and abandoning their homes to anyone who wished to break in, ran to the Great Church. The thoroughfare, overflowing with people, was a sight to behold!

Why were they all seeking refuge in the Great Church? Many years before they had heard from some false prophets that the city was fated to be surrendered to the Turks, who would enter with great force, and that the Romans would be cut down by them as far as the Column of Constantine the Great. Afterward, however, an angel, descending and holding a sword, would deliver the empire and the sword to an unknown man, extremely plain and poor, standing at the column. "Take this sword," the angel would say, "and avenge the people of the Lord." Then the Turks would take flight and the Romans would follow hard upon them, cutting them down. They would drive them from the city and from the West, and from the East as far as the borders of Persia, to a place called Monodendrion. This was the cause then of the flight into the Great Church. In one hour's time that enormous temple was filled with men and women. There was a throng too many to count, above and below, in the courtyards and everywhere. They bolted the doors and waited, hoping to be rescued by the anonymous savior.

Pillaging, slaughtering, and taking captives on the way, the Turks reached the temple before the termination of the first hour. The gates were barred, but they broke them with axes. They entered with swords flashing and, beholding the myriad populace, each Turk caught and bound his own captive. There was no one who resisted or who did not surrender himself like a sheep. Who can recount the calamity of that time and place? Who can describe the wailing and the cries of the babes, the mothers' tearful screams and the fathers' lamentations? The commonest Turk sought the most tender maiden. The lovely nun, who heretofore belonged only to the one God, was now seized and bound by another master. The rapine caused the tugging and pulling of braids of hair, the exposure of bosoms and breasts, and outstretched arms. The female slave was bound with her mistress, the master with his slave, the archimandrite with the doorkeeper, tender youths with virgins, who had never been exposed to the sun and hardly ever seen by their own fathers, were dragged about, forcibly pushed together and flogged. The despoiler led them to a certain spot and, placing them in safekeeping, returned to take a second and even a third prize. The abductors, the avengers of God, were in a great hurry. Within one hour they had bound everyone, the male captives with cords and the women with their own veils. The infinite chains of captives who like herds of cattle and flocks of sheep poured out of the temple and the temple sanctuary made an extraordinary spectacle! They wept and wailed and there was none to show them mercy.

What became of the temple treasures? What shall I say and how shall I say it? My tongue is stuck fast in my larynx. I am unable to draw breath through my sealed mouth. In that same hour the dogs hacked the holy icons to pieces, removing the ornaments. As for the chains, candelabra, holy altar coverings, and lamps, some they destroyed and the rest they seized. All the precious and sacred vessels of the holy sacristy, fashioned from gold and silver and other valuable materials, they collected in an instant, leaving the temple desolate and naked; absolutely nothing was left behind.

The frightful day on which the city fell was the feast day of the holy martyr Theodosia. All these events took place between the first hour of the day and the eighth hour. Setting aside his suspicions and fears, the Turkish sultan Mehmed II made his entry into the city with his viziers and satraps, preceded and followed by his fire-eating slaves, all of whom were archers superior to Apollo, youthful Heracleidae eager to challenge ten men. Proceeding to the Great Church, he dismounted from his horse and went inside. He marveled at the sight! When he found a Turk smashing a piece of marble pavement, he asked him why he was demolishing the floor. "For the faith," he replied. He extended his hand and struck the Turk a blow with his sword, remarking "You have enough treasure and captives. The city's buildings are mine." When the tyrant beheld the treasures that had been collected and the countless captives, he regretted his compact. The Turk was dragged by the feet and cast outside half dead. He summoned one of his vile priests who ascended the pulpit to call out his foul prayer. The son of iniquity, the forerunner of the Antichrist, ascending the holy altar, offered the prayer.

The morning following the black day on which the utter destruction of our nation took place, the entire city was desolate. Within, neither man nor beast nor fowl was heard to cry out or utter a sound. Only they were left who were too weak to pillage. Many were killed as one dragged away the spoils of another. He who was able seized, and he who was unable to resist received a mortal blow and succumbed. On the second day, the thirtieth of May, the Turkish troops entered and collected whatever had been abandoned. And the city was desolate, lying dead, naked, soundless, having neither form nor beauty.

Ducas, *from* Decline and Fall of Byzantium to the Ottoman Turks. *After defending Constantinople from Huns, Slavs, Persians, Franks, and Venetians, the Byzantine Empire was overrun by the Ottomans under the command of Mehmed II, whom Byzantine historians named the Antichrist. Ducas, who served the royalty of Lesbos on diplomatic missions to the Ottoman court, advocated the union of the Byzantine and Latin empires, criticizing the Byzantine orthodoxy for not appealing to the West in its fight against the Turks. His history covers the years 1341 to 1462.*

Dust Storm, Fifth Avenue, by John Sloan, 1906.

1915: Chicago

HELEN REPA INTO THE BREACH

I was on a trolley car at Lake Street when I heard what I thought must be screams. I could hear them even above the noise of the car and the noises on the street. Just then a mounted policeman galloped up and stopped all the traffic, shouting, "Excursion boat capsized—look out for the ambulance!"

I ran to the front of the car to get off. The motorman tried to stop me, but I slipped past him and jumped off just as one of the ambulances came up. It had to slow up on account of the congestion, and I managed to jump on the back step. I had my uniform on

and so was allowed to stay on until we got to the dock.

I don't know how I got on the dock, or on the *Eastland*. Indeed, there are a good many things that happened that day that I am still hazy about. All I remember is climbing up the slippery side of the boat, losing my footing, and being shoved up by somebody from behind. I finally got to where I could stand up on the side of the boat, which was lying out of water.

I shall never be able to forget what I saw. People were struggling in the water, clustered so thickly that they literally covered the surface of the river. A few were swimming; the rest were floundering about, some clinging to a life raft that had floated free, others clutching at anything they could reach—at bits of wood, at each other, grabbing each other, pulling each other down, and screaming! The screaming was the most horrible of all.

They were already pulling them out from below when I got there, out of the water and out through the portholes. People were being dragged out, wet, bleeding, and hysterical, by the scores. Most of those from the decks and the inside of the boat were cut more or less severely, because the chairs and benches had slid down on top of them when the boat went over.

Those who had no injuries beyond the wetting and the shock were sent to the various hotels. I started working, first on the boat itself and then on the dock, helping to try and resuscitate those who were unconscious. The pulmotors had not yet arrived, and we had to try what first-aid measures we could.

The injured were taken to the Iroquois Memorial Hospital. Remembering that this is only an emergency hospital, and is not equipped to handle a large number of cases at once, I asked a policeman how many nurses were on duty there. He said that there were only two. Knowing that I would be more needed there than at the dock, for the present, I hurried over. I went back and forth between the hospital and the dock several times during the day and had no trouble in making the journey quickly. I simply jumped on a patrol wagon or an ambulance and being, as I have said, in uniform, was able to make the trip without being questioned. The one place I did have trouble, and a great deal of it, was at the dock. The police had evidently received orders to keep everybody back, and so zealously did they perform their work that I was held up several times until I could be identified. I finally remembered the armbands that we nurses had received to wear at the picnic. These were of red, white, and blue cloth, with a red cross on them. After I had put mine on I had no further trouble.

By this time the hospital was so full of people that we had no place to put the less seriously injured while they were drying off. Luckily, just at this time, word came from men working in the boiler room of a large building nearby that they would care for as many people as we cared to send over.

Camels before an oil fire, Kuwait, 1991. Photograph by Steve McCurry.

I must say that the people of Chicago showed a wonderful spirit. Everyone did all he could to help. As soon as my patients were sufficiently recovered, I would send them home, thinking it better to have them with their families as soon as possible. In order to do this, I would simply go out into the street, stop the first automobile that came along, load it up with people, and tell the owner or driver where to take them. And not one driver said no, or seemed anything but anxious to help out. When the women would be brought off the boat dripping wet, the men standing by simply took off their coats and put them around them.

About nine or half past I started back to the dock. When I got to Clark Street the crowd was so dense that I simply couldn't walk a step further. So I got on a hook-and-ladder truck that was going down.

When I got to the dock they had begun to bring the bodies up from the hold, and it was pouring rain. The bodies came out faster than we could handle them. By this time a number of outside nurses and doctors were at work on the victims. Most of them were dead, but a few still showed signs of life. I saw that if any of these were to be saved we must get them away from the dock. The crowding and confusion were terrible. The bodies were laid out on the dock, on the bridges, some on a boat, others on the sidewalk. A crowd of willing but ignorant volunteers kept getting in the way and made our attempts at resuscitation almost useless.

I asked a policemen, "Isn't there some building where we can take these people? Some of them have a fighting chance if we can get them out of the rain and away from this crowd."

He promised to see what could be done and went away. A little later he returned, saying that we could take the bodies over to Reid & Murdoch's warehouse. We took the bodies we had, and all the others that came out, over there but it was too late. Out of hundreds that we took to the warehouse, only four were revived.

By this time I had on my armband and so was able to go from the dock to the warehouse and back without being stopped. What made the confusion at the dock still worse was the fact that many of the people who had been pulled out of the water uninjured were still so dazed that they were wandering up and down without knowing where they were or what they were doing. I found one man up a little alley nearby. He was wandering up and down, with a ghastly, expressionless face, repeating over and over again, "I lost them all, I lost them all." His wife and three children were somewhere in the hold of the *Eastland.*

About twelve o'clock they reached the bodies in the inner cabins, and after that time all

Perhaps catastrophe is the natural human environment, and even though we spend a good deal of energy trying to get away from it, we are programmed for survival amid catastrophe.
—Germaine Greer, 1984

the bodies that came up seemed to be women and children. It had begun to drizzle just before the boat was to start, and the mothers had taken their children inside to be out of the wet.

When I started out in the morning I had had on a white uniform and white shoes. By noon, what with dressing wounds and kneeling on the dock, I was covered with bloodstains and caked with mud from head to foot. I had lost my coat. A fireman threw a woman's skirt over my shoulders, and I kept the rain out with that.

At four o'clock I went home. There was nothing left to do. I had been on my feet since seven thirty that morning, and I felt that if I ever sat down I would never get up again. I came home in the streetcar, with the skirt wrapped around my shoulders and my brother's raincoat over that.

"The Experiences of a Hawthorne Nurse." Workers of the Western Electric Company and their families boarded the Eastland *on July 24, 1915, for a company-sponsored day trip on Lake Michigan. The ship, sailing just three years after the sinking of the* Titanic, *was carrying thirty-seven life rafts and eleven lifeboats (though it was designed to carry just six); the weight of the emergency crafts is thought to have caused the ship to capsize. Eight hundred and forty-four people died in the accident.*

1874: Wessex

SHEEP TO SLAUGHTER

One night, when farmer Gabriel Oak had returned to his house, believing there would be no further necessity for his attendance on the down, he called as usual to the dogs, previously to shutting them up in the outhouse till next morning. Only one responded—old George; the other could not be found, either in the house, lane, or garden. Gabriel then remembered that he had left the two dogs on the hill eating a dead lamb (a kind of meat he usually kept from them, except when other food ran short), and concluding that the young one had not finished his meal he went indoors to the luxury of a bed, which latterly he had only enjoyed on Sundays.

It was a still, moist night. Just before dawn he was assisted in waking by the abnormal reverberation of familiar music. To the shepherd, the note of the sheep bell, like the ticking of the clock to other people, is a chronic sound that only makes itself noticed by ceasing or altering in some unusual manner from the well-known idle tinkle which signifies to the accustomed ear, however distant, that all is well in the fold. In the solemn calm of the awakening morn that note was heard by Gabriel, beating with unusual violence and rapidity. This exceptional ringing may be caused in two ways—by the rapid feeding of the sheep bearing the bell, as when the flock breaks into new pasture, which gives it an intermittent rapidity, or by the sheep starting off in a run, when the sound has a regular palpitation. The experienced ear of Oak knew the sound he now heard to be caused by the running of the flock with great velocity.

He jumped out of bed, dressed, tore down the lane through a foggy dawn, and ascended the hill. The forward ewes were kept apart from those among which the fall of lambs would be later, there being two hundred of the latter class in Gabriel's flock. These two hundred seemed to have absolutely vanished from the hill. There were the fifty with their lambs, enclosed at the other end as he had left them, but the rest, forming the bulk of the flock, were nowhere. Gabriel called at the top of his voice the shepherd's call:

"Ovey, ovey, ovey!"

Not a single bleat. He went to the hedge; a gap had been broken through it, and in the gap were the footprints of the sheep. Rather surprised to find them break fence at this season, yet putting it down instantly to their great fondness for ivy in wintertime, of which a great deal grew in the plantation, he followed through the hedge. They were not in the plantation. He called again; the valleys and furthest hills resounded as when the sailors invoked the lost Hylas on the Mysian shore; but no sheep. He passed through the trees and along the ridge of the hill. On the extreme summit, where the ends of the two converging hedges of which we have spoken were stopped short by meeting the brow of the chalk pit, he saw the younger dog standing against the sky—dark and motionless as Napoleon at St. Helena.

A horrible conviction darted through Oak. With a sensation of bodily faintness he advanced; at one point the rails were broken through, and there he saw the footprints of his ewes. The dog came up, licked his hand, and made signs implying that he expected some great reward for signal services rendered. Oak looked over the precipice. The ewes lay dead and dying at its foot—a heap of two hundred mangled carcasses, representing in their condition just now at least two hundred more.

Oak was an intensely humane man; indeed, his humanity often tore in pieces any politic intentions of his which bordered on strategy, and carried him on as by gravitation. A shadow in his life had always been that his flock ended in mutton—that a day came and found every shepherd an arrant traitor to his defenseless sheep. His first feeling now was one of pity for the untimely fate of these gentle ewes and their unborn lambs.

It was a second to remember another phase of the matter. The sheep were not insured. All the savings of a frugal life had been dispersed at a blow; his hopes of being an independent farmer were laid low—possibly forever. Gabriel's

energies, patience, and industry had been so severely taxed during the years of his life between eighteen and twenty-eight, to reach his present stage of progress, that no more seemed to be left in him. He leaned down upon a rail and covered his face with his hands.

Stupors, however, do not last forever, and Farmer Oak recovered from his. It was as remarkable as it was characteristic that the one sentence he uttered was in thankfulness:

"Thank God I am not married. What would she have done in the poverty now coming upon me!"

Oak raised his head and, wondering what he could do, listlessly surveyed the scene. By the outer margin of the pit was an oval pond, and over it hung the attenuated skeleton of a chrome-yellow moon, which had only a few days to last—the morning star dogging her on the left hand. The pool glittered like a dead man's eye, and as the world awoke a breeze blew, shaking and elongating the reflection of the moon without breaking it, and turning the image of the star to a phosphoric streak upon the water. All this Oak saw and remembered.

As far as could be learned it appeared that the poor young dog, still under the impression that since he was kept for running after sheep, the more he ran after them the better, had at the end of his meal off the dead lamb, which may have given him additional energy and spirits, collected all the ewes into a corner, driven the timid creatures through the hedge, across the upper field, and by main force of worrying had given them momentum enough to break down a portion of the rotten railing, and so hurled them over the edge.

George's son had done his work so thoroughly that he was considered too good a workman to live, and was in fact taken and tragically shot at twelve o'clock that same day—another instance of the untoward fate which so often attends dogs and other philosophers who follow out a train of reasoning to its logical conclusion, and attempt perfectly consistent conduct in a world made up so largely of compromise.

Gabriel's farm had been stocked by a dealer—on the strength of Oak's promising look and character—who was receiving a percentage from the farmer till such time as the advance should be cleared off. Oak found that the value of stock, plant, and implements which were really his own would be about sufficient to pay his debts, leaving himself a free man with the clothes he stood up in, and nothing more.

Thomas Hardy, *from* Far from the Madding Crowd. *Born in the English county of Dorset in 1840, Hardy first published* Madding Crowd *as a serial in* Cornhill Magazine. *Some reviewers mistook the writing for that of George Eliot. He would later recall that with his next novel,* The Hand of Ethelberta, *he "had the satisfaction of proving, amid the general disappointment at the lack of sheep and shepherds, that he did not mean to imitate anybody, whatever the satisfaction might have been worth." Hardy died in 1928 a few miles from his birthplace.*

AFTERMATH

c. 2030: San Bernardino County

CLAIRE VAYE WATKINS IN GEOLOGICAL TIME

Naturally, there were efforts to stop the desert's spread. The Essex town board planted the wild grasses they were told would deter the steady intrusion of sand. With seeds donated by the Sierra Club, FEMA funding, and meltwater from glaciers tugged down from Alaska, the town surrounded itself with thousands of acres of hearty, supposedly indigenous grassland. Still came the dune, rolling over the grasses like so many swaths of peach fuzz, the world's most invasive species no species at all.

Baker and Ludlow erected fifty-foot retaining walls, Baker's made of high-tech perforated flexfoam developed at the Jet Propulsion Laboratory in Pasadena, Ludlow's old-fashioned concrete and rebar. The dune buckled both.

Windbreaks were constructed, tree lines were sowed, thousands of truckloads of gravel were dumped. Scrappy Needles—a town of three hundred truck drivers and rock hounds and recovering alcoholics—offered the mightiest fight, or at least the best-documented, sta-tioning Caltrans trucks and the tanker from the county volunteer fire department at the edge of town and continually spraying the advancing sand wall with oil. Still came the dune.

Still came sand in sheets, sand erasing the sun for hours then days, sand softening the corners of stucco strip malls, sand whistling through the holes bored in the ancient adobe of mission churches. Still came the wind. Still came ceaseless badland bluster funneled by the Sierra Nevada. Still came all the wanderlusting topsoil of Brigham Young's aerated Southwest free at last, the billowing left behind of tilled scrub, the aloft fertilizer crust of manifest destiny. Ashes in the plow's wake, Mulholland's America.

Still came the scientists: climatologists, geologists, volcanologists, soil experts, agriculturists, horticulturists, conservationists. In fluxed new-booted, khaki-capped men and women from the Northeast, stalking tenure in L.L. Bean. Still came journalists, deadline-hungry, sense of subtlety atrophied. Still came

Train wreck at the Gare Montparnasse, Paris, 1895.
One person was killed after a brake failure caused the train to overrun its buffer stop.

BLM and EPA and NWS and USGS, all assigned to determine why a process that ought to have taken 500,000 years had happened in fifty. All tasked with determining how to stop the mountain's unrelenting march. All of them failed.

Or half failed. How it happened they could explain, a micro-chronicle even the layest Mojav might recite: drought of droughts, wind of winds.

Unceasing drought indifferent to prayer, and thanks to it rivers, lakes, reservoirs, and aquifers drained, crops and ranches succumbed, vegetation withered, leaving behind deep, dry beds of loose alkali evaporate.

Scraping wind, five-hundred-year wind, the desert's primal inhale raking the expired floodplain, making a wind tunnel of California's Central Valley. In came particulate, swelling simultaneously Dumont Dunes and their southerly cousins, Kelso Dunes. In barely a blink of desertification's encrusted eye, the two conjoined across the eighty miles that had long separated them, creating a vast dune field over one hundred miles wide, instantly the longest dune in North America.

But knowing how it came would not stop it from coming. Still came the wind, hoarding sand and superlatives: widest dune in North America, tallest dune in North America, largest dune in the Western Hemisphere. The dune field overtook I-15 in a weekend, reaching a corpulent four hundred square miles, insisting upon its reclassification from dune field to dune sea.

Still rose the dune sea, and like a sea now making its own weather. Sparkling white slopes superheated the skies above, setting the air achurn with funnels, drawing hurricanes of dust from as far away as Saskatchewan. Self-perpetuating then, the sand a magnet for its own mixture of clay, sulfates, and carbonate particles from the

Meteorite from the K–T extinction event, a period of massive species extinction that occurred about 66 million years ago. SEM micrograph by Edward Kinsman.

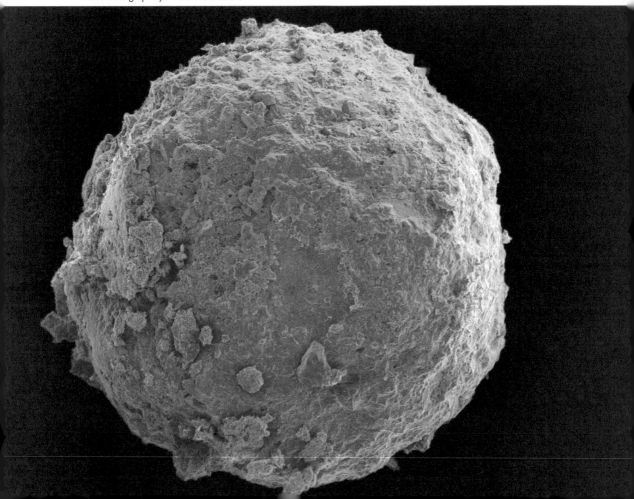

pulverized bodies of ancient marine creatures, so high in saline that a sample taken from anywhere on the dune will be salty on the tongue.

So came the name, *amargo* being the Spanish word for bitter; Amargosa being the name of the first mountain range the dune sea interred.

In the blurred background of the Pulitzer Prize–winning photograph, the remaining citizens of Needles, nine men and three women—the Needles Dozen, as they will be briefly known—are frosty with sand mortared to their oil-slickened bodies, white specters with dark holes demarking gas masks or goggles, handkerchiefs pulled over mouths, a dish sponge tied to a face with a shoelace. They look to the dune, perhaps rather than acknowledge each other stepping backward across the besieged playground they've vowed to protect. In the foreground a toddler—the caption called him "the forgotten child of the Mojave"—squats naked in a sandbox. A plastic bulldozer lies on its side at his feet, rumored the photographer's salt. The child's crusted face is tilted skyward, to the ration jug he holds inverted over his head. His tongue is a violent belt of glistening red, the last drop of water dangling from the lip of the jug. A wink of light in the droplet, too pure to be digital.

Still those once of Needles lingered, stationing themselves at the foot of the dune for three weeks after the town was buried, accepting only rations from Red Cross, wanting perhaps to stay as close as they could to their interred lives. They looked to the hot white whale glittering in the sun and saw their homes, shops, their football field entombed in sand. Preserved. Like those quaint towns they'd read about, long ago drowned by dams but re-emerged, mud-logged and algaed and alien-looking, as the reservoirs drained.

But the base of the dune was not sand, reporters reminded the Needles Dozen at a press conference held in a tent with generators shuddering behind it, and had not been sand for some time. Question: Did they realize that the dune now behaved more like a glacier, albeit a vastly accelerated glacier? Question: Were they

aware that geologists had ascertained that the base of the dune—the foot, they called it—was rock? That it carved the land more than covered it? Question: Did they wish to comment on the fact that the buildings they envisioned, in which they had spent the entirety of their short lives—their homes, say, or their twelve-step club—had already been crushed, were now but fossil flecks in banded sandstone?

And so retreated even the hard-nosed dreamers of Needles, California. So dispersed the last of the true Mojavs, though the term

I think we are inexterminable, like flies and bedbugs. —Robert Frost, 1959

had already outgrown them. They were reabsorbed by New England, the Midwest, the South, all those moist and rich-soiled places their wild-eyed forefathers once fled. Some were granted temporary asylum in the petite verdant kidney of the Pacific Northwest. In retreat, the stalwarts of Needles comforted themselves by categorizing the dune as a natural disaster, though by then it had become increasingly difficult to distinguish the acts of God from the endeavors of men. The wind was God; of this they were confident. As were the mountains funneling the wind.

But the sand, all that monstrous, infinite sand. Who had latticed the Southwest with a network of aqueducts? Who had drained first Owens Lake then Mono Lake, Mammoth Lake, Lake Havasu, and so on, leaving behind wide white smears of dust? Who had diverted the coast's rainwater and sapped the Great Basin of its groundwater? Who had tunneled beneath Lake Mead, installed a gaping outlet at its bottommost point, and drained it like a sink? Who had sucked up the Ogallala Aquifer, the Rio Grande aquifer, the snowpack of the Sierras and the Cascades? If this was God he went by new names: Los Angeles City Council, Los Angeles Department of Water and Power, City of San Diego, City of Phoenix, Arizona Water and Power, New Mexico Water Commission,

1825: Paris

SUDDEN MOVEMENTS

The repeated eruptions and retreats that have left the earth as we now find it have not all been gradual, not all uniform. On the contrary, the greater portion of these catastrophes have been sudden, and that is easily proved by the last of these events, that which by a twofold action inundated and then left dry our present continent, or at least a great portion of the soil that now composes it. It also left in the northern countries carcasses of large quadrupeds frozen in the ice, which have been preserved down to the present period with their skin, hair, and flesh. If they had not been frozen as soon as killed, putrefaction would have decomposed them. And besides, this eternal frost did not previously exist in those parts in which they were frozen, for they could not have existed in such a temperature. The same instant that these animals were bereft of life, the country that they inhabited became frozen. This event, was sudden, momentary, without gradation. What is so clearly proved as to this last catastrophe equally applies to that which preceded it. The convulsions, the alterations, the reversings of the most ancient layers, leave not a doubt on the mind but that sudden and violent causes reduced them to their present state, and even the powerful action of the mass of waters is proved by the accumulation of relics and round flints that in many places intervene between the solid layers. Existence has thus been often troubled on this earth by appalling events. Living creatures without number have fallen victims to these catastrophes. Some, the inhabitants of dry land, have been swallowed up by a deluge; others, which peopled the depths of the waters, have been cast on land by the sudden receding of the waters, their very race become extinct, and only a few remains left of them in the world, scarcely recognized by the naturalist.

Georges Cuvier, *from* Discourse on the Revolutionary Upheavals on the Surface of the Globe. *French zoologist Cuvier brought new prestige to the old concept of catastrophism, which claimed that the present features of Earth were established through a series of "revolutions"—abrupt upheavals of land and floods. Honoré de Balzac, a great admirer of his, wrote in 1831 that through Cuvier "dead things live anew and lost worlds are unfolded before us!" Cuvier's catastrophism was supplanted in the mid-nineteenth century by uniformitarian theories regarding consistent geological processes.*

Las Vegas Housing and Water Authority, Bureau of Land Management, United States Department of the Interior.

Metaphors were unavoidable. The Amargosa was a disease: a cancer, a malignancy, a tumor. A steamroller, a plow. A hungry beast, a self-spawning corpulence, a bloated blob gobbling land, various images of appetite, projections of our ugly, innermost selves.

The Amargosa was angry, cruel, or uncaring—personification inevitable and forgivable too, for at times the mass did seem to move with discernment. Witnesses describe occasions when it seemed to pause its march, or reach its steady foot around a town rather than atop it, as though in embrace, allowing the citizens time to hitch their trailers to their trucks and haul them from harm. Its storms once lifted a child playing jacks in his yard and deposited him unscathed atop the dumpster behind the Terrible's gas station where his mother worked. But just as effortlessly, a sandalanche humming ten miles away veered to take an entire town in minutes. It has been called the devil incarnate, but also the wide, open eye of God.

With the Needles Dozen, the last of the newspapermen, the lingering specialists from this institute and that withdrew. Civilization retreated; the frontier reasserted itself. Their staff and charges evacuated, local sheriffs' offices disbanded de facto. Sinkholes gulped the interstate, rendering highway patrol moot. State troopers ceded jurisdiction to the Department of the Interior, whose last vestige of authority is a fee booth at the northwest entrance to Death Valley National Park, a shack with a busted mechanical arm flopping out front, a bulletin board tacked with maps bleached blank and disintegrating.

USGS concluded its modest survey efforts when an SUV with government plates was ransacked, stripped, and set on fire, the assessors found four days later, wandering the edge of the dune naked and nearly insane. As the *New York Times* put it, AMARGOSA DUNE SEA INTERNATIONAL WATERS.

No complete map of the Amargosa Dune Sea exists. Partial maps of one face or another are etched almost immediately to obsolescence by the ever-shifting sands. The most informed estimate of the terrain describes "nearly exponential exaggeration of features," wherein each chain of dunes gives way to another taller, wider, hotter, until these crescendo at the Six Sisters, a chain of crestcentric dunes whose sandstone feet are estimated to be as wide as they are tall. Any one of the Sisters would easily be the tallest sand dune in the world. Atop these, the hypothesis goes, reclines the summit: a nameless five-crested star dune, entirely unmapped and ever shawled in rainless clouds. Though never scaled, the summit is suspected to be the second tallest mountain in North America. At last count, geologists estimate seven thousand individual peaks and crestlines accumulated to form the dune sea, though sandalanches and extremely hostile environs make an accurate count impossible. And anyway, funding's dried up.

No one has circumnavigated the Amargosa, no one has ventured into its interior, and no one has crossed it. Unmanned IMQ-18A Hummingbird drones sent on scouting patterns inevitably encountered a "severe electromagnetic anomaly," transmitting back only an eerie white throb. Satellite-imaging attempts were similarly frustrated, yielding only ghostly blurs.

BLM's *Survey of the Area Surrounding and Encompassing the Amargosa Dune Sea* reports a population of zero. The one-page document—the Bureau's shortest survey to date—is itself salted with words like *inhospitable*, *barren*, *bleak*, and *empty*.

A desert deserted, the official line.

Flight of Sultan Bahadur During Humayun's Campaign in Gujarat in 1535 (detail), miniature from a sixteenth-century edition of the *History of Akbar*, by Abu'l Fazl.

Yet stories circulated the stuffed cities, rumors whipped around the social networks, urban legends rippled through the besieged green East: amassed at the foot of the dune was perhaps a colony.

Some versions people the colony with stubborn Mojavs, the calculation being that for every thousand fleeing the Amargosa, one stayed. A welder from Needles with fifteen years of sobriety refused to board the National Guard lorry with his wife and twin daughters. A high school geography teacher, supposedly a descendent of Meriwether Lewis, insisted on staying to finish the new maps. The ranger who once manned the fee booth at Death Valley National Park built himself a yurt and lived there with three teenage girls he called his wives-in-Christ.

The versions circling among the professional set populate the colony with refugees of the bourgeoisie. A spinster assistant professor failed to submit her tenure box in the fall. The environment desk lost contact with its Ivy League greenhorn. The anal-retentive manager of the illustrious lab failed to renew his grant application. A brilliant but antisocial postdoc did not return to his carrel at the institute.

Underclass iterations have the colony an assemblage of shrewd swindlers, charlatans, and snake-oil salesmen, hearts inherited from the forty-niners, awaiting the oil bonanza when the tremendous sand mass squeezes out its inevitable pods of petro, or the adventure bonanza when the summit outgrows Denali and helicopter rides to base camp go to the highest bidder, when brightly clothed cadres of

Pogroms, by an unknown artist, c. 1915.

the stubbled wealthy stand atop their piles of money to be the first to summit.

On the left it is a survivalist outpost, vindicated doomsayers with homes of abandoned freight cars of rusty oranges and reds and clear crisp blues and stockpiled with guns and canned goods and bottled water and military rations. Home to libertarian drifters and vagabonds, tramps, wanderers preferring not to have an address, a garrison for the familiar cast of trigger-happy vigilantes scowling and squirting tobacco juice across the New Old West.

On the right it is ground zero of the eco-revolution, vital utopia where the beatniks of the Enchanted Circle have relocated from Big Sur—or the aging acidheads of Atlas City from Tucson, or the free rangers of No Where Ranch from Santa Fe, or the wispy vegans of Gaia Village from Taos, or the kinky paramours of Agape from Sebastopol, or the anarchist pinkos of Ant Hill Collective from Oakland, or the burnouts of Alpha Farm from Grass Valley, or the lesbo Amazons of Girlhouse from Portland, or the junkies of the Compound from Santa Monica, or the burners of New Black Rock City from Minden, or the shorn monks of the Shamanic Living Center from Ojai, or the jam band Technicolor Tree Tribe from Santa Cruz—all with their wheeled zero-footprint Earthships made of tires and bottles and clay.

Rumors of a colony are nourished by the many who saw the dune sea firsthand and thereafter ascribed to it a curious energy. While it's a fact that certain places woo, the Amargosa's pull was said to be far beyond topographic charm. It was chemical, pheromonal, elemental, a tingle in the ions of the brain, a tug in the iron of the blood. The dune beckoned the chosen, they said. "I was overcome with this very powerful feeling," one Mojav refugee told CNN of the first time she saw the dune sea. "A feeling of, well, belonging."

Another refugee said, "I miss it. Sounds strange, I realize. But I do. I truly do."

Another described the Amargosa as "a feeling, like that swelling inside you when you hear a song perfectly sung."

"I saw it from the air, from far off, back when there were flights out West," wrote a mirage-chasing New York stockbroker on his blog.

The PWI [Palisades Water Index] had been banging against the ceiling for weeks, so of course I'm flying to pitch water derivatives in Silicon Valley, or what was left of it. A lot of my guys had gone back to Boston when Stanford closed, but there were still some whales floating around. I was polishing my presentation when the captain came on the intercom and said if we looked out our windows we could see the Amargosa. I thought, Bullshit. We were hundreds of miles north. But I looked out my window real quick and there it was, glowing. It was so bright, like a light I'd never seen before. I felt very full then, and couldn't take my eyes off it. When we passed out of sight I felt just bereft, like someone I loved was dead. I've come to realize I need that full feeling. Very full but also incredibly calm, like heaven, or the rush of warmth before you freeze to death.

This last simile, those parting words of the stockbroker's final post before he disappeared, was perhaps especially apt, for among the called the Amargosa is both siren and jagged reef, its good vibes a blessing, its curse just as likely. Fickle, it is said to be, false and traitorous. Others, wounds less fresh, describe it simply as an arbiter, allude only vaguely to its methods of exiting the unwelcome. You might have heard it on the eastbound evac lorry: *The dune is rejecting me.* Or later, among the jilted devotees in the Mojav camps: *The mountain has turned its back on me.*

From Gold Fame Citrus. *Claire Vaye Watkins' first novel, which takes place in an uninhabitable, drought-wrecked California, was published in 2015. "Drought is fascinating to me because it's a collision of human time with geologic time," Watkins has said. "We're saying, 'There's always been water here!' But geologic time knows: not so." An assistant professor at the University of Michigan, Watkins is also co-director of the Mojave School, a creative-writing workshop for teenagers in rural Nevada.*

1759: Glasgow

Let us suppose that the great empire of China, with all its myriads of inhabitants, was suddenly swallowed up by an earthquake, and let us consider how a man of humanity in Europe, who had no sort of connection with that part of the world, would be affected upon receiving intelligence of this dreadful calamity. He would, I imagine, first of all, express very strongly his sorrow for the misfortune of that unhappy people. He would make many melancholy reflections upon the precariousness of human life and the vanity of all the labors of man, which could thus be annihilated in a moment. He would too, perhaps, if he was a man of speculation, enter into many reasonings concerning the effects which this disaster might produce upon the commerce of Europe, and the trade and business of the world in general. And when all this fine philosophy was over, when all these humane sentiments had been once fairly expressed, he would pursue his business or his pleasure, take his repose or his diversion, with the same ease and tranquility as if no such accident had happened. The most frivolous disaster which could befall himself would occasion a more real disturbance. If he was to lose his little finger tomorrow, he would not sleep tonight. But, provided he never saw them, he will snore with the most profound security over the ruin of a hundred million of his brethren, and the destruction of that immense multitude seems plainly an object less interesting to him than this paltry misfortune of his own. To prevent, therefore, this paltry misfortune to himself would a man of humanity be willing to sacrifice the lives of a hundred million of his brethren, provided he had never seen them? Human nature startles with horror at the thought, and the world, in its greatest depravity and corruption, never produced such a villain as could be capable of entertaining it. But what makes this difference? When our passive feelings are almost always so sordid and so selfish, how comes it that our active principles should often be so generous and so noble? When we are always so much more deeply affected by whatever concerns ourselves than by whatever concerns other men, what is it which prompts the generous, upon all occasions, and the mean upon many, to sacrifice their own interests to the greater interests of others? It is not the soft power of humanity, it is not that feeble spark of benevolence which nature has lighted up in the human heart that is thus capable of counteracting the strongest impulses of self-love. It is a stronger power, a more forcible motive, which exerts itself upon such occasions. It is reason, principle, conscience, the inhabitant of the breast, the man within, the great judge and arbiter of our conduct. It is he who, whenever we are about to act so as to affect the happiness of others, calls to us with a voice capable of astonishing the most presumptuous of our passions that we are but one of the multitude, in no respect better than any other in it; and that when we prefer ourselves so shamefully and so blindly to others, we become the proper objects of resentment, abhorrence, and execration. It is from him only that we learn the real littleness of ourselves, and of whatever relates to ourselves, and the natural misrepresentations of self-love can be corrected only by the eye of this impartial spectator. It is he who shows us the propriety of generosity and the deformity of injustice; the propriety of resigning the greatest interests of our own for the yet greater interests of others, and the deformity of doing the smallest injury to another in order to obtain the greatest benefit to ourselves. It is not the love of our neighbor, it is not the love of mankind, which upon many occasions prompts us to the practice of those divine virtues. It is a stronger love, a more powerful affection which generally takes place upon such occasions, the love of what is honorable and noble, of the grandeur and dignity and superiority of our own characters.

Adam Smith, *from* The Theory of Moral Sentiments. *Smith was born in a Scottish fishing village in 1723; according to his first biographer, at the age of four he was abducted by a band of gypsies. In the first sentence of* Moral Sentiments, *Smith's first book, he puts forth his theory of sympathy: "However selfish man may be supposed, there are evidently some principles in his nature, which interest him in the fortune of others."*

1998: Middletown, CT

BOOK OF NUMBERS

We have dated waves, as well as clouds. On April 30, 1991—on that one day—138,000 people drowned in Bangladesh. At dinner I mentioned to our daughter, who was then seven years old, that it was hard to imagine 138,000 people drowning.

"No, it's easy," she said. "Lots and lots of dots, in blue water."

How are we doing in numbers, we who have been alive for this most recent verse of human life? How many people have lived and died?

"The dead outnumber the living," Harvard's Nathan Keyfitz wrote in a 1991 letter to Justin Kaplan. "Credible estimates of the number of people who have ever lived on earth run from 70 billion to over 100 billion." Averaging those figures puts the total persons ever born at about 85 billion. By these moderate figures, the dead outnumber us by about 14 to 1. None of these figures is certain, and Keyfitz wrote that the ratio "could be as high as 20 to 1." The dead will always outnumber the living.

Dead Americans, however, if all proceeds, will not outnumber living Americans until the year 2030, because the nation is young. Many of us will be among the dead then. Will we know or care, we who once owned the still bones under the quick ones, we who spin inside the planet with our heels in the air? The living might well seem foolishly self-important to us, and overexcited.

In the beginning, according to Rabbi Isaac Luria, God contracted himself—*zimzum*. The divine essence withdrew into itself to make room for a finite world. Evil became possible: those genetic defects that dog cellular life, those clashing forces that erupt in natural catastrophes, and those sins human minds invent and human hands perform.

Luria's Kabbalist creation story, however baroque, accounts boldly for both moral evil and natural calamity. The creator meant his light to emanate, ultimately, to man. Grace would flow downward through ten holy vessels, like water cascading. Cataclysm—some say creation itself—disrupted this orderly progression. The

David Bowie in a scene from *Merry Christmas Mr. Lawrence*, directed by Nagisa Oshima, 1983.

holy light burst the vessels. The vessels splintered and scattered. Sparks of holiness fell to the depths, and the opaque shards of the broken vessels (*qelippot*) imprisoned them. This is our bleak world. We see only the demonic shells of things. It is literally sensible to deny that God exists. In fact, God is hidden, exiled, in the sparks of divine light the shells entrap. So evil can exist, can continue to live: the spark of goodness within things, the Gnostic-like spark that even the most evil tendency encloses, lends evil its being.

"The sparks scatter everywhere," Martin Buber said. "They cling to material things as in sealed-up wells, they crouch in substances as in caves that have been bricked up, they inhale darkness and breathe out fear; they flutter about in the movements of the world, searching where they can lodge to be set free."

Only redemption—restoration, *tikkun*—can return the sparks of light to their source in the primeval soul; only redemption can restore God's exiled presence to his being in eternity. Only redemption can reunite an exiled soul with its root. The holy person, however, can hasten redemption and help mend heaven and earth.

Another dated wave: In northeast Japan, a seismic sea wave killed 27,000 people on June 15, 1896. Do not fail to distinguish this infamous day from April 30, 1991, when typhoon waves drowned 138,000 Bangladeshi.

On the dry Laetoli plain of northern Tanzania, Mary Leakey found a trail of hominid footprints. The three barefoot people—likely a short man and woman and child *Australopithecus*—walked closely together. They walked on moist volcanic tuff and ash. We have a record of those few seconds from a day about 3.6 million years ago—before hominids even chipped stone tools. More ash covered the footprints and hardened like plaster. Ash also preserved the pockmarks of the raindrops that fell beside the three who walked; it was a rainy day. We have almost ninety feet of the three's steady footprints intact. We do not know where they were going or why. We do not know why the woman paused and turned left, briefly, before continuing. "A remote ancestor," Leakey said, "experienced a moment of doubt." Possibly they watched the Sadiman volcano erupting, or they took a last look back before they left. We do know we cannot make anything so lasting as these three barefoot ones did.

Jeremiah, walking toward Jerusalem, saw the smoke from the Temple's blaze. He wept; he saw the blood of the slain. "He put his face close to the ground and saw the footprints of sucklings and infants who were walking into captivity" in Babylon. He kissed the footprints.

Who were these individuals? Who were the three who walked together and left footprints in the rain? Who was the Baal Shem Tov, who taught, danced, and dug clay? He survived among the children of exiles whose footprints on the bare earth Jeremiah kissed. Centuries later, Emperor Hadrian destroyed another such son of exile, Rabbi Akiva, in Rome. Russian Christians and European Christians alike tried to wipe all those survivors of children of exile from the ground of the earth as a man wipes a plate—survivors of exiles whose footprints on the ground we might well kiss, and whose feet.

Who and of what import were the men whose bones bulk the Great Wall, the thirty million Mao starved, or the thirty million children not yet five who die each year now? Why, they are the insignificant others, of course; living or dead, they are just some of the plentiful others. A newborn slept in a shell of aluminum foil; a Dutchman watched a crab in the desert; a punch-drunk airport skycap joined me for a cigarette. And you? To what end were we billions of oddballs born?

Annie Dillard, *from* For the Time Being. *In 1974 Dillard published her first book, the poetry collection* Tickets for a Prayer Wheel, *as well as* Pilgrim at Tinker Creek, *for which she received a Pulitzer Prize. After the 2004 Indian Ocean tsunami, Dillard read an essay on National Public Radio adapted from* Time Being. The Abundance, *a collection of her narrative essays, was published in March 2016.*

c. 1750 BC: Egypt

SOCIETAL COLLAPSE

Lo, hearts are violent, storm sweeps the land,
There's blood everywhere, no shortage of dead,
The shroud calls out before one comes near it.
Lo, many dead are buried in the river,
The stream is the grave, the tomb became stream.
Lo, nobles lament, the poor rejoice,
Every town says, "Let us expel our rulers."
Lo, the land turns like a potter's wheel,
The robber owns riches, the noble is a thief.
The citizen says, "Woe, what shall I do!"
Lo, the river is blood,
As one drinks of it one shrinks from people
And thirsts for water.
Towns are ravaged, Upper Egypt became wasteland.
Lo, crocodiles gorge on their catch,
People go to them of their own will.
The land is injured,
One says, "Don't walk here, there's a net,"
People flap like fish,
The scared does not discern it in his fright.
Lo, the desert claims the land,

The Prairie Burial, by William Ranney, 1848.

Boy struggling against a typhoon, Ha Long, Vietnam, 2000. Photograph by John Vink.

The nomes are destroyed,
Foreign bowmen have come into Egypt.
Lo, everyone's hair has fallen out,
One can't distinguish the son of a man from the pauper.
Lo, one is numb from noise,
No voice is straight in years of shouting,
No end of shouting.
Lo, all beasts, their hearts weep,
Cattle bemoan the state of the land.
Lo, children of nobles are dashed against walls,
Infants are put out on high ground.
Citizens come and go in desolation,
If only this were the end of man,
No more conceiving, no births!
Then the land would cease to shout,
Tumult would be no more!

> *From* The Admonitions of Ipuwer. *This wisdom text addressing a state of widespread Egyptian disorder has been thought variously by scholars to be: "the direct and natural response to a real national calamity"; possible evidence of the biblical plagues; description of the geophysical result of a volcanic eruption; or a historical romance, a literary form said to be "always popular in Ancient Egypt." Only one heavily damaged papyrus, with the text inscribed several centuries after its original composition, survives. "Every page," according to its translator, "has large lacunae."*

1906: Palo Alto, CA

WILLIAM JAMES TAKES NOTE OF THE HUMAN RESPONSE

I realize now better than ever how inevitable were men's earlier mythologic versions of such catastrophes, and how artificial and against the grain of our spontaneous perceiving are the later habits into which science educates us. It was simply impossible for untutored men to take earthquakes into their minds as anything but supernatural warnings or retributions.

A good instance of the way in which the tremendousness of a catastrophe may banish fear was given me by a Stanford student. He was in the fourth story of Encina Hall, an immense stone dormitory building. Awakened from sleep, he recognized what the disturbance was and sprang from the bed, but was thrown off his feet in a moment, while his books and furniture fell around him. Then, with an awful, sinister, grinding roar, everything gave way, and with chimneys, floor beams, walls and all, he descended through the three lower stories of the building into the basement. "This is my end, this is my death," he felt, but all the while no trace of fear. The experience was too overwhelming for anything but passive surrender to it.

Arrived at the bottom, he found himself with rafters and debris around him, but not pinned in or crushed. He saw daylight and crept toward it through the obstacles. Then, realizing that he was in his nightgown, and feeling no pain anywhere, his first thought was to get back to his room and find some more presentable clothing. The stairways at Encina Hall are at the ends of the building. He made his way to one of them and went up the four flights, only to find his room no longer extant. Then he noticed pain in his feet, which had been injured, and came down the stairs with difficulty. When he talked with me ten days later he had been in hospital a week, was very thin and pale, and went on crutches, and was dressed in borrowed clothing.

So much for Stanford, where all our experiences seem to have been very similar. Nearly all our chimneys went down, some of them disintegrating from top to bottom; parlor floors were covered with bricks; plaster strewn the floors; furniture was everywhere upset and dislocated; but the wooden dwellings sprang back to their original position, and in house after house not a window stuck or a door scraped at top or bottom. Wood architecture was triumphant! Everybody was excited, but the excitement at first, at any rate, seemed to be almost joyous. Here at last was a *real* earthquake after so many years of harmless waggle! Above all, there was an irresistible desire to talk about it and exchange experiences.

Most people slept outdoors for several subsequent nights, partly to be safer in case of a recurrence, but also to work off their emotion and get the full unusualness out of the experience. The vocal babble of early-waking girls and boys from the gardens of the campus, mingling with the birds' songs and the exquisite weather, was for three or four days a delightful sunrise phenomenon.

Now turn to San Francisco, thirty-five miles distant, from which an automobile ere long brought us the dire news of a city in ruins, with fires beginning at various points, and the water supply interrupted. I was fortunate enough to board the only train of cars—a very small one—that got up to the city; fortunate enough also to escape in the evening by the only train that left it. This gave me and my valiant feminine escort some four hours of observation. My business is with "subjective" phenomena exclusively, so I will say nothing of the material ruin that greeted us on every hand—the daily papers and the weekly journals have done full justice to that topic. By midday, when we reached the city, the pall of smoke was vast and the dynamite detonations had begun, but the troops, the police, and the firemen seemed to have established order, dangerous neighborhoods were roped off everywhere and picketed, saloons closed, vehicles impressed, and everyone at work who *could* work.

It was indeed a strange sight to see an entire population in the streets, busy as ants in an uncovered anthill scurrying to save their eggs and larvae. Every horse and everything on wheels in the city, from hucksters' wagons to automobiles, was being loaded with what effects could be scraped together from houses which the advancing flames were threatening. The sidewalks were covered with well-dressed men and women carrying baskets, bundles, valises, or dragging trunks to spots of greater temporary safety, soon to be dragged farther, as the fire kept spreading!

In the safer quarters, every doorstep was covered with the dwelling's tenants, sitting surrounded with their more indispensable chattels, and ready to flee at a minute's notice. I think everyone must have fasted on that day, for I saw no one eating. There was no appearance of general dismay, and little of chatter or of incoordinated excitement.

The mind is its own place, and in itself
Can make a heaven of hell, a hell of heaven.
                                    —John Milton, 1667

Everyone seemed doggedly bent on achieving the job which he had set himself to perform; and the faces, although somewhat tense and set and grave, were inexpressive of emotion. I noticed only three persons overcome, two Italian women, very poor, embracing an aged fellow countrywoman, and all weeping. Physical fatigue and seriousness were the only inner states that one could read on countenances.

With lights forbidden in the houses and the streets lit only by the conflagration, it was apprehended that the criminals of San Francisco would hold high carnival on the ensuing night. But whether they feared the disciplinary methods of the United States troops, who were visible everywhere, or whether they were themselves solemnized by the immensity of the disaster, they lay low and did not "manifest," either then or subsequently.

The only very discreditable thing to human nature that occurred was later, when hundreds of lazy "bummers" found that they could keep camping in the parks, and make alimentary storage-batteries of their stomachs, even in some cases getting enough of the free rations in their huts or tents to last them well into the summer. This charm of pauperized vagabondage seems all along to have been Satan's most serious bait to human nature. There was theft from the outset, but confined, I believe, to petty pilfering.

Cash in hand was the only money, and millionaires and their families were no better off in this respect than anyone. Whoever got a vehicle could have the use of it, but the richest often went without and spent the first two nights on rugs on the bare ground, with nothing but what their own arms had rescued. Fortunately, those nights were dry and comparatively warm, and Californians are accustomed to camping conditions in the summer, so suffering from exposure was less great than it would have been elsewhere. By the fourth night, which was rainy, tents and huts had brought most campers under cover.

I went through the city again eight days later. The fire was out and about a quarter of the area stood unconsumed. Intact skyscrapers dominated the smoking level majestically and superbly—they and a few walls that had survived the overthrow. Thus has the courage of our architects and builders received triumphant vindication!

Two things in retrospect strike me especially, and are the most emphatic of all my impressions. Both are reassuring as to human nature.

The first of these was the rapidity of the improvisation of order out of chaos. It is clear that just as in every thousand human beings there will be statistically so many artists, so many athletes, so many thinkers, and so many potentially good soldiers, so there will be so many potential organizers in times of emergency. In point of fact, not only in the great city but in the outlying towns, these natural ordermakers, whether amateurs or officials, came to the front immediately. There seemed to be no possibility which there was not someone there to think of, or which within twenty-four hours was not in some way provided for.

The completeness of organization at Palo Alto, a town of ten thousand inhabitants close to Stanford University, was almost comical. People feared exodus on a large scale of the rowdy elements of San Francisco. In point of fact, very few refugees came to Palo Alto. But within twenty-four hours rations, clothing, hospital, quarantine, disinfection, washing, police, military, quarters in camp and in houses, printed information, employment, all were provided for under the care of so many volunteer committees.

Much of this readiness was American, much of it Californian; but I believe that every country in a similar crisis would have displayed it in a way to astonish the spectators. Like soldiering, it lies always latent in human nature.

The second thing that struck me was the universal equanimity. We soon got letters from the East, ringing with anxiety and pathos; but I now know fully what I have always believed, that the pathetic way of feeling great disasters belongs rather to the point of view of people at a distance than to the immediate victims. I heard not a single really pathetic or sentimental word in California expressed by anyone.

"An Abandoned Farm," by Arthur Rothstein, 1936.

A scene from *Deep Impact*, directed by Mimi Leder, 1998.

The terms *awful*, *dreadful* fell often enough from people's lips, but always with a sort of abstract meaning, and with a face that seemed to admire the vastness of the catastrophe as much as it bewailed its cuttingness. When talk was not directly practical, I might almost say that it expressed (at any rate in the nine days I was there) a tendency more toward nervous excitement than toward grief. The hearts concealed private bitterness enough, no doubt, but the tongues disdained to dwell on the misfortunes of self, when almost everybody one spoke to had suffered equally.

Surely the cutting edge of all our usual misfortunes comes from their character of loneliness. We lose our health, our wife or children die, our house burns down, or our money is made way with, and the world goes on rejoicing, leaving us on one side and counting us out from all its business. In California everyone to some degree was suffering, and one's private miseries were merged in the vast general sum of privation and in the all-absorbing practical problem of general recuperation. The cheerfulness, or, at any rate, the steadfastness of tone, was universal. Not a single whine or plaintive word did I hear from the hundred losers whom I spoke to. Instead of that there was a temper of helpfulness beyond the counting.

It is easy to glorify this as something characteristically American, or especially Californian. Californian education has, of course, made the thought of all possible recuperations easy. In an exhausted country, with no marginal resources, the outlook on the future would be much darker. But I like to think that what I write of is a normal and universal trait of human nature. In our drawing rooms and offices we wonder how people ever *do* go through battles, sieges, and shipwrecks. We quiver and sicken in imagination, and think those heroes superhuman. Physical pain, whether suffered alone or in company, is always more or less unnerving and intolerable. But mental pathos and anguish, I fancy, are usually effects of distance. At the place of action, where all are concerned together, healthy animal insensibility and heartiness take their place.

From "On Some Mental Effects of the Earthquake." Psychologist and philosopher William James was teaching at Stanford for a semester when the 1906 San Francisco earthquake occurred. He lectured on the Lisbon earthquake and the eruptions of Mount Pelée, arguing that such disasters incite humans to extraordinary behavior. To his brother Henry, who back east had expressed some squeamishness, he wrote, "All the earthquake anguish has been yours. Taking it so lightly ourselves, how could we suppose that you would take it so hard?"

1692: Port Royal

FEAR AND TREMBLING

Dear Friend,

I doubt not but you have heard of the dreadful calamity that has befallen this island by a terrible earthquake on the seventh instant, which has thrown down almost all the houses, churches, sugarworks, mills, and bridges in the island.

I had been at prayers, which I did every day since I was rector of Port Royal, to keep up some show of religion among a most ungodly and debauched people, and was gone to a place near the church, where the merchants used to meet, and where the president of the council then was.

To this gentleman's friendship, under the direction of the gracious and overruling will of Providence, I ascribe my own happy and, I may add, miraculous escape; for by his pressing instances, I was prevailed upon to decline an invitation, which I had before accepted, to dine with Captain Rudend, whose house upon the first concussion sunk into the sea, and with it his wife, his children, himself, and all that were with him, who every soul perished in this general, this dreadful devastation. Had I been of the number of his guests, my fate had been involved in theirs. But, to return, we had scarce dined at the president's before I felt the earth begin to heave and roll under me. Said I, "Lord, Sir, what's this?" He replied, very composedly, "It is an earthquake, be not afraid, it will soon be over." But it increased and we heard the church and tower fall, upon which we ran to save ourselves. I quickly lost him and made toward Morgan's Fort, which, being a wide open place, I thought to be there secure from the falling houses. But as I made toward it, I saw the earth open and swallow up a multitude of people, and the sea mounting in upon us over the fortifications.

I then laid aside all thoughts of escaping and resolved to make toward my own lodging, there to meet death in as good a posture as I could. From the place where I was, I was forced to cross and run through two or three very narrow streets. The houses and walls fell on each side of me; some bricks came rolling over my shoes but none hurt me. When I came to my lodging, I found all things in the order I had left them. I then went to my balcony to view the street in which our house stood, and saw never a house down there, nor the ground so much as cracked. The people seeing me cried out to come and pray with them. When I came into the street, everyone laid hold on my clothes and embraced me, so that I was almost stifled with their kindness. I persuaded them at last to

It is not light that is needed, but fire; it is not the gentle shower, but thunder. We need the storm, the whirlwind, and the earthquake.
—Frederick Douglass, 1852

kneel down and make a large ring, which they did. I prayed with them near an hour, when I was almost spent with the heat of the sun and the exercise. They then brought me a chair, the earth working all the while with new motions and tremblings, like the rollings of the sea.

By that time I had been half an hour longer with them, in setting before them their sins and heinous provocations, and seriously exhorting them to repentance, there came some merchants of the place who desired me to go aboard some ship in the harbor and refresh myself, telling me that they had a boat to carry me off. I found the sea had swallowed up the wharf. I continued in the ship that night, but could not sleep for the returns of the earthquake almost every hour, which made all the guns in the ship to jar and rattle.

For every day this terrible earthquake happened, as soon as night came on, a company of lewd rogues, whom they call privateers, fell to breaking open warehouses and houses deserted, to rob and rifle their neighbors, while the earth trembled under them, and the houses fell on some of them in the act; and those audacious whores, who remain still upon the place, are as impudent and drunken as ever.

I have been twice on shore to pray with bruised and dying people, where I met too many

Men being attacked by bees after attempting to steal the honey on which the infant Zeus was fed, Attic amphora, c. 540 BC.

drunk and swearing. I did not spare them, nor the magistrates either, who have suffered wickedness to grow to such a height. In the last sermon I delivered in the church, I set before them what would be the issue of their impenitence and wickedness so clearly that they have since acknowledged it more like a prophecy than a sermon. I had, I confess, an impulse on me to do it, and many times I have preached in this pulpit things which I never premeditated at home, and could not, methought, do otherwise.

Dear Friend,

Ever since that fatal day, the most terrible that ever I had in my life, I have lived on board a ship; for the shaking of the earth returns every now and then. Yesterday we had a very great one, but it seems less terrible on shipboard than on shore; yet I have ventured to Port Royal no less than three times among the shattered houses to bury the dead, pray with the sick, and christen the children.

It is a sad sight to see this harbor, one of the fairest I ever saw, covered with the dead bodies of people of all conditions, floating up and down without burial. For our burying place was destroyed by the earthquake, which dashed to pieces the tombs; the sea washed the carcasses of those who had been buried out of their graves. We have had accounts from several parts of this island, but none suffered like Port Royal, where whole streets, with their inhabitants, were swallowed up by the opening of the earth, which when shut in upon them, squeezed the people to death. And in that manner several are left with their heads above ground; only some heads the dogs have eaten; others are covered with dust and earth by the people who yet remain in the place, to avoid the stench.

Thus I have told you a long story, and God knows what worse may happen yet. I am afraid to stay, and yet know not how, in point of conscience, at such a juncture, to quit my station.

I am, Sir, yours,

> **Emmanuel Heath**, *from his correspondences. On June 7, 1692, an earthquake destroyed the Jamaican city of Port Royal, a buccaneer's paradise described by Cotton Mather as "a very Sodom for wickedness." Heath, the Anglican rector of Port Royal, had arrived in Jamaica only a short while before the earthquake; he afterward promulgated the widely held belief that the town's devastation was evidence of divine retribution. Aftershocks dissuaded residents from rebuilding, and the city of Kingston was founded in July for survivors.*

2011: Yellowstone

BEARING WITNESS

Before that heartbreaking night at the end of July, she was a ghost bear tramping the backwoods shade, a scared specter at her wit's end. She and her three cubs, all woefully thin and eking out a diet from grass and shoots, were so unwell that they wore their winter coats through the full, high heat of summer. In a lean year for grizzlies, they stood last in line, going without a solid meal of deer or elk or the staple of Yellowstone's bears, whitebark pine seeds. Those seeds, rich and fleshy, had grown for centuries on the crowns of the staunchest trees in North America: gnarled, obdurate pines that survived 50-below winters and laughed off killing winds on western peaks. Nothing could slay those trees, neither fire nor ice, until the region started warming around 1980. Now 80 percent of the Rockies' whitebark pine groves stand dead or dying in ghost-gray swaths, and the bears who ate their fruit and kept out of harm's way have bumbled down the hills in search of food. Among their number was the sow with three cubs and teats running dry of milk. With winter two months off, she had to somehow bulk up fast or watch her yearlings starve.

Sometime after midnight on a streamside slope near the northeast end of the park, the sow and her three cubs entered Soda Butte Campground, drawn by the lingering smell of broiled fish. After trying in vain to pry the tamper-proof lids off food bins and garbage cans, the sow poked her nose under the fly of a tent. She bit the leg of its occupant, Ronald Singer, who managed to drive her off with panicked blows. A short while later, around 2:15 A.M., Deborah Freele awoke in her tent at No. 11 to find the sow gnawing on her arm. She shrieked and fought back, but the bear bit down harder, snapping bones. By now, there was tumult in adjacent sites, people dashing around and honking car horns in warning, and the sow let go of Freele and ran away. A couple of hours later, rangers and deputies scoured the pitch-dark camp. Near

the western end, 600 yards from Freele's tent, they came upon the gnawed remains of a man named Kevin Kammer. Kammer, a medic from Grand Rapids, Michigan, whose lifelong dream was to fish Yellowstone's streams, had been dragged from his tent, killed by several bites, then consumed from chest to groin. There were several sets of prints on his flattened tent—the sow's and at least one of her cubs'.

Over the next days and weeks, all manner of havoc ensued. The media descended from as far away as Finland, asking pointed questions about "killer bears" and the safety of the park's guests. Park Service wardens, who trapped the sow and dispatched her via lethal injection, denounced her as a rogue whose "predatory" act was indefensible

Those least responsible for climate change are worst affected by it.
—Vandana Shiva, 2008

but rare. (Her cubs were transported across the state for permanent residence in a zoo.) Test after test was conducted, postmortem, to establish her motivation. Was she rabid? No. Exotic diseases? None. Maddened by injury or wounds? The federal Interagency Grizzly Bear Study Team, which took charge of the investigation, needed a month to conclude that there was "no clear explanation for the behavior of this bear," though a lucid possibility fairly leaped off her chart. Her weight at the time of death was 216 pounds, or about 80 pounds less than average for a full-grown sow. Like her cubs, called malnourished by the zoo's curator, and countless other bears forced downhill by hunger, she was a forerunner of the turmoil that awaits us all: species pushed to breaking by climate change.

One very warm week in early October, I took a four-day tour of Yellowstone's peaks and ravines with people who love the park dearly. My principal guide was an attorney with the Natural Resources Defense Council named Matt Skoglund. We hiked toward Packsaddle Peak, the split-rock summit high above tree line on the humpbacked mountain. The farther

Risky Business

Scope (Cosmic?)		Global catastrophic risks	Existential risks
Trans-generational	Loss of one species of beetle	Drastic loss of biodiversity	Human extinction
Global	Global warming by 0.001° C	Spanish flu pandemic	Aging
Local	Congestion from one extra vehicle	Recession in a country	Genocide
Personal	Loss of one hair	Car is stolen	Fatal car crash
	Imperceptible	Endurable	Terminal → Intensity (Hellish?)

From Global Catastrophic Risks. *Philosopher Nick Bostrom and physicist Milan Ćirković proposed this graph in 2008 as a way to evaluate the potential severity of human disasters. The upper right corner holds risks capable of inflicting serious damage to global human well-being—including risks to existence itself. "We cannot allow even one existential disaster to happen," wrote the authors. "There would be no opportunity to learn from the experience."*

we went, though, the bleaker things got: stand after stand of rust-colored pine, the red hue both a last sign of life and a coating of bug-shit and sawdust. Equally distressing was the absence of birds—most important, Clark's nutcrackers, who built these woods. Unlike other pines, whitebarks can't spread their seeds, which are locked inside tightly woven cones. For that they need nutcrackers to pierce the cones, then bury the seeds under the rocky soil to eat at a later time. It's an arrangement that's served everyone well for eons: The birds get a store of food for the winter, new pines are born from the seeds they forget, and at the end of every summer, so many new cones have sprouted that bears swarm up here to raid the stashes that red squirrels hide in the dirt. But the few healthy trees now were far too young to produce and drop their seeds, and the only cones we saw were decomposed husks that lay on the ground like mulch

In the end, of course, there won't be a national day of mourning if or when the whitebark dies out. It's a commercially useless tree, too far up to interest loggers or summon camera-snapping tourists from Dallas. But among its unsung vir-

tues, whitebark shelters the shrinking snowpack that feeds the water table in the West. Without the deep shade of its wide-armed canopy, the high snow would melt in torrents each spring, causing floods and mudslides in April and May and hellacious drought each summer. And whitebark matters to the millions of people who fish the gin-clear waters of the Rockies. Early, heavy snowmelt makes for raging spring rapids—and streams too thin to fly-fish by mid-August.

All this affects the grizzlies. The park's bears used to fish for trout at the end of summer before heading up the hills to gorge on pine seeds. Now they're reduced to squirrels and berries and the occasional road-kill deer. A hundred years ago, there were roughly 50,000 bears living west of the Mississippi River. These days, there are maybe 1,500, and it's hard to imagine how Yellowstone's bruins will make it to the end of this century. So desperate have they become that they run *toward* gunfire, having learned that hunters leave gut piles after a kill. Their main chance may lie in one day quitting the park and heading north toward the Yukon Territory. There's a consensus building among wildlife groups to try to carve out a corridor to western Canada, in which bears, wolves, and lynx could come and go freely, roaming where there's food and cover. It's a plan fraught with peril—they'd have to cross three states, four superhighways, and two Canadian provinces—and opposed by a formidable cast of lobbies, primarily big ranchers and mining firms. But the winters there are arctic, the forests are robust, and the glacier-fed lakes teem with fighting trout and pike the size of beagles. They'd better start now, though, to beat the rush. We'll all be heading north soon enough.

Paul Solotaroff, *from "The Ghost Park." The son of storied editor Ted Solotaroff—who fled book publishing during its period of corporatization and wrote a critique for* The New Republic *in 1987 called "The Literary-Industrial Complex"—Paul Solotaroff is a contributing editor at* Men's Journal, *where this story first appeared. In 2010 he published* The Body Shop *about his time with bodybuilding and steroids in 1970s New York. "It was very rare from our culture of Upper West Side Jewish intellectuals," said his brother. "There was nobody else who went this way."*

c. 1520: Mexico

JOURNAL OF THE PLAGUE YEARS

God struck and chastened with ten terrible plagues this land and all who dwelled in it, both natives and foreigners.

The first was a plague of smallpox, and it began in this manner. When Hernán Cortés was captain and governor, there was in one of his ships a Negro stricken with smallpox, a disease that had never been seen here. At this time New Spain was extremely full of people, and when the smallpox began to attack the Indians it became so great a pestilence among them throughout the land that in most provinces more than half the population died; in others the proportion was little less. For as the Indians did not know the remedy for the disease and were very much in the habit of bathing fre-

quently, whether well or ill, and continued to do so even when suffering from smallpox, they died in heaps, like bedbugs. Many others died of starvation, because, as they were all taken sick at once, they could not care for each other. In many places it happened that everyone in a house died, and, as it was impossible to bury the great number of dead, they pulled down the houses over them in order to check the stench that rose from the dead bodies, so that their homes became their tombs.

The second plague was the great number of those who died in the conquest of New Spain, especially around Mexico. For you must know that when Hernán Cortés landed on the coast of this country, with the energy which he always showed, he scuttled his ships to rouse the courage of his men and plunged into the interior. After marching forty leagues he entered the land of Tlaxcallan, one of the largest provinces

Flood victims scrambling for food rations while struggling against downwash from a Pakistan Army helicopter during a relief operation, Goza, Pakistan, 2010. The floods submerged one-fifth of the country. Photograph by Daniel Berehulak.

The *Lusitania* eighteen minutes after being torpedoed by a German U-boat, 1915.

of the country and most thickly populated. Entering the inhabited part of it, he established himself in some temples of the devil in a little town called Tecoautzinco and while there he fought for two weeks with the Indians roundabout. A great number of them came together, for the country is thickly populated. In this war, because of the great numbers who died in both armies, men compared the number of the dead and say that it is greater than the number of those who died in Jerusalem when it was destroyed by Titus and Vespasian.

The third plague was a very great famine that came immediately after the taking of the city of Mexico. As they were unable to plant because of the great wars, some of them defending the land and helping the Mexicans and others fighting on the side of the Spaniards, and as what was planted by one side was cut down and laid waste by the other, they had nothing to eat.

The fourth plague was that of the *calpixques* [tribute collectors] and the Negroes. As soon as the land was divided, the conquerors put into their allotments and into the towns granted to them servants or Negroes to collect the tributes and to look after their various affairs. These men lived, and still live, in the villages, and though for the most part they are peasants from Spain, they have taken possession of the land and order the native lords around as if the latter were their slaves. In the first years these overseers were absolute in their maltreatment of the Indians, overloading them, sending them far from their land, and giving them many other tasks, so that many Indians died because of them and at their hands.

The fifth plague was the great taxes and tributes that the Indians paid. As they had in the temples of their idols and in the possession of their lords and chief men and in many tombs a great quantity of gold, the accumulation of many years, the Spaniards began to exact heavy tributes from them, and the Indians, terrified of the Spaniards ever since the war, gave everything they had. As the tributes, however, were so continuous that they scarcely paid one when they were obliged to pay another, they sold children and their lands to the moneylenders in order to meet obligations. When they were unable to do so many died because of it, some under torture and some in cruel prisons, for the Spaniards treated them brutally and considered them less than beasts.

The sixth plague was the gold mines, for in addition to the taxes and tributes paid by the towns that had been granted to the Spaniards, the latter began to seek for mines, and it would be impossible to count the number of Indians who have died in these mines. Gold of this country was a second golden calf, worshiped as a god, for they came all the way from Castile through many dangers and difficulties to adore it.

The seventh plague was the building of the great city of Mexico, which, in the first years, employed more people than the building of Jerusalem. So many were the people engaged in the work that one could scarcely make his way along some streets and highways, broad as they are. In the construction some were crushed by beams, others fell from heights, others were caught beneath buildings that were being torn down in one place to be built up again in another. Many Indians died when they tore down the principal temples of the devil. It was many years before they completely demolished the temples, from which they obtained an enormous amount of stone.

The eighth plague was the slaves whom the Spaniards made in order to put them to work in the mines. So great was their haste to make slaves that from all parts of Mexico they brought in great herds of them, like flocks of sheep, in order to brand them. They hurried the Indians so as to produce slaves in tribute—so many every eighty days—that, having exhausted the supply of slaves, they brought their children and their *macehuales* (who are of a low social class, like farmer-vassals) and all whom they could get together, and brought them in, terrifying them into saying they were slaves.

The ninth plague was the service of the mines, to which the heavily laden Indians traveled sixty leagues or more to carry provisions. The food they carried for themselves gave out when they reached the mines and sometimes on the way back before they reached home. Sometimes they were kept by the miners for several days to help them get out the mineral or to build houses for them or to serve them, and when their food gave out they died, either at the mines or on the road, for they had no money to buy food and there was no one to give it to them. For half a league around these mines and along a great part of the road one could scarcely avoid walking over dead bodies or bones, and the flocks of birds and crows that came to feed upon the corpses were so numerous that they darkened the sun.

The tenth plague was the divisions and factions that existed among the Spaniards in Mexico. This was the one that most endangered the country, had it not been that the

Catastrophe is indeed already the condition of language, the condition of the ruins of time.
—Harold Bloom, 1982

Lord kept the Indians blinded. These dissensions were the cause of the execution of some Spaniards and the injury and exile of others. The few Spaniards left in Mexico were all passionate adherents of one party or the other, and the friars had to go out sometimes to prevent their fighting, and sometimes to separate them after they had started, exposing themselves to the shots and weapons of the combatants and the hoofs of the horses. They had to be kept from fighting both because it endangered the Spanish possession of the country and because it was known that the Indians were ready for war and had made provision of arms and were only awaiting the arrival of an expected piece of news. Here in Mexico the Indians were waiting for one party of Spaniards to defeat the other in order to fall upon those who should be left and put them all to the sword.

Toribio de Benavente Motolinia, *from the* History of the Indians of New Spain. *After conquering the Aztecs, Hernán Cortés requested that religious men from Spain be sent to him in Tenochtitlán. He did not trust the church with his plunder and asked specifically for Franciscans, who had taken vows of poverty. Motolinia was among the first dozen Franciscans to arrive in Mexico, where he became an advocate for the indigenous people. "Whatever was given to him," wrote Bernal Díaz del Castillo, "he gave to the Indians, and sometimes was left without food."*

1917: Slateford War Hospital

SHELL SHOCK

Since the war I have experienced two distinct and recurrent specimens of war dream. Neither of them expressed any dislike of high explosive. I have never had nightmares about being shelled, though I must confess to a few recent ones about being bombed from the air, but that was probably caused by reading the newspapers.

The two recurrent dreams: First, I was with my battalion in some slough of despond, from which it seemed there was no way back. We were all doomed to perish in the worst possible of all most hopeless "dud shows." Our only enemy was mud. This was caused by hearing about the Ypres salient, and by the haunting fear that sooner or later I should find myself in some such "immortal morass," as it might be designated by one of those lofty-minded persons who prefer to let bygones be bygones—one might call them "the Unknown Warrior School of Unrealists"—"these men perished miserably, but the spirit in which they did it lives forever," and so on. Measured in terms of unmitigated horror, this dream was, I think, quite good peace propaganda. But the queer thing about it was that while in the thick of my dream despair, I sometimes thought, "Anyhow, I am adding a very complete piece of war experience to my collection." This dream did not recur after I had written my account of military service.

The second dream still recurs, every two or three months. It varies in context and background, but always amounts to the same thing. The war is still going on and I have got to return to the front. I complain bitterly to myself because it hasn't stopped yet. I am worried because I can't find my active-service kit. I am worried because I have forgotten how to be an officer. I feel that I can't face it again, and sometimes I burst into tears and say, "It's no good. I can't do it." But I know that I can't escape going back, and search frantically for my lost equipment.

Sometimes I actually find myself "out there" (though the background is always in England—the Germans have usually invaded half Kent).

And, as in the first dream, I am vaguely gratified at "adding to my war experience." I take out a patrol and am quite keen about it.

This dream obviously dates from the autumn of 1917, when I made the choice which seemed like a "potential death sentence." If it proves anything it is this; the fact that it was everybody's business to be prepared to die for his country did not alter the inward and entirely personal grievance one had against being obliged to do it. The instinct of self-preservation automatically sank below all arguments put forward by one's "higher self." "I don't want to die," it insisted. "I want to be a middle-aged man writing memoirs, and not a 'glorious name' living forevermore on a block of stone subject to the inevitable attritions and obfuscations caused by climate." "But your deathless name will be invisibly inscribed in the annals of your imperishable race," argued some celestial leader-writer. "I prefer to peruse tomorrow's *Times* in normal decrepitude," replied ignoble self-preservation.

It would be an exaggeration if I were to describe Slateford Hospital as a depressing place by daylight. The doctors did everything possible to counteract gloom, and the wrecked faces were outnumbered by those who were emerging from their nervous disorders. But the War Office had wasted no money on interior decoration; consequently the place had the melancholy atmosphere of a decayed hydro, redeemed only by its healthy situation and pleasant view of the Pentland Hills. By daylight the doctors dealt successfully with these disadvantages, and Slateford, so to speak, "made cheerful conversation."

But by night they lost control and the hospital became sepulchral and oppressive with saturations of war experience. One lay awake and listened to feet padding along passages which smelled of stale cigarette smoke; for the nurses couldn't prevent insomnia-ridden officers from smoking half the night in their bedrooms, though the locks had been removed from all doors. One became conscious that the place was full of men whose slumbers were morbid and terrifying—men muttering uneasily or suddenly crying out in their sleep. Around me was that underworld of

Gaza Border, by Rina Castelnuovo, 2009.

dreams haunted by submerged memories of warfare and its intolerable shocks and self-lacerating failures to achieve the impossible. By daylight each mind was a sort of aquarium for the psychopath to study. In the daytime, sitting in a sunny room, a man could discuss his psychoneurotic symptoms with his doctor, who could diagnose phobias and conflicts and formulate them in scientific terminology. Significant dreams could be noted down, and Dr. Rivers could try to remove repressions. But by night each man was back in his doomed sector of a horror-stricken front line, where the panic and stampede of some ghastly experience was re-enacted among the livid faces of the dead. No doctor could save him then, when he became the lonely victim of his dream disasters and delusions.

Shell shock. How many a brief bombardment had its long-delayed aftereffect in the minds of these survivors, many of whom had looked at their companions and laughed while inferno did its best to destroy them. Not then was their evil hour, but now; now, in the sweating suffocation of nightmare, in paralysis of limbs, in the stammering of dislocated speech.

Worst of all, in the disintegration of those qualities through which they had been so gallant and selfless and uncomplaining—this, in the finer types of men, was the unspeakable tragedy of shell shock; it was in this that their humanity had been outraged by those explosives which were sanctioned and glorified by the churches; it was thus that their self-sacrifice was mocked and maltreated—they who in the name of righteousness had been sent out to maim and slaughter their fellow men. In the name of civilization these soldiers had been martyred, and it remained for civilization to prove that their martyrdom wasn't a dirty swindle.

Siegfried Sassoon, *from* Sherston's Progress. *Poet and novelist Sassoon's near-suicidal heroism on the Western Front inspired his fellow soldiers to award him the nickname Mad Jack. In 1917, while recovering from being wounded by a sniper, Sassoon published a declaration against the war, calling it a "deception"; his statements of pacifism prompted higher-ranking military authorities to place him in the asylum on which the fictional Slateford War Hospital is based. Sassoon published the first volume of his semiautobiographical trilogy in 1928, completing the set with* Sherston's Progress *in 1936.*

1942: Lake Ladoga

FROZEN IN TIME

It was nearly dawn this morning when a sentry announced that rockets were being fired into the sky above the "bridge." I made my way with some officers on to a promontory, from which the eye ranges far across the lake; and after a few moments I was able to distinguish clearly five, nine, twelve red and green rockets. They appeared in rapid succession, and were spaced out at intervals of about half a mile. Evidently a convoy was trying to cross the lake. But something must have gone wrong, because after about ten minutes the signals were repeated, this time at much shorter intervals.

Is all our fire of shipwreck wood?
—Robert Browning, 1862

Now the convoys are becoming less frequent; and soon they will cease entirely. Already the "bridge" is starting to creak, already the ice at the edge of the shore is splitting, becoming opaque, streaked with white scars, its surface is getting less wrinkled. As the snow melts, so the transparent crust beneath is exposed, and through it one can discern the slimy bed of the lake. (Lake Ladoga is not very deep; sixteen or twenty feet at the most.) Owing to the action of the waves the mud is all corrugated, like a starched petticoat. At some points, where the water is particularly shallow, the crust of ice touches the bottom. One sees whole families of fish imprisoned in the crystal, trapped in that gigantic refrigerator. The soldiers go fishing with picks, they break the ice with hammers and chisels, they extract the fish from it as from an icebox.

With the beginning of the thaw the lake reveals its mysteries, its extraordinary secrets. The other day I passed near a shallow bay shaded by a dense clump of silver birches. A party of soldiers was smashing into fragments, with violent yet compassionate strokes of their picks, what looked like a large block of green crystal, within which were embedded the pitiful remains of some Finnish soldiers. (In the same way, last January, when I visited the salt mine at Wieliczka, in Poland, I saw numbers of small fish, marine plants, and shells trapped in the crystals.) And yesterday morning, as I wandered along the shore of Lake Ladoga, near the mouth of a stream that rises in Raikkola Forest, I noticed at a certain point that I was actually walking on the roof of ice that covers the river. I heard below me the gurgling of the water, the dull murmur of the current. I looked down and saw the stream flowing tumultuously beneath my feet. I seemed to be walking on a sheet of glass. I felt as if I were suspended in space. And suddenly I was assailed by a kind of giddiness.

Imprinted in the ice, stamped on the transparent crystal beneath the soles of my shoes, I saw a row of exquisitely beautiful human faces: a row of diaphanous masks, like Byzantine icons. They were looking at me, gazing at me. Their lips were thin and shriveled, their hair was long, they had sharp noses and large, very brilliant eyes. (They were not human bodies, they were not corpses. If they had been I should have refrained from mentioning the incident.) That which was revealed to me in the sheet of ice was a row of marvelous images, full of a tender, moving pathos: as it were the delicate, living shadows of men who had been swallowed up in the mysterious waters of the lake.

War and death sometimes partake of these exquisite mysteries, which are imbued with a sublimely lyrical quality. At certain times Mars is at pains to transform his most realistic images into things of beauty, as if there came a moment when even he was overwhelmed by the compassion that man owes to his like, which nature owes to man. Beyond a doubt, I was looking at the images of some Russian soldiers who had fallen in an attempt to cross the river. The pitiful corpses, after remaining trapped as in a block of crystal all the winter, had been carried away by the first spring tides that followed the river's liberation from its icy shackles. But their faces had remained imprinted on that sheet of glass, stamped on that clear, cold,

Monju Bosatsu, bodhisattva of wisdom, surrounded by eight sacred utterances, Kyoto, Japan, mid-to-late fourteenth century. The hanging scroll was used in rituals intended to ward off natural disasters.

greeny-blue crystal. They looked at me with serene attention, they seemed almost to be following me with their eyes.

I was bending over the ice. On a sudden impulse I kneeled down and gently passed my hand across those diaphanous masks. The sun's rays were already warm, they passed through those faces and were reflected from the chuckling stream beneath, kindling as it were flames of light about those pale, transparent brows.

I returned to the glass sepulcher in the afternoon to find that the sun had almost melted those dead images. By now only the memory, only the shadow of the faces remained. Even thus does man disappear, even thus is he blotted out by the sun. Such is the transitoriness of his life. (This morning I could not bring myself to shave in front of the mirror. No, I just could not do it. I had to close my eyes, I had to shave with my eyes tight shut.)

Curzio Malaparte, *from* The Volga Rises in Europe. *Banished from the Fascist party for writing works critical of Mussolini, Malaparte was exiled to an Aeolian island in 1933, where he served a year of solitary confinement. From 1941 to 1943 he wrote a series of articles on the eastern front for the* Corriere della Sera, *from which this piece on the siege of Leningrad is taken. Before his death in 1957, Malaparte had announced a plan, never executed, to cross the United States on his bicycle.*

Scapegoats

Who takes the blame?

Scapegoat	Descendants of King Saul
Where/When	Israel, c. 1000 BC
Blamed for	A three-year famine throughout the nation
Blamed by	King David

Reason given	When David asked his oracle about the famine's cause, blame was placed on King Saul and the copious amount of innocent blood he had shed during his reign.
Incident	Saul was long dead, so David rounded up seven of Saul's sons and hanged them in the spring, at the beginning of the barley harvest. The mother of two of the boys sat under the gallows tree the entire summer to ward off scavenging creatures. Rain reportedly came in the autumn.

Scapegoat	Justinian I
Where/When	Byzantine Empire, c. 530
Blamed for	Earthquakes at Antioch, floods along the Nile, plague
Blamed by	Procopius

Reason given	In his *Secret History* Procopius held a "demon who had become incarnate in Justinian" responsible for these calamities, which he considered a sign of divine disfavor.
Incident	Procopius claimed Justinian inflicted these disasters on "men by means of a hidden power," even though several of them occurred during the last reigning years of Justinian I's predecessor and uncle, Justin, whom Procopius described as "simple-minded" and "like a stupid donkey."

Scapegoat	Ningzong
Where/When	China, 1201
Blamed for	A four-day fire that destroyed 52,000 houses in Lin'an
Blamed by	Himself

Reason given	As emperor of the southern Song dynasty, Ningzong claimed his own lack of virtue was the cause of the burning of Lin'an, capital of the Song state.
Incident	After Lin'an's burning, the emperor released a proclamation condemning himself. In contrition, he confined himself to his apartments and curbed daily luxuries.

Scapegoat	Jews
Where/When	Toulon, 1348
Blamed for	Black Death
Blamed by	European Gentiles

Reason given	Guild artisans felt that the loans of Jewish creditors were usurious and unnecessarily impoverishing debtors. Jews were also continually blamed for Christ's death and subsequent afflictions of Christians.
Incident	Rumors proliferated attributing the Black Death's spread to Jews poisoning the wells. A mob ransacked the Jewish quarter in Toulon the night before Palm Sunday, murdering 40 residents. Persecution escalated throughout Europe, including in Barcelona, Flanders, and Basel, where 600 Jews were burned alive and their 130 children taken to be baptized.

Scapegoat	Gay men
Where/When	United States, 1981
Blamed for	AIDS crisis
Blamed by	Christian fundamentalists, fueling wider indictments

Reason given	According to Pat Buchanan, the AIDS crisis was caused by the "willful refusal of homosexuals to cease indulging in the immoral, unnatural, unsanitary, unhealthy, and suicidal practice of anal intercourse."
Incident	Before it was called AIDS, the autoimmune disorder was termed "gay-related immune deficiency" by researchers and the "Gay Plague" by the media. Suggested containment strategies at the time included quarantine, reinstating sodomy laws, and tattooing those infected.

Scapegoat	Promiscuous women
Where/When	Iran, 2010
Blamed for	Past and future earthquakes
Blamed by	Islamic clerics

Reason given	"When promiscuity spreads, earthquakes increase," said cleric Hojatoleslam Kazem Sedighi. An earthquake in the city of Bam had killed 31,000 people in 2003.
Incident	In response, an American college student organized "Boobquake," during which participants wore revealing clothing. Weeks later Sedighi explained in a sermon that Western nations are not immediately punished by God: "He allows them" to sin "so that they go to the bottom of Hell" eventually.

1864: Columbia, SC

HARD AS STONES

August 29

I take my hospital duty in the morning. I am so glad to be a hospital nurse once more. I had excuses enough, but at heart I felt a coward and a skulker. Something inside of me kept calling out, "Go, you shabby creature; you can't bear to see what those fine fellows have to bear."

I have excellent servants; no matter for their shortcomings behind my back. They are so kind, attentive, and quiet. They must know what is at hand if Sherman is not hindered from coming here—"Freedom! My masters!" But these sphinxes give no sign, unless it be increased diligence and absolute silence.

September 2

The battle has been raging at Atlanta, and our fate hanging in the balance. Atlanta, indeed, is gone. Well, that agony is over. Like David, when the child was dead, I will get up from my knees, will wash my face and comb my hair. No hope; we will try to have no fear.

At the Prestons' I found them drawn up in line of battle every moment looking for the doctor on his way to Richmond. Now, to drown thought, for our day is done, read Dumas' *Maîtres d'armes*. Russia ought to sympathize with us. We are not as barbarous as this, even if Mrs. Stowe's word be taken. Brutal men with unlimited power are the same all over the world. See Russell's India—Bull Run Russell's. They say General Morgan has been killed. We are hard as stones; we sit unmoved and hear any bad news chance may bring. Are we stupefied?

September 19

My pink silk dress I have sold for $600, to be paid for in installments, $200 a month for three months. And I sell my eggs and butter from home for $200 a month. Does it not sound well—$400 a month regularly. But in what? In Confederate money. *Hélas!*

September 21

Went with Mrs. Rhett to hear Dr. Palmer. I did not know before how utterly hopeless was our situation. This man is so eloquent, it was hard to listen and not give way. Despair was his word, and martyrdom. He offered us nothing more in this world than the martyr's crown. He is not for slavery, he says; he is for freedom, and the freedom to govern our own country as we see fit. He is against foreign interference in our state matters. That is what Mr. Palmer went to war for, it appears. Every day shows that slavery is doomed the world over; for that he thanked God. He spoke of our agony, and then came the cry, "Help us, O God! Vain is the help of man." And so we came away shaken to the depths.

The end has come. No doubt of the fact. Our army has so moved as to uncover Macon and Augusta. We are going to be wiped off the face of the earth. What is there to prevent Sherman taking General Lee in the rear? We have but two armies, and Sherman is between them now.

September 24

These stories of our defeats in the valley fall like blows upon a dead body. Since Atlanta fell I have felt as if all were dead within me forever. Captain Ogden, of General Chesnut's staff, dined here today. Had ever a brigadier, with little or no brigade, so magnificent a staff? The reserves, as somebody said, have been secured only by robbing the cradle and the grave—the men too old, the boys too young. Isaac Hayne, Edward Barnwell, Bacon, Ogden, Richardson, Miles are the picked men of the agreeable world.

Mary Chesnut, *from her diary. The daughter of a South Carolina governor, the author married James Chesnut, the son of a wealthy landowner, in 1840, when she was seventeen. Her husband's election to the U.S. Senate in 1858 brought the family to Washington, DC, where they became acquaintances of Jefferson Davis; they returned to South Carolina after Lincoln's election. Mary's account of the Confederacy during the Civil War spans February 1861 to July 1865. "This diary is an extraordinary document," wrote literary critic Edmund Wilson a century later, "in its informal department, a masterpiece."*

1986: Pripyat

FALLOUT

We were newlyweds. We still walked around holding hands, even if we were just going to the store. I would say to him, "I love you." But I didn't know then how much. I had no idea. We lived in the dormitory of the firehouse where he worked. On the second floor. There were three other young couples, we all shared a kitchen. On the first floor they kept the trucks. The red fire trucks. That was his job. So I always knew what was happening—where he was, how he was.

Whenever feasible, everything possible should be done to head off a conflict or disaster.
—Bertrand Ramcharan, 2008

One night I heard a noise. I looked out the window. He saw me.

"Close the window and go back to sleep. There's a fire at the reactor. I'll be back soon."

I didn't see the explosion itself. Just the flames. Everything was radiant. The whole sky. A tall flame. And smoke. The heat was awful. And he's still not back.

The smoke was from the burning bitumen, which had covered the roof. He said later it was like walking on tar. They tried to beat down the flames. They kicked at the burning graphite with their feet. They weren't wearing their canvas gear. They went off just as they were, in their shirtsleeves. No one told them. They had been called for a fire, that was it.

Four o'clock. Five. Six. At six we were supposed to go to his parents' house. Seven o'clock. At seven I was told he was in the hospital. I ran there, but the police had already encircled it, and they weren't letting anyone through. Only ambulances. The policemen shouted, "The ambulances are radioactive, stay away!" I wasn't the only one there, all the wives whose husbands were at the reactor that night had come. I started looking for a friend, she was a doctor at that hospital. I grabbed her white coat when she came out of an ambulance.

"Get me inside!"

"I can't. He's bad. They all are." I held on to her.

"Just to see him!"

"All right," she said. "Come with me. Just for fifteen or twenty minutes."

I saw him. He was all swollen and puffed up. You could barely see his eyes.

"He needs milk, lots of milk," my friend said. "They should drink at least three liters each." Many of the doctors and nurses in that hospital, and especially the orderlies, later got sick themselves and died. But we didn't know that then.

I said, "Vasya, what should I do?"

"Get out of here! Go! You have our child." But how can I leave him? He's telling me, "Go! Leave! Save the baby."

"First I need to bring you some milk, then we'll decide what to do."

My friend Tanya Kibenok comes running in—her husband's in the same room. Her father's with her, he has a car. We get in and drive to the nearest village for some milk. It's about three kilometers from town. We buy a bunch of three-liter bottles, six, so it's enough for everyone. But they started throwing up from the milk. They kept passing out, they got put on IVs. The doctors kept telling them they'd been poisoned by gas. No one said anything about radiation. And the town was inundated right away with military vehicles, they closed off all the roads. The trolleys stopped running, and the trains. They were washing the streets with some white powder. Only the military people wore surgical masks. The people in town were carrying bread from the stores, just open sacks with the loaves in them. People were eating cupcakes on plates.

I couldn't get into the hospital that evening. There was a sea of people. I stood under his window, he came over and yelled something to me. It was all so desperate! Someone in the crowd heard him—they were being taken to Moscow that night. All the wives got together in one group. We decided we'd go with them. The soldiers—there were already soldiers—pushed us back. Then the doctor came out and said, Yes, they were flying to Moscow, but we needed to bring them their clothes. The clothes they'd worn at the station had been burned. The buses had stopped running already and we ran across the city. We came running back with their bags, but the plane was already gone. They tricked us. So that we wouldn't be there yelling and crying.

It's night. On one side of the street there are buses, they're already preparing the town for evacuation, and on the other side, hundreds of fire trucks. They came from all over. And the whole street is covered in white foam. We're walking on it, just cursing and crying. Over the radio they tell us they might evacuate the city for three to five days, take your warm clothes with you, you'll be living in the forest. In tents. People were even glad—a camping trip! We'll celebrate May Day

like that, a break from routine. People got barbecues ready. They took their guitars with them, their radios. Only the women whose husbands had been at the reactor were crying.

In Moscow we asked the first police officer we saw, Where did they put the Chernobyl firemen, and he told us. We were surprised, too, everyone was scaring us that it was top secret. "Hospital No. 6. At the Shchukinskaya stop."

It was a special hospital, for radiology, and you couldn't get in without a pass. I gave some money to the woman at the door, and she said, "Go ahead." Then I had to ask someone else, beg. Finally I'm sitting in the office of the head radiologist, Angelina Vasilyevna Guskova. But I didn't know that yet, what her name was, I didn't remember anything. I just knew I had to see him. Right away she asked, "Do you have kids?"

What should I tell her? I can see already I need to hide that I'm pregnant. They won't

View of Market Street from the Union Ferry Building after the San Francisco earthquake of 1906.

1542: Greenland

THE LAST MAN

In the memory of living men, Jon Graen-lendingur, who was for a long time associated with German merchants from Hamburg, testified that on one occasion, when they were driven to Greenland, the ship was carried near crags and high cliffs and they thought it would strike the rocks. But a single passage opened there; when they entered this, they saw the bay was so wide and large that they could not see where it would end, and in this bay or fjord were several islands. This bay was sheltered from storms and rough seas. They cast anchor at a small, uninhabited, outlying island, but avoided those that were inhabited. They saw, however, that the land was inhabited, and also many of the islands. They put out a boat and stepped onto the little island at which they lay. There were ship shelters and some fishing booths and many drying sheds made of stone, like those here. They found there a dead man, lying face down. He had on his head a well-sewn hood, and his clothing was both of wadmal and sealskin. Beside him lay a crooked carving knife, very much ground and wasted; they took this knife with them to show. This Jon was called Graenlendingur because he was thrice driven to Greenland with sailors and had much to report thence.

Björn Johnson of Skardso, *from the* Annals of Greenland. *Described by scholars as an "Icelandic yeoman," Johnson compiled his history of Greenland between the years 1623 and 1625. Icelandic settlers first arrived in Greenland circa 984; their settlements on the world's largest island endured for nearly half a millennium. This description of Jon Graenlendingur's visit came after a long period during which the colony had lost contact with Europe. When Norsemen returned to the colony in 1605, the only people they encountered were Inuits.*

let me see him! It's good I'm thin, you can't really tell.

"Yes," I say.

"How many?"

I'm thinking, I need to tell her two. If it's just one, she won't let me in.

"A boy and a girl."

"So you don't need to have anymore. All right, listen, his central nervous system is com-pletely compromised, his skull is completely compromised."

Okay, I'm thinking, so he'll be a little fidgety.

"And listen, if you start crying, I'll kick you out right away. No hugging or kissing. Don't even get near him. You have half an hour."

But I knew already that I wasn't leaving. *If I leave, then it'll be with him,* I swore to myself!

He looks so funny, he's got pajamas on for a size forty-eight, and he's a size fifty-two. The sleeves are too short, the pants are too short. But his face isn't swollen anymore. They were given some sort of fluid.

I say, "Where'd you run off to?"

He wants to hug me, the doctor won't let him.

"Sit, sit," she says. "No hugging in here."

We turned it into a joke somehow. And then everyone comes over, from the other rooms too, everyone from Pripyat. There were twenty-eight of them on the plane. What's going on? How are things in town? I tell them they've begun evacuating everyone, the whole town is being cleared out for three or five days.

I wanted to be with him alone, if only for a minute. The guys felt it, and each of them thought of some excuse, and they all went out into the hall. Then I hugged and kissed him. He moved away.

"Don't sit near me. Get a chair."

The next day they were lying by themselves, each in his own room. They were banned from going in the hallway, from talking to each other. The doctors explained that everyone's body reacts differently to radiation, one person can handle what another can't. They moved out all the sick people from the floor below and the floor above. There was no one left in the place.

He started to change—every day I met a brand-new person. The burns started to come to the surface. In his mouth, on his tongue, his cheeks—at first there were little lesions, and then they grew. It came off in layers—as white film…the color of his face…his body…blue…red…gray-brown. And it's all so very mine!

It's impossible to describe! The only thing that saved me was, it happened so fast; there wasn't any time to think, there wasn't any time to cry.

It was a hospital for people with acute radiation poisoning. Fourteen days. In fourteen days a person dies.

My father, sister, and brother flew out to Moscow. They brought me my things. And money. It was the ninth of May. He always used to say to me, "You have no idea how beautiful Moscow is! Especially on V-Day, when they set off the fireworks. I want you to see it."

I'm sitting with him in the room, he opens his eyes.

"Is it day or night?"

"It's nine at night."

"Open the window! They're going to set off the fireworks!"

I opened the window. We're on the eighth floor, and the whole city's there before us! A bouquet of fire was exploding in the air.

"Look at that!" I said.

"I told you I'd show you Moscow."

The other biochambers, where our boys were, were tended to by soldiers, because the orderlies on staff refused, they demanded protective clothing. The soldiers carried the sanitary vessels. They wiped the floors down, changed the bedding. They did everything. Where did they get those soldiers? We didn't ask. But he—he—every day I would hear: Dead. Dead. Tischura is dead. Titenok is dead. Dead. It was like a sledgehammer to my brain.

He was producing stool twenty-five to thirty times a day. With blood and mucous. His skin started cracking on his arms and legs. He became covered with boils. When he turned his head, there'd be a clump of hair left on the pillow. I tried joking, "It's convenient, you don't need a comb." Soon they cut all their hair. I did it for him myself. I wanted to do everything for him myself. If it had been physically possible I would have stayed with him all twenty-four hours.

One night, everything's quiet. We're all alone. He looked at me very, very carefully and suddenly he said, "I want to see our child so much. How is he?"

"What are we going to name him?"

"You'll decide that yourself."

"Why myself, when there's two of us?"

"In that case, if it's a boy, he should be Vasya, and if it's a girl, Natasha."

I had no idea then how much I loved him! I was like a blind person! I couldn't feel the little pounding underneath my heart. Even though I was six months in. I thought that my little one was inside me, that he was protected.

I tell the nurse on duty, "He's dying." And she says to me: "What did you expect? He got sixteen hundred roentgen. Four hundred is a lethal dose. You're sitting next to a nuclear reactor." It's all mine…it's my love. When they all

The Thin Red Line, color reproduction of a painting by Robert Gibb, 1881.
A depiction of the stand of the Ninety-Third (Highlanders) Regiment of Foot at the Battle of Balaclava, Crimean War.

The Flood (detail), by Hans Baldung, 1516.

died, they renovated the hospital. They scraped down the walls and dug up the parquet.

And then—the last thing. I remember it in flashes, all broken up.

I'm sitting on my little chair next to him at night. At eight I say, "Vasenka, I'm going for a little walk." He opens his eyes and closes them, lets me go. I just walk to the dorm, go up to my room, lie down on the floor, I couldn't lie on the bed, everything hurt too much, when already the cleaning lady is knocking. "Go! Run to him! He's calling for you like mad!" That morning Tanya Kibenok pleaded with me: "Come to the cemetery, I can't go there alone." They were burying Vitya Kibenok and Volodya Pravik.

They were friends of my Vasya. Our families were friends. There's a photo of us all in the building the day before the explosion. Our husbands are so handsome! And happy! It was the last day of that life. We were all so happy!

I came back from the cemetery and called the nurse's post right away.

"How is he?"

"He died fifteen minutes ago."

What? I was there all night. I was gone for three hours! I came up to the window and started shouting, "Why? Why?" I looked up at the sky and yelled. The whole building could hear me. They were afraid to come up to me. Then I came to: I'll see him one more time!

Once more! I run down the stairs. He was still in his biochamber, they hadn't taken him away yet. His last words were "Lyusya! Lyusenka!" "She's just stepped away for a bit, she'll be right back," the nurse told him. He sighed and went quiet. I didn't leave him anymore after that. I escorted him all the way to the gravesite. Although the thing I remember isn't the grave, it's the plastic bag. That bag.

At the morgue they said, "Want to see what we'll dress him in?" I do! They dressed him up in formalwear, with his service cap. They couldn't get shoes on him because his feet had swelled up. They had to cut up the formal wear too, because they couldn't get it on him, there wasn't a whole body to put it on. It was all—wounds. The last two days in the hospital—I'd lift his arm, and meanwhile the bone is shaking, just sort of dangling, the body has gone away from it. Pieces of his lungs, of his liver, were coming out of his mouth. He was choking on his internal organs. I'd wrap my hand in a bandage and put it in his mouth, take out all that stuff. It's impossible to talk about. It's impossible to write about. And even to live through. It was all mine. My love. They couldn't get a single pair of shoes to fit him. They buried him barefoot.

Right before my eyes—in his formalwear—they put him in that cellophane bag of theirs and tied it up. And then they put this bag in the wooden coffin. And they tied the coffin with another bag. The plastic is transparent, but thick, like a tablecloth. And then they put all that into a zinc coffin. They squeezed it in. Only the cap didn't fit.

Everyone came—his parents, my parents. They all bought black handkerchiefs in Moscow. The Extraordinary Commission met with us. They told everyone the same thing: it's impossible for us to give you the bodies of your husbands, your sons, they are very radioactive and will be buried in a Moscow cemetery in a special way. In sealed zinc caskets, under cement tiles. And you need to sign this document here.

We sat in the hearse. The relatives and some military people. A colonel and his regiment. They tell the regiment, "Await your orders!" We drive around Moscow for two or three hours, around the beltway. We're going back to Moscow again. They tell the regiment, "We're not allowing anyone into the cemetery. The cemetery's being attacked by foreign correspondents. Wait some more." The parents don't say anything. Mom has a black handkerchief. I sense I'm about to black out. "Why are they hiding my husband? He's—what? A murderer? A criminal? Who are we

Society is not a disease, it is a disaster: what a stupid miracle that one can live in it!
—*E.M. Cioran, 1949*

burying?" My mom: "Quiet. Quiet, daughter." She's petting me on the head. The colonel calls in, "Let's enter the cemetery. The wife is getting hysterical." At the cemetery we were surrounded by soldiers. We had a convoy. And they were carrying the coffin. No one was allowed in. It was just us. They covered him with earth in a minute. "Faster! Faster!" the officer was yelling. They didn't even let me hug the coffin. And—onto the bus. Everything on the sly.

Right away they bought us plane tickets back home. For the next day. The whole time there was someone with us. God forbid we might talk with someone—especially me. As if I could talk by then. I couldn't even cry. When we were leaving, the woman on duty counted all the towels and all the sheets. She folded them right away and placed them in a polyethylene bag. They probably burned them. We paid for the dormitory ourselves. For fourteen nights. It was a hospital for radiation poisoning. Fourteen nights. That's how long it takes a person to die.

Svetlana Alexievich, *from* Voices from Chernobyl. *On April 26, 1986, during a test conducted before a routine maintenance outage, a power transient destroyed the Chernobyl 4 reactor, causing the worst nuclear-reactor accident ever recorded. More than thirty operators and firemen died of acute radiation poisoning. A native of Ukraine, Alexievich interviewed hundreds of people affected by the meltdown, including Lyudmilla Ignatenko, whose husband's fire brigade was the first to arrive at the scene. Alexievich won the Nobel Prize for literature in 2015.*

2100: Rome

GOODBYE TO ALL THAT

Have any of you, my readers, observed the ruins of an anthill immediately after its destruction? At first it appears entirely deserted of its former inhabitants; in a little time you see an ant struggling through the upturned mold; they reappear by twos and threes, running hither and thither in search of their lost companions. Such were we upon the earth, wondering aghast at the effects of pestilence. Our empty habitations remained, but the dwellers were gathered to the shades of the tomb.

Things fall apart; the center cannot hold.
—*W.B. Yeats, 1919*

As the rules of order and pressure of laws were lost, some began with hesitation and wonder to transgress the accustomed uses of society. Palaces were deserted, and the poor man dared at length, unreproved, intrude into the splendid apartments, whose very furniture and decorations were an unknown world to him. It was found that, though at first the stop put to all circulation of property, had reduced those before supported by the factitious wants of society to sudden and hideous poverty, yet when the boundaries of private possession were thrown down, the products of human labor at present existing were more, far more, than the thinned generation could possibly consume. To some among the poor this was matter of exultation. We were all equal now; magnificent dwellings, luxurious carpets, and beds of down were afforded to all. Carriages and horses, gardens, pictures, statues, and princely libraries, there were enough of these even to superfluity; and there was nothing to prevent each from assuming possession of his share. We were all equal now; but near at hand was an equality still more leveling, a state where beauty and strength, and wisdom, would be as vain as riches and birth. The grave yawned beneath us all, and its prospect prevented any of us from enjoying the ease and plenty which in so awful a manner was presented to us.

Where could we turn and not find a desolation pregnant with the dire lesson of example? The fields had been left uncultivated, weeds and gaudy flowers sprung up—or where a few wheat fields showed signs of the living hopes of the husbandman, the work had been left halfway, the plowman had died beside the plow; the horses had deserted the furrow, and no seedsman had approached the dead; the cattle unattended wandered over the fields and through the lanes; the tame inhabitants of the poultry yard, balked of their daily food, had become wild—young lambs were dropped in flower gardens, and the cow stalled in the hall of pleasure. Sickly and few, the country people neither went out to sow nor reap, but sauntered about the meadows, or lay under the hedges, when the inclement sky did not drive them to take shelter under the nearest roof. Many of those who remained secluded themselves; some had laid up stores which should prevent the necessity of leaving their homes—some deserted wife and child, and imagined that they secured their safety in utter solitude. Such had been one man's plan, and he was discovered dead and half-devoured by insects, in a house many miles from any other, with piles of food laid up in useless superfluity. Others made long journeys to unite themselves to those they loved, and arrived to find them dead.

London did not contain above a thousand inhabitants, and this number was continually diminishing. Most of them were country people, come up for the sake of change; the Londoners had sought the country. The busy eastern part of the town was silent, or at most you saw only where, half from cupidity, half from curiosity, the warehouses had been more ransacked than pillaged: bales of rich India goods, shawls of price, jewels, and spices, unpacked, strewn the floors. In some places the possessor had to the last kept watch on his store and died before the barred gates. The massy portals of the churches swung creaking on their hinges, and some few lay dead on the pavement. The wretched female, loveless victim of vulgar brutality, had wandered to the

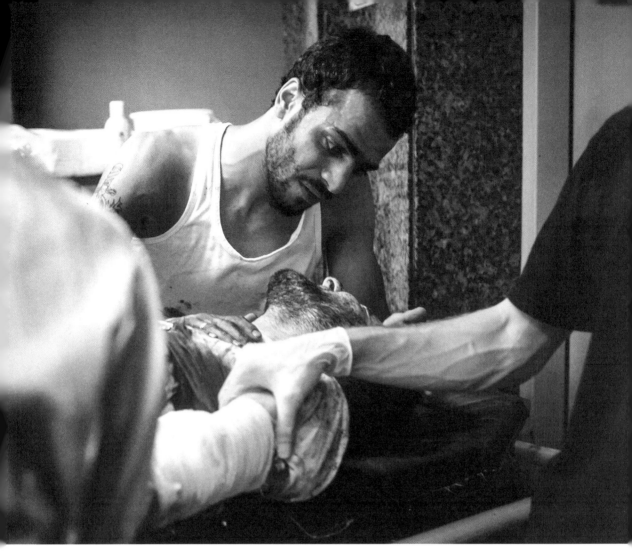

Man comforting a wounded friend at a field hospital, Aleppo, Syria, 2012. Photograph by Edouard Elias.

toilet of high-born beauty and, arraying herself in the garb of splendor, had died before the mirror which reflected to herself alone her altered appearance. Women whose delicate feet had seldom touched the earth in their luxury had fled in fright and horror from their homes till, losing themselves in the squalid streets of the metropolis, they had died on the threshold of poverty.

The hunger of Death was now stung more sharply by the diminution of his food; or was it that before, the survivors being many, the dead were less eagerly counted? Now each life was a gem, each human breathing form of far, oh far more worth than subtlest imagery of sculptured stone; and the daily, nay, hourly decrease visible in our numbers visited the heart with sickening misery. This summer extinguished our hopes, the vessel of society was wrecked, and the shattered raft, which carried the few survivors over the sea of misery, was riven and tempest tossed. Man existed by twos and threes; man, the individual who might sleep and wake and perform the animal functions; but man, in himself weak, yet more powerful in congregated numbers than wind or ocean; man, the queller of the elements, the lord of created nature, the peer of demigods, existed no longer.

Farewell to the patriotic scene, to the love of liberty and well-earned meed of virtuous aspiration! Farewell to crowded senate, vocal with the councils of the wise, whose laws were keener than the sword blade tempered at Damascus! Farewell to kingly pomp and warlike pageantry; the crowns are in the dust, and the wearers are in their graves! Farewell to the desire of rule, and

Block from a relief depicting a battle, reused in the foundation of the Theban mortuary temple of Ramses IV, c. 1400 BC.

the hope of victory; to high vaulting ambition, to the appetite for praise, and the craving for the suffrage of their fellows! The nations are no longer! No senate sits in council for the dead; no scion of a time-honored dynasty pants to rule over the inhabitants of a charnel house; the general's hand is cold, and the soldier has his untimely grave dug in his native fields, unhonored, though in youth. The marketplace is empty, the candidate for popular favor finds none whom he can represent. To chambers of painted state farewell! To midnight revelry, and the panting emulation of beauty, to costly dress and birthday show, to title and the gilded coronet, farewell!

Farewell to the giant powers of man—to knowledge that could pilot the deep-drawing bark through the opposing waters of shoreless ocean, to science that directed the silken balloon through the pathless air, to the power that could put a barrier to mighty waters, and set in motion wheels and beams and vast machinery, that could divide rocks of granite or marble and make the mountains plain!

Farewell to the arts—to eloquence, which is to the human mind as the winds to the sea, stirring and then allaying it. Farewell to poetry and deep philosophy, for man's imagination is cold, and his inquiring mind can no longer expatiate on the wonders of life, for "there is no work, nor device, nor knowledge, nor wisdom in the grave whither thou goest!"—to the graceful building, which in its perfect proportion transcended the rude forms of nature! Farewell to sculpture, where the pure marble mocks human flesh, and in the plastic expression of the culled excellencies of the human shape shines forth the god! Farewell to painting, the high wrought sentiment and deep knowledge of the artist's mind in pictured canvas! Farewell to music, and the sound of song, to the marriage of instruments, where the concord of soft and harsh unites in sweet harmony and gives wings to the panting listeners, whereby to climb heaven and learn the hidden pleasures of the eternals! Farewell to the well-trod stage; a truer tragedy is enacted on the world's ample scene that puts to shame mimic grief. To highbred comedy and the low buffoon, farewell! Man may laugh no more.

Mary Wollstonecraft Shelley, *from* The Last Man. *A science-fiction novel published in 1826,* The Last Man *purports to tell of a late twenty-first-century England consumed by plague. Even though it was one of the* Frankenstein *author's favorite books,* The Last Man *was met with critical derision upon publication—"the offspring of a diseased imagination, and of a most polluted taste," read one contemporary review—and only sporadically kept in print until a 1965 American edition. Shelley died in London in 1851 at the age of fifty-three.*

1912: South Pole

My Dear Mrs. Wilson,

If this letter reaches you, Bill and I will have gone out together. We are very near it now, and I should like you to know how splendid he was at the end—everlastingly cheerful and ready to sacrifice himself for others, never a word of blame to me for leading him into this mess. He is not suffering, luckily, at least only minor discomforts.

His eyes have a comfortable blue look of hope and his mind is peaceful with the satisfaction of his faith in regarding himself as part of the great scheme of the Almighty. I can do no more to comfort you than to tell you that he died as he lived, a brave, true man—the best of comrades and staunchest of friends.

My whole heart goes out to you in pity,
Yours,
R. Scott

My Dear J.M. Barrie,

We are pegging out in a very comfortless spot. Hoping this letter may be found and sent to you, I write a word of farewell. More practically I want you to help my widow and my boy—your godson. We are showing that Englishmen can still die with a bold spirit, fighting it out to the end. It will be known that we have accomplished our object in reaching the pole, and that we have done everything possible, even to sacrificing ourselves in order to save sick companions. I think this makes an example for Englishmen of the future, and that the country ought to help those who are left behind to mourn us. I leave my poor girl and your godson, Wilson leaves a widow, and Edgar Evans also a widow in humble circumstances. Do what you can to get their claims recognized. Goodbye. I am not at all afraid of the end, but sad to miss many a humble pleasure which I had planned for the future on our long marches. I may not have proved a great explorer, but we have done the greatest march ever made and come very near to great success. Goodbye, my dear friend.

Yours ever,
R. Scott

We are in a desperate state, feet frozen, etc. No fuel and a long way from food, but it would do your heart good to be in our tent, to hear our songs and the cheery conversation as to what we will do when we get to Hut Point.

Later—We are very near the end, but have not and will not lose our good cheer. We have four days of storm in our tent and nowhere's food or fuel. We did intend to finish ourselves when things proved like this, but we have decided to die naturally in the track.

As a dying man, my dear friend, be good to my wife and child. Give the boy a chance in life if the state won't do it. He ought to have good stuff in him. I never met a man in my life whom I admired and loved more than you, but I never could show you how much your friendship meant to me, for you had much to give and I nothing.

My Dear Sir Francis,

I fear we have shipped up; a close shave; I am writing a few letters which I hope will be delivered some day. I want to thank you for the friendship you gave me of late years, and to tell you how extraordinarily pleasant I found it to serve under you. I want to tell you that I was *not* too old for this job. It was the younger men that went under first. After all we are setting a good example to our countrymen, if not by getting into a tight place, by facing it like men when we were there. We could have come through had we neglected the sick.

Goodbye, and goodbye to dear Lady Bridgeman.

Yours ever,
R. Scott

Excuse writing—it is -40 degrees and has been for nigh a month.

My Dear Sir George,

I fear we have shot our bolt—but we have been to pole and done the longest journey on record.

A Sudden Appearance Out of the Sea of a Race of Amphibious Monsters, Capable of Sweeping Men Out of Existence, illustration from *Pearson's Magazine,* by Warwick Goble, 1900.

I hope these letters may find their destination someday. Subsidiary reasons of our failure to return are due to the sickness of different members of the party, but the real thing that has stopped us is the awful weather and unexpected cold toward the end of the journey.

This traverse of the Ice Barrier has been quite three times as severe as any experience we had on the summit. There is no accounting for it, but the result has thrown out my calculations, and here we are little more than a hundred miles from the base and petering out.

Goodbye. Please see my widow is looked after as far as Admiralty is concerned.

R. Scott

To My Widow,

Dearest darling—we are in a very tight corner and I have doubts of pulling through. In our short lunch hours I take advantage of a very small measure of warmth to write letters preparatory to a possible end—the first is naturally to you on whom my thought mostly dwells, waking or sleeping.

If anything happens to me I shall like you to know how much you have meant to me and that pleasant recollections are with me as I depart.

I should like you to take what comfort you can from these facts also—I shall not have suffered any pain but leave the world fresh from harness and full of good health and vigor. Therefore you must not imagine a great tragedy—we are very anxious, of course, and have been for weeks, but in splendid physical condition, and our appetites compensate for all discomfort. The cold is biting and sometimes angering, but here again the hot food which drives it forth is so wonderfully enjoyable that we would scarcely be without it.

We have gone downhill a good deal since I wrote the above. Poor Titus Oates has gone—he was in a bad state—the rest of us keep going and imagine we have a chance to get through, but the cold weather doesn't let up at all—we are now only twenty miles from a depot, but we have very little food or fuel.

Well dear heart, I want you to take the whole thing very sensibly, as I am sure you will—the boy will be your comfort.

I had looked forward to helping you to bring him up, but it is a satisfaction to feel that he is safe with you. I think both he and you ought to be specially looked after by the country for which after all we have given our lives with something of spirit which makes for example.

I must write a little letter for the boy if time can be found to be read when he grows up—dearest, that you know I cherish no sentimental rubbish about remarriage—when the right man comes to help you in life, you ought to be your happy self again.

I hope I shall be a good memory. Certainly the end is nothing for you to be ashamed of, and I like to think that the boy will have a good start in parentage of which he may be proud. Dear it is not easy to write because of the cold—70 degrees below zero and nothing but the shelter of our tent.

You know I have loved you—you know my thoughts must have constantly dwelled on you, and, oh dear me, you must know that quite the worst aspect of this situation is the thought that I shall not see you again.

The inevitable must be faced—you urged me to be leader of this party and I know you felt it would be dangerous—I've taken my place throughout, haven't I?

Since writing the above we have got to within eleven miles of our depot, with one hot meal and two days' cold food, and we should have got through but have been held for four days by a frightful storm—I think the best chance has gone. We have decided not to kill ourselves but to fight it to the last for that depot, but in the fighting there is a painless end, so don't worry.

I have written letters on odd pages of this book—will you manage to get them sent? You see I am anxious for you and the boy's future—make the boy interested in natural history if you can, it is better than games—they encourage it at some schools—I know you will keep him out in the open air—try and make him believe in a God, it is comforting.

Oh my dear, my dear, what dreams I have had of his future, and yet, oh my girl, I know you will face it stoically—your portrait and the boy's will be found in my breast and the one in the little red morocco case given by Lady Baxter. There is a piece of the Union flag I put up at the South Pole in my private kit bag together with Amundsen's black flag and other trifles—give a small piece of the Union flag to the king and a small piece to Queen Alexandra and keep the rest a poor trophy for you!

What lots and lots I could tell you of this journey. How much better it has been than lounging in comfort at home—what tales you would have for the boy, but oh what a price to pay—to forfeit the sight of your dear, dear face.

Robert Falcon Scott, *from letters found with his diary. After his first polar expedition returned in 1904, British naval officer Scott became a national celebrity. In 1909 he heard news that Ernest Shackleton had come close to reaching the South Pole, and he announced his own expedition, on the* Terra Nostra, *later that year. In January 1912 Scott finally reached the pole; a team of Norwegians had preceded him there by thirty-four days. The bodies of Scott and his men were found in November. "Nothing in our time," proclaimed one newspaper, "has touched the whole nation so instantly and so deeply as the loss of these men."*

1894: Alexandria

ONLY THIS

You said: "I'll go to some other land, I'll go to some other sea
There's bound to be another city that's better by far.
My every effort has been ill-fated from the start;
my heart—like something dead—lies buried away;
How long will my mind endure this slow decay?
Wherever I look, wherever I cast my eyes,
I see all around me the black rubble of my life
where I've spent so many ruined and wasted years."
You'll find no new places, you won't find other shores.
The city will follow you. The streets in which you pace
will be the same, you'll haunt the same familiar places,
and inside those same houses you'll grow old.
You'll always end up in this city. Don't bother to hope
for a ship, a route, to take you somewhere else; they don't exist.
Just as you've destroyed your life, here in this
small corner, so you've wasted it through all the world.

> **C.P. Cavafy**, *"The City." Born in Alexandria in 1863 to Turkish Greeks,
> Cavafy lived in Liverpool for seven years before returning to Egypt to
> begin a thirty-year career in its ministry of public works. "The City" is one
> of only a handful of poems he published during his lifetime; he circulated
> the majority of them among his acquaintances in homemade booklets
> bound with pins. In 1919 his friend E.M. Forster helped introduce his
> work to the English-speaking world in an essay that described Cavafy as
> "standing absolutely motionless at a slight angle to the universe."*

Stalemate, by Richard Mosse, 2011. United Nations excavator stuck in mud during the rainy season, Masisi Territory, North Kivu, Democratic Republic of Congo. Numerous armed groups fight for control of the mineral-rich Masisi Territory.

1984: Ghana

DISASTER CAPITALISM

"Frankly," he said through the electronic glass partition, "it will be a sad day for some of us when this catastrophic drought is over. Fortunately," he snapped a finger, "it will go on. And on."

I'd noticed the fellow at the last three conferences I'd covered for my magazine, the struggling satirical sheet *Sic Transit*. A lot of people writing to the editor spell the first part of our magazine's name *Sick*. The publisher normally owes the small staff three months' wages. Still, I keep searching out the humorous vein hidden somewhere under life's jugular, writing pieces I hope are funny, but which in my heart I know are merely ridiculous. Besides, it's possible to earn short-order income at conferences doubling as a translator. That's how I came to develop such a keen interest in conferences. And that's how I met Christian Mohamed Tumbo.

Yes of course, I asked him how he came to possess such perfectly ecumenical names. Were they pseudonyms he'd chosen himself?

"No," he answered readily. "My mother was a good Christian, my father an equally good Muslim."

"So you became…"

"A compromise."

It was our first conversation. I knew at once I'd hit the hidden vein. In spite of everything, there was something likeable about this rotund fellow. His charm was indeterminate, but I knew it had something to do with the liveliness of his tiny eyes. They were like trapped sparks. There

1978: Bucharest

GOVERNMENT OVERSIGHT

According to careful estimates, in the last earthquake to strike Bucharest 2,500 people lost their lives; exact calculations, however, have shown that some 4,000 people perished beneath the ruins. This number would have been reduced by 500 if the city had acted contrary to the express orders of the official of the Bucharest administration responsible for these things to bulldoze the rubble of the hotel that was totally destroyed rather than to clear it away, and had actually cleared the rubble away. For a whole week after the earthquake, people could still hear the cries of hundreds of those who had been buried coming from the rubble. The official of the city administration had the area around the hotel cordoned off until he received reports that absolutely nothing more was stirring beneath the rubble and not a single sound was still to be heard from the rubble. Not until two and a half weeks after the earthquake were the people of Bucharest permitted to view the heap of rubble, which was completely bulldozed in the third week. The official is said to have refused, on grounds of expense, to rescue some 500 guests of the hotel who had been buried. Rescuing them would have cost a thousand times more than bulldozing, even without taking into account the fact that probably hundreds of severely injured people would have been brought out from the rubble who would then have had to be supported by the state for the rest of their lives. According to reports, the official had, in the nature of things, assured himself of the support of the Romanian government. His promotion to a higher position in the civil service is said to be imminent.

Thomas Bernhard, *"Decision." Bernhard grew up in Salzburg, where as a teenager he dropped out of school and went to work in a grocery store. This report on the aftermath of the Romanian earthquake of March 4, 1977, was included in his 1978 collection, The Voice Imitator. When Bernhard died in 1989 his will forbade any publication or performance of his work in his native Austria, which he once called "a common hell in which the intellect is incessantly defamed and art and science are destroyed."*

---

was also the incongruous smoothness of his baby cheeks. His teeth were ugly and uncared-for. But he bared them so often, and in such a pleased smile, that in the end one got used to

them, like frequent, affectionate visitors. He spoke a voluble, jovial French. It was he who said, right in the middle of a solemn-sounding speech about the present threat of famine, that conference sessions were excellent for working up a thirst, in preparation, come break time, for the real objective of such gatherings: drinking. He'd aroused laughter that time, with his slightly dangerous sense of humor. He said it was all a technique, the technique of the griot: take a bantering attitude to truths others prefer to bury under taciturn official masks.

At least once, though, his humorous technique had backfired. In a moment of absentmindedness, participants at the end of a development-strategies conference had asked him to give the vote of thanks. He gave a honeyed speech, full of francophone marshmallows and admiration for the organizers' many superlative qualities. The last, but not the least of these super qualities, he concluded, was the chairman's enviable ability to appear chronically overworked even while riding on the Nirvana line. After this joke I noticed conference officials and participants avoided him. I sought him out.

I found him exceedingly open, eager, in fact, to talk. He seemed to have had to keep to himself something he wanted to share—a huge joke. Finally he'd found a friendly female ear, mine. Still, I doubt if he'd ever have opened up so totally except for an accident.

Because we talked frequently during breaks, we often sat near each other during sessions. Conferences are not hard work, but they are tedious, and when poorly organized they can be exhausting in a wasteful way. I'd noticed that Christian Mohamed Tumbo never seemed crushed by the monotonous drudgery of all these speeches. At the end of each session, he could be seen far ahead of the others, bounding joyfully toward the cocktail bar, a manic spirit unchained.

The secret of his energy, when I discovered it, surprised me with the elegance of its sheer simplicity: during most conference sessions, Christian Mohamed Tumbo slept. He had the priceless political gift of being able to sleep with his eyes open; not wide open—that was the beauty of it—just a shade narrowed, like the eyes of an alert person paying receptive, benevolently critical attention to whatever was going on.

Participants were being asked when they wanted to go on a field trip to a disaster area: 1500 hours or 1700 hours. The usual practice at conferences is for the organizers to fix all important decisions. The participants endorse them by acclamation. This was an unimportant matter, however, and individual preferences were being canvassed. The chairman called Christian Mohamed Tumbo twice, a third time. Tumbo sat there looking particularly intelligent and smart, but hearing nothing. I nudged him awake as the chairman repeated the question. Christian Mohamed Tumbo said, "1700 hours," then turned to ask me what it was all about. I knew why he trusted me: I was on the conference circuit, without being part of the conference establishment. He had nothing to fear from me. There may have been an additional, more frivolous reason. Perhaps he wished we'd get to be closer friends.

For a period Christian Mohamed Tumbo suffered no further embarrassment in his sleep. On at least three occasions, though, he came close. It was inevitable that catastrophe would strike one day. What floored me was the way it happened. I'd imagined Christian Mohamed Tumbo sleeping his way through a conference session and the chairman, innocent soul, asking the usual earthshaking question: What, in the opinion of your delegation, would be the implementational modalities for achieving the objective of the total eradication of poverty and injustice in Africa by, at the latest, the year 4000? Instead it was Christian Mohamed Tumbo himself who took the initiative and spoke in his sleep. Loud and clear, as in a ringing peroration.

The conference, incidentally, was another one on the drought. The chairman, a somber fellow from the Cosmic Meteorological Organization, had gone through the part of his closing speech about the present drought being an

The Rescue, by Maurice Poirson, c. 1880.

unprecedented threat requiring unprecedented measures. He had come to the part about the urgent need for further conferences to promote reflection on the problem that had been discussed for the past ten years. The shout came, bold and clear: "*Vive la Sécheresse!*"

The chairman, embarrassed by the interruption, wound up in a hurry. Two of the organizers leaned forward, apparently uncertain whether there was a heckler to be bounced, or a gaffe to be diplomatically ignored. But Christian Mohamed Tumbo had fallen quiet again.

We were so close together that I felt the eyes turned on him were glaring at me too. To cover my embarrassment, no doubt, but so spontaneously I was astonished at my presence of mind, I did Christian Mohamed Tumbo a service he claims he'll never forget. I rose, loudly applauding the chairman's speech as if here at last was the international bureaucrat who had found the magic words for solving the world's problems.

The chairman was sitting as I rose. One of the organizers pointed to me, thinking I was

Katrina X-Codes

After Hurricane Katrina made landfall in Louisiana on August 29, 2005, teams directed by the Federal Emergency Management Agency embarked on a building-by-building search of every structure in the city of New Orleans. The teams adapted a system outlined in FEMA manuals and spray-painted X-codes to indicate the results of their searches. Eighty percent of the city's buildings were marked with these Katrina crosses.

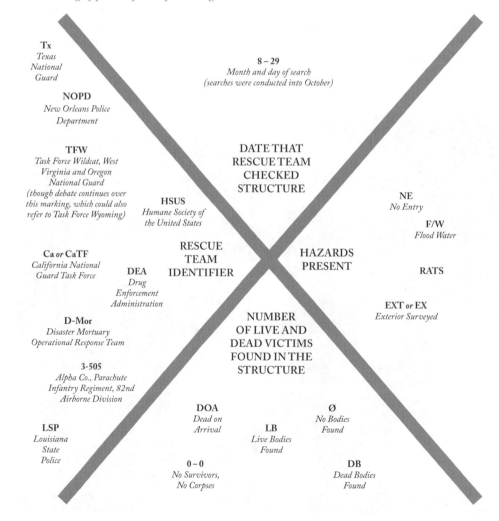

Tx
Texas National Guard

NOPD
New Orleans Police Department

8 – 29
Month and day of search (searches were conducted into October)

TFW
Task Force Wildcat, West Virginia and Oregon National Guard (though debate continues over this marking, which could also refer to Task Force Wyoming)

DATE THAT RESCUE TEAM CHECKED STRUCTURE

HSUS
Humane Society of the United States

NE
No Entry

F/W
Flood Water

Ca *or* CaTF
California National Guard Task Force

DEA
Drug Enforcement Administration

RESCUE TEAM IDENTIFIER

HAZARDS PRESENT

RATS

D-Mor
Disaster Mortuary Operational Response Team

EXT *or* EX
Exterior Surveyed

NUMBER OF LIVE AND DEAD VICTIMS FOUND IN THE STRUCTURE

3-505
Alpha Co., Parachute Infantry Regiment, 82nd Airborne Division

LSP
Louisiana State Police

DOA
Dead on Arrival

LB
Live Bodies Found

Ø
No Bodies Found

0 – 0
No Survivors, No Corpses

DB
Dead Bodies Found

asking for the floor. In the intense confusion, the chairman gave me the floor. I flew at the chance.

"*Comme notre collègue vient de le dire,*" I said, putting such a desperate roll on the francophone *r* in the next word that I bruised the lining of my throat, "*vivre la sécheresse, c'est notre problème numéro un. Monsieur le Président, nous vous félicitons vivement pour votre exposé.*"

The tension eased. A sigh of relief came from someone, probably a participant now convinced he had misheard the shout after all.

On the way down to the poolside restaurant for dinner, a couple of people came to congratulate me. At the cocktail bar just before the restaurant entrance, Christian Mohamed Tumbo was uncharacteristically morose.

"I spoke in my sleep, didn't I?" he asked me. "Yes."

He winced, but couldn't suppress his curiosity. "What did I say?"

"*Vive la sécheresse.* You must have been having a nightmare."

He smiled enigmatically: "A nightmare first, then a dream. In the nightmare Africa's deserts became forests and gardens. It was frightening. Luckily, the nightmare ended. The deserts regained their dryness. Familiar signs of famine reappeared: skeletons in the Sahel sand. I recognized our continent. I suppose that's when I shouted, '*Vive la sécheresse.*'"

"Long live the drought?" I queried.

"I know what you're thinking," he said, staring at me as at a beloved but retarded sibling. "The man makes his living working for an antidrought organization. But this same man thinks the end of the drought would be a disaster. Right?"

"More or less."

He took a moment deciding whether I was worth his confidence. Then his eyes took on a hundred–watt intensity. "You're looking at a man who'd have died ten years ago if frustration could kill. I taught secondary-school geography for fifteen years. Every year I earned starvation wages, and watched my students come back five years later with academic degrees and salaries that gave me a headache just

to imagine. I was getting to be a sick man, bitter as a dwarf lemon.

"There's no better work than teaching, but in time I realized what I needed was not a better job but more money and a bit of respect from the swinish society.

"'Try Nirvana,' a friend advised me. I thought Nirvana was some new version of Transcendental Meditation, or a drug to cure hypertension. A cure for frustrated greed. Green in every way, that's what I was. The

> *It really seems to me that in the midst of great tragedy there is always the horrible possibility that something terribly funny will happen.*
> —*Philip K. Dick, 1996*

friend explained Nirvana: the UN System in one seamless phrase: European salaries diplomatic status tax exemption duty-free goodies travel galore clean paperwork cool hotels, per diems in dollars. A smooth talker, my friend.

"I tried the Nirvana Highway, and ran into a wall. The wall has secret holes in it, and only those already on the other side can pull you through. Besides, I don't even have a bachelor's degree. Everyone in Nirvana has to have that. At least.

"I'd practically given up on getting near Nirvana at all when the same friend told me about the NGO approach. Nongovernmental organizations. Well, I found the NGO road open even if the Nirvana highway was blocked. My friend introduced me to a Swede with a permanent crease in his forehead and foundation money behind him, looking for an African assistant to help him set up an agency to Fight the Drought.

"I went to the Swede and listened to him for four hours. He could have been a regular missionary, if he'd been a shade less intelligent. I listened to his absurd litany of strategies and solutions. I know droughts and floods have been part of African history for thousands of years. But he kept saying The Drought was an unprecedented disaster. I agreed absolutely with

The Burning of the Houses of Lords and Commons, October 16, 1834, by Joseph Mallord William Turner, c. 1835.

him. Between this strange Swede and me, why shouldn't there be a perfect identity of views?

"The Swede found his African assistant, and I found my NGO, halfway to Nirvana. The Anti-Drought Organization. Nice acronym, ADO. Since that day, four years ago, I've changed from a man of problems into a man of solutions. I've forgotten what it feels like to be in debt. I have three villas. Two are embassy residences. Rent paid a year in advance. In dollars. The third I live in myself. ADO pays me a handsome rent for living in my own house. Every month I travel abroad. When I'm on the move my salary stays intact, while per diems compensate me for my dedicated suffering in hotels and nightclubs as I move from capital to capital, conference to seminar, fighting the drought.

"I didn't mean to shout. The words escaped me, but I know I'd live a lot less well if there were no drought or famine."

We'd finished dinner, except for the liqueur. As I drained the small, sweet glass, it caught the light from the swimming pool outside and broke it into a frail, momentary indoor rainbow. I put the tiny glass against the menu, propped up against a twin rose in a vase.

Langouste mayonnaise
Potage de légumes
Salade niçoise
Entrecôte aux échalottes
Plateau de fromage
Coupe Mont Blanc
Café Liégeois

"Nice meal, eh?" Christian Mohamed Tumbo asked.

I nodded, then rose to go to the poolside area. He wanted to go up to his room. Perhaps he'd hoped, but he swallowed his regret as we shook hands, parting. He pressed mine like a tyro conspirator, winked into the bargain and, as I walked toward the electronic glass partition, called out softly: "*Vive la sécheresse.*"

Ayi Kwei Armah, *"Halfway to Nirvana." A native of Ghana, Armah worked as a scriptwriter, translator, and teacher in Europe, Africa, and the United States. "It is not every age or every continent which can boast of fiery revolutionaries who have never ventured within the smelling distance of a revolution, of freedom fighters whose suits are made in Paris," Armah lamented in 1967. "This is Africa's heroic age." His first novel,* The Beautyful Ones Are Not Yet Born, *was published the following year. He currently resides in Senegal.*

1889: St. Louis, MO

WATER OVER THE DAM

Those who have been over to Johnstown and witnessed the operations that are going on at this writing, of trying to loosen an enormous mass of debris and get through it by the use of dynamite, every other means having failed, will be ready to accept the contrary conclusion and admit that water can do a great deal of mischief and pile up a great mass of earth, stones, trees, houses, railway locomotives, cars, human bodies and whatnot in a very few minutes, and make the pile very deep and the mass very solid if it only tries. If those dynamiters would cease their work, some future geologist might discover in that pile of debris another Neanderthal skull.

But this brings us to the law of the case. What is the responsibility of a corporation or person who collects on his land a vast body of water, and does not sufficiently restrain it as to prevent its being turned loose by means of an extraordinary freshet upon the unsuspecting inhabitants below? The general answer would be that the authors of such mischief are liable on the principle of negligence. That answer is good enough, if the judge will only turn them over to a common jury. In the hands of twelve good and honest men such a rule of law will answer every practical purpose. But unfortunately we have judges who think that on questions of ordinary care and questions of what is reasonable and unreasonable in practical life one legal scholar (although a poor one) knows more than twelve practical men in the jury box. So that the law tries to give an answer; and what answer has it given? The best answer that has ever yet been given was given in one of the best considered cases which ever went through the courts of England. That answer was given by Justice Blackburn in his judgment in the Court of Exchequer Chamber in the great case of *Fletcher v. Bylands*:

We think that the true rule of law is that the person who, for his own purposes, brings on his lands and collects and keeps there any-

thing likely to do mischief if it escapes must keep it in at his peril, and if he does not do so is *prima facie* answerable for all the damage that is the natural consequence of its escape. He can excuse himself by showing that the escape was owing to the plaintiff's default; or perhaps that the escape was the consequence of *vis major*, or the act of God.

This dictum was approved in the same case in the House of Lords, and must be accepted as the law of England upon this question. It has been, in terms, adopted by several American courts, though denied by some. It is good enough for the practical purpose of charging with damages a company of gentlemen who have maintained a vast reservoir of water behind a rotten dam, for the mere pleasure of using it for a fishing pond, to the peril of thousands of honest people dwelling in the valley below. It is enough that they are *prima facie* answerable. That takes the question to the jury. The jury will do the rest. They can be safely trusted to say whether or not it was the plaintiff's default, that is the fault of some poor widow in Johnstown, whose husband and children were drowned while she was cast ashore and suffered to live. They can also be trusted to say whether it was in consequence of a *vis major*, or the act of God. A jury of Pennsylvania Lutherans, Reformed Dutch, Presbyterians, Methodists, Baptists, or Catholics will not take readily to the attempt to cast the responsibility of such a catastrophe from the shoulders of the fine, rich gentlemen who owned the fishpond and the rotten dam to the shoulders of God.

From an article in The American Law Review. *The editors of this influential law journal—which had recently included Oliver Wendell Holmes—took up the "law of bursting reservoirs" shortly after the Johnstown flood in Pennsylvania. The South Fork dam held back the pleasure lake of the South Fork Fishing and Hunting Club, which counted as members Andrew Carnegie, Henry Frick, and Andrew Mellon. On May 31, 1889, the dam broke; more than two thousand people died in the ensuing flood. Bodies were found as far away as Cincinnati and as late as 1911. No lawsuit against the club was successful and no damages were ever paid.*

c. 60 BC: Rome

THE CENTER NEVER HOLDS

After the time the world was born, and the first
Day of the sea and the earth and the sun had dawned,
Much matter was added from beyond, seeds added
Around us, which the great All flung into union;
From these the sea and the earth can grow, from these
The heavens extend their demesne and lift still higher
Their lofty towers; from these the winds arise.
For driven from all quarters the atoms are sorted
Each to his own, and settle into kinds:
Water settles with water, from atoms of earth the earth
Grows; fire flints out the fire and air the air;
Until to the utmost limit of growth all things
Are led, made perfect by Creating Nature.
That happens when no more is fed into
Life-giving veins than that which ebbs away.
This is the age at which all things must stand,
When mighty Nature reins in all increase.
For whatever you see grow big with hearty addition,
Mounting the steps to maturity one by one,
Takes on more atoms than it loses while
The veins are freely fed, and their bodies are
Not yet so tattered they lose their atoms and
Expend more than their time of life restores.
You must surrender the point, that atoms flood
Into and ebb from things. But more must enter
Till things have touched their pinnacle of growth.
Then slowly and softly the solid trunk of adulthood
Breaks, and we melt into the lesser age.
And that's no wonder: the fuller and broader a thing
When you exhaust the source of its increase,
The sooner will it scatter and lose its atoms,
Nor will its veins be nourished easily,
Nor is there enough to shore up and restore
The ample exhalations of the old.
By rights they pass away, made thin and porous
In the dwindle of atoms, laid low by blows from without,
When finally in their great age all food fails them
And the outside atoms, hammering, never cease
Till they rule with their rain of pounding and crush the thing.
So also the great battlements of the world,
Besieged and battered, will crumble into ruin.
For food it is that makes things whole and new,
Food shores them up, holds all things in repair—
In vain; enough will not be suffered to enter

The Horseman, flayed and preserved man and horse by Honoré Fragonard, c. 1770.

The blood; Nature will not supply what's needed.
And now, so crippled is our age that the earth,
Worn out by labor, scarce makes tiny creatures—
Which once made all, gave birth to giant beasts.
What's more, at first she made, of her own prompting,
The glossy corn and the glad vine for us mortals,
And gave, of her own, sweet offspring and glad pasture.
Yet these now hardly grow for all our work:
We sweat our oxen thin and the strength of our farmhands
We crush; for our fields the plow is not enough.
So full of labor and so spare of birth!
Now the old plowman shakes his head and sighs
That all of his hard work has come to nothing,
Compares the present days to days gone by
And over and over touts his father's luck.
Disheartened, the planter of stooped and shriveled vines
Curses this bent of our age, and rattles on
With his reproach: our elders, full of reverence,
Managed to live with ease in narrow bounds,
With much less acreage to a man; he doesn't
Grasp that, slowly, wasting away, all things
Go to the tomb, worn out by the long years.

Lucretius, *from* On the Nature of Things. *The first time Lucretius describes religion in this poem, it assumes the form of a monster in the sky; early Christians considered him an enemy of the church. About Epicurus, whose philosophy Lucretius expounds in* On the Nature of Things, *the poet wrote that the ancient Greek showed "what disaster exists everywhere in human life, how it comes into being and flies about in different ways, whether through chance or force of nature."*

1960: Hampstead

EXIT STRATEGY

The flight crowd is created by a threat. Everyone flees; everyone is drawn along. The danger which threatens is the same for all. It is concentrated at a definite point and makes no distinctions there. It can threaten the inhabitants of a city, or all those who belong to a particular faith, or speak a particular language.

People flee together because it is best to flee that way. They feel the same excitement and the energy of some increases the energy of others; people push each other along in the same direction. So long as they keep together they feel that the danger is distributed, for the

I see America spreading disaster. I see America as a black curse upon the world. I see a long night settling in and that mushroom which has poisoned the world withering at the roots.
—Henry Miller, 1936

ancient belief persists that danger springs at one point only. They argue that, while the enemy is seizing one of them, all the others can escape. The flanks of the flight are uncovered but, since they are extended, they think it impossible for danger to attack all of them at the same time. No one is going to assume that he, out of so many, will be the victim and, since the sole movement of the whole flight is toward salvation, each is convinced that he personally will attain it.

For the most striking thing about a mass flight is the force of its direction. The crowd has, as it were, become all direction, away from danger. Since the goal of safety and the distance from it are the only things which matter, all the previously existing distances between men become unimportant. Strange and widely dissimilar creatures who have never come near each other before suddenly find themselves together. In their flight all the distances between them disappear, though the differences

of course do not. The flight crowd is the most comprehensive of all crowds. It contains absolutely everybody and the picture of diversity that it thus presents is further complicated by the differing speeds of the fugitives: there are young and old among them, strong and weak, those less and those more burdened. But the picture is misleading. Its motley colors are only incidental and, measured against the overpowering force of direction, utterly insignificant.

The impetus of the flight continues to multiply so long as everyone recognizes that there are others fleeing with him. He may press them forward, but he must not push them aside. The moment he starts to think only of himself and to regard those around him purely as obstacles, the character of the mass flight changes completely and it turns into its exact opposite; it becomes a panic, a struggle of each against all who stand in his way. This reversal generally occurs when the direction of the flight has been repeatedly impeded. To block the crowd's way is enough to make it break out in another direction. If its way is repeatedly blocked, it soon no longer knows where to turn. It grows confused about its direction and thus loses its coherence. The danger that, till then, had united its members and given them wings, now sets each man up as an enemy of the next. Everyone is intent only on saving himself.

The mass flight, on the other hand, contrary to the panic, derives its energy from its coherence. As long as it remains one powerful and undivided river and does not allow itself to be dispersed and split, so long does the fear by which it is driven remain bearable. Once a mass flight is underway it is characterized by a kind of exaltation—the exaltation of common movement. No one person is in any less danger than any other and, though he continues to run or ride with all his might to save his own life, he still occupies a recognized place among all the others and sticks to it throughout the turmoil.

The flight can last for days or weeks and, during it, some remain behind, either stricken by the enemy, or because their strength is gone.

Admirable Act of Valor: Stoker Saves Girl near Ancona by Lying Over Her Under an Oncoming Train (detail), illustration from *La Domenica del Corriere*, by Achille Beltrame, 1909.

Everyone who falls by the way acts as a spur to the others. Fate has overtaken him and exempted them. He is a sacrifice offered to danger. However important he may have been to some of them as a companion in flight, by falling he becomes important to all of them. The sight of him gives new strength to the weary; he has proved weaker than they are; the danger was aimed at him and not at them. The isolation in which he remains behind, and in which they still see him for a short time, heightens for them the value of their being together. Anyone who falls has thus an incalculable importance for the cohesion of the flight.

The natural end of the flight is the attainment of the goal; once this crowd is in safety it dissolves. But the danger can also be arrested at its source. An armistice may be declared and the city from which people were fleeing be no longer in danger. They fled together, but they return singly, and soon everything is again as separate as it used to be. But there is also a third possibility, which may be called the oozing away of the flight in sand. The goal is too far off, the surroundings are hostile and the people starve and grow exhausted. It is no longer only a few, but hundreds and thousands who collapse and remain behind. This physical disintegration sets in only gradually, for the original impetus lasts for a long time; people crawl on even when every chance of salvation has vanished. Of all types of crowd, the flight crowd is the one which exhibits the greatest tenacity; its remnants keep together until the very last moment.

Elias Canetti, *from* Crowds and Power. *A Sephardic Jew born in Bulgaria, Canetti was inspired to write* Crowds *after being caught in a battle between workers and police on a Viennese street in 1927. Almost ninety rioters died in the so-called July Revolt, and the Palace of Justice was set on fire. Canetti, wrote W.G. Sebald, "linked the fascination of power in its purest form to the growing number of its accumulated victims." In 1981 Canetti won the Nobel Prize in Literature.*

2003: Halifax

REBECCA SOLNIT AMONG THE RUINS

I landed in Nova Scotia shortly after a big hurricane tore up the city in October 2003. The man in charge of taking me around told me about the hurricane—not about the winds that roared at more than a hundred miles an hour and tore up trees, roofs, and telephone poles, or about the seas that rose nearly ten feet, but about the neighbors. He spoke of the few days when everything was disrupted, and he lit up with happiness as he did so. In his neighborhood all the people had come out of their houses to speak with each other, aid each other, improvise a community kitchen, make sure the elders were okay, and spend time together, no longer strangers. His joy struck me powerfully.

A friend told me of being trapped in a terrible fog, one of the dense tule fogs that overtakes California's Central Valley periodically. On this occasion the fog mixed with dust from the cotton fields created a shroud so perilous that the highway patrol stopped all traffic on the highway. For two days she was stranded with many others in a small diner. She and her husband slept upright, shoulder to shoulder with strangers, in the banquettes of the diner's booths. Although food and water began to run short, they had a marvelous time. The people gathered there had little in common, but they all opened up, began to tell each other the stories of their lives, and by the time the road was safe, my friend and her husband were reluctant to leave. But they went onward, home to New Mexico for the holidays, where everyone looked at them perplexedly as they told the story of their stranding with such ebullience. That time in the diner was the first time ever her partner, a Native American, had felt a sense of belonging in a society at large. Such redemption amid disruption is common.

What More Can One Do?, from the series *The Disasters of War*, by Francisco de Goya, c. 1815.

It reminded me of how many of us in the San Francisco Bay Area had loved the Loma Prieta earthquake that took place three weeks before the Berlin Wall fell in 1989. Or loved not the earthquake but the way communities had responded to it. It was alarming for most of us as well, devastating for some, and fatal for sixty people (a very low death count for a major earthquake in an area inhabited by millions). When the subject of the quake came up with a new acquaintance, she too glowed with recollection about how her San Francisco neighborhood had, during the days the power was off, cooked up all its thawing frozen food and held barbecues on the street; how gregarious everyone had been, how people from all walks of life had mixed in candlelit bars that became community centers. Another friend recently remembered with unextinguished amazement that when he traveled the several miles from the World Series baseball game at Candlestick Park in the city's southeast to his home in the central city, someone was at every blacked-out intersection, directing traffic. Without orders or centralized organization, people had stepped up to meet the needs of the moment, suddenly in charge of their communities and streets.

When that earthquake shook the central California coast on October 17, 1989, I was surprised to find that the person I was angry at no longer mattered. The anger had evaporated along with everything else abstract and remote, and I was thrown into an intensely absorbing present. I was more surprised to realize that most of the people I knew and met in the Bay Area were also enjoying immensely the disaster that shut down much of the region for several days, the Bay Bridge for months, and certain unloved elevated freeways forever—as if *enjoyment* is the right word for that sense of immersion in the moment and solidarity with others caused by the rupture in everyday life, an emotion graver than happiness but deeply positive.

When I ask people about the disasters they have lived through, I find on many faces that retrospective basking as they recount tales of Canadian ice storms, Midwestern snow days,

New York City blackouts, oppressive heat in southern India, fire in New Mexico, the great earthquake in Mexico City, earlier hurricanes in Louisiana, the economic collapse in Argentina, earthquakes in California and Mexico, and a strange pleasure overall. It was the joy on their faces that surprised me. And with those whom I read rather than spoke to, it was the joy in their words that surprised me. It should not be so, is not so, in the familiar version of what disaster brings, and yet it is there, arising from rubble,

Nothing's going to happen to you; it wouldn't be the end of the world if anything did.
—*George Bernard Shaw, 1905*

from ice, from fire, from storms and floods. The joy matters as a measure of otherwise neglected desires, desires for public life and civil society, for inclusion, purposes, and power.

Disasters are, most basically, terrible, tragic, grievous, and no matter what positive sides effects and possibilities they produce, they are not to be desired. But by the same measure, those side effects should not be ignored because they arise amid devastation. The desires and possibilities awakened are so powerful they shine even from wreckage, carnage, and ashes. What happens here is relevant elsewhere. And the point is not to welcome disasters. They do not create these gifts, but they are one avenue through which the gifts arrive. Disasters provide an extraordinary window into social desire and possibility, and what manifests there matters elsewhere, in ordinary times and in other extraordinary times.

Most social change is chosen—you want to belong to a co-op, you believe in social safety nets or community-supported agriculture. But disaster doesn't sort us out by preferences; it drags us into emergencies that require we act, and act altruistically, bravely, and with initiative in order to survive or save the neighbors, no matter how we vote or what we do for a living. The positive emotions that arise in those unpromising circumstances demonstrate that social ties and meaningful work are deeply desired, readily improvised, and intensely rewarding. The very structure of our economy and society prevents these goals from being achieved. The structure is also ideological, a philosophy that best serves the wealthy and powerful but shapes all of our lives, reinforced as the conventional wisdom disseminated by the media, from news hours to disaster movies. The facets of that ideology have been called individualism, capitalism, and social Darwinism, and have appeared in the political philosophies of Thomas Hobbes and Thomas Malthus, as well as the work of most conventional contemporary economists, who presume we seek personal gain for rational reasons and

Strange (is it not?) that battles, martyrs, agonies, blood, even assassination should condense—perhaps only really, lastingly condense—a nationality.
—*Walt Whitman, 1879*

refrain from looking at the ways a system skewered to that end damages much else we need for our survival and desire for our well-being. Disaster demonstrates this, since among the factors determining whether you will live or die are the health of your immediate community and the justness of your society.

Since postmodernism reshaped the intellectual landscape, it has been problematic to even use the term *human nature*, with its implication of a stable and universal human essence. The study of disasters makes it clear that there are plural and contingent natures—but the prevalent human nature in disaster is resilient, resourceful, generous, empathic, and brave. The language of therapy speaks almost exclusively of the consequence of disaster as trauma, suggesting a humanity that is unbearably fragile, a self that does not act but is acted upon, the most basic recipe of the victim. Disaster movies and the media continue to portray ordinary people as hysterical or vicious in the face of calamity. We believe these sources telling us we are victims or brutes more than we trust our own experience. Most people know this other human nature from experience,

that rising from the ruins that is the ordinary human response to disaster—a subject that slips between the languages we have been given to talk about who we are when everything goes wrong.

To understand both that rising and what hinders and hides it, there are two other important subjects to consider. One is the behavior of the minority in power, who often act savagely in a disaster. The other is the beliefs and representations of the media, the people who hold up a distorting mirror to us in which it is almost impossible to recognize these paradises and our possibilities. Beliefs matter, and the overlapping beliefs of the media and the elites can become a second wave of disaster—as they did most dramatically in the aftermath of Hurricane Katrina. These three subjects are woven together in almost every disaster, and finding the one that matters most—this glimpse of paradise—means understanding the forces that obscure, oppose, and sometimes rub out that possibility.

This social desire and social possibility go against the grain of the dominant stories of recent decades. You can read recent history as a history of privatization not just of the economy but also of society, as marketing and media shove imagination more and more toward private life and private satisfaction, as citizens are redefined as consumers, as public participation falters and with it any sense of collective or individual political power, as even the language for public emotions and satisfactions withers. There is no money in what is aptly called free association: we are instead encouraged by media and advertising to fear each other and regard public life as a danger and a nuisance, to live in secured spaces, communicate by electronic means, and acquire our information from media rather than each other. But in disaster people come together, and though some fear this gathering as a mob, many cherish it as an experience of a civil society that is close enough to paradise. In contemporary terms, *privatization* is largely an economical term, for the consignment of jurisdictions, goods, services, and powers—railways, water rights, policing, education—to the private sector and the vagaries of the marketplace. But this

"A Man in Four Million," 1946. One of over four million Japanese repatriated by the U.S. Navy after World War II from Far Eastern ports and Pacific Islands, the boy is wearing a label on his coat to prevent his becoming lost.

economic privatization is impossible without the privatization of desire and imagination that tells us we are not each other's keeper. Disasters, in returning their sufferers to the public and collective life, undo some of this privatization, which is a slower, subtler disaster all its own. In a society in which participation, agency, purposefulness, and freedom are all adequately present, a disaster would be only a disaster.

Few speak of paradise now, except as something remote enough to be impossible. The ideal societies we hear of are mostly far away or long ago or both, situated in some primordial society before the Fall or a spiritual kingdom in a remote Himalayan vastness. The implication is that we here and now are far from capable of living such ideals. But what if paradise flashed up among us from time to time—at the worst of times? What if we glimpsed it in the jaws of hell? These flashes give us, as the long ago and far away do not, a glimpse of who else we ourselves may be and what else our society could become. This is a paradise of rising to the occasion that points out by contrast how the rest of the time most of us fall down from the heights of possibility, down into diminished selves and dismal societies. Many now do not even hope for a better society, but they recognize it when they encounter it, and that discovery shines out even through the namelessness of their experience. Others recognize it, grasp it, and make something of it, and long-term social and political transformation, both good and bad, arise from the wreckage. The door to this era's potential paradises is in hell.

From A Paradise Built in Hell. "*Disaster makes it clear that our interdependence is not only an inescapable fact but a fact worth celebrating,*" Solnit *wrote in "The Uses of Disaster," published in* Harper's Magazine *in 2005, "that the production of civil society is a work of love, indeed the work that many of us desire most." That essay was expanded into* A Paradise Built in Hell, *which was published in 2009. Discussion around her essay "Men Explain Things to Me" led others to coin the term* mansplaining.

PRESSURE DROP

by Simon Winchester

Naval officers of advanced rank are usually a circumspect group, their caution born of many years of doing battle with the caprices of the sea. But in March 2013 Adm. Samuel Locklear III, the American four-star flag officer who at the time was in charge of all American forces in and around the Pacific Ocean—328,000 Navy, Army, Marine, and Air Force personnel, stationed in docks and barracks and airdromes ranged around 52 percent of the planet's surface—made an unusual pronouncement.

Usually, and in common with his predecessors as the chief of U.S. Pacific Command, the admiral, just winding up his fortieth year with the senior service, would recite at briefings and at hearings on Capitol Hill from a Pentagon-approved hymn sheet of threats to regional peace. There were always, in the short term, the villainous generals of North Korea, the devious graybeards of China, and the architects of various territorial disputes involving pointless islands claimed by Japan on the one hand, and by Russia, South Korea, and China on the other, all likely to trigger some kind of a brouhaha sooner or later. There were also the manifold possibilities for mayhem from the jihadists or Maoists or others known to be bent on destabilizing matters in Jakarta, or Dhaka, or southern Mindanao, or a score of other Pacific places known for their feverish political dispositions.

But in the spring of 2013, these usual suspects were not for Admiral Locklear, and at a defense conference at Harvard that spring, he broke form. Political disputations were not, he said, the principal threat to his area of responsibility (which stretches from Karachi to San Diego, from Nome to Hobart, and includes 64 million square miles of sea). Most critical was, in fact, the climate.

Significant upheaval related to the warming planet, Locklear declared, "is probably the most likely thing that is going to happen that will cripple the security environment, probably more likely than the other scenarios we all often talk about."

Simon Winchester is the author of more than twenty books, including Atlantic, The Man Who Loved China, Krakatoa, The Men Who United the States, The Professor and the Madman, *and, most recently,* Pacific. *His last essay for* Lapham's Quarterly *appeared in the Summer 2013 issue,* The Sea.

He promptly bolstered his claim. His staff officers—most especially his weather analysts—had detected significant changes in the frequency and violence of recent Pacific typhoons. "Weather patterns are more severe than they have been in the past," he told his now-rapt listeners. "We are on super-typhoon twenty-seven or twenty-eight this year in the western Pacific. The average is about seventeen." And such new typhoon clusterings suggest major changes to the climate in the region—changes that pose the greatest of all security threats in the region.

Whether the admiral spoke with authority or not—he did so just as the latest El Niño event began to show signs of creating another episode of meteorological madness around the eastern Pacific—has never been

The more we learn about asteroid impacts, the clearer it becomes that the human race has been living on borrowed time.

—Brian May, 2014

properly addressed. No Pentagon official has repudiated his assertion; but on the other hand, while it had once been thought possible that Locklear's career might continue upward—that he might become chief of naval operations or chairman of the Joint Chiefs of Staff, quite natural progressions for many of the previous PACOM commanders—it never did. So he now lives in blameless retirement, with his distinguished maritime career culminating in five sentences about climate that mark the only memorable public remarks he ever made.

But was he right? Eight months after he made his remarks, a fast-developing and monumentally destructive storm named Haiyan suggested that there may be legitimacy to his claim.

Haiyan was first spotted by four duty officers who arrived for their night shift on the early evening of November 1, 2013, in the drab Pearl Harbor building that houses the offices of Pacific Command's Joint Typhoon Warning Center. The center's official remit is to provide storm warnings for Admiral Locklear's fleet of warships, and on November 2 satellite images showed a disorganized cluster of squalls about 250 miles to the southeast of the tiny island of Pohnpei, in Micronesia—and that it was changing its appearance fast. Within twenty-four hours the clouds had formed into the cyclonic appearance that betokens danger. The suddenness of its appearance and the fast lowering of pressure all struck the weather analysts as noteworthy.

They promptly sent a message to the operations room of Pacific Fleet headquarters: U.S. Navy ships in the area might want to know that wind and rain could affect any vessels heading for that quarter of the sea.

By November 4, the now swirling clouds had been designated Tropical Storm 31W. The next day the swirls had grown much more powerful, and the storm was upgraded to full typhoon status. It was given the pre-assigned name *Haiyan*—the Chinese word for petrel, a bird that in mariners' lore is associated with foul weather. The fast-gathering beast by now appeared to be traveling directly toward the barrier wall of the Philippine islands—where the local weather agency, following its own naming rules, had perversely decided to call the storm Yolanda.

The situation was becoming alarming. The American and Japanese weather forecasters, and later those watching the big weather radars in China and Hong Kong, were giving the local civil defense agencies at least some days' warning, allowing them to prepare for what was clearly going to be a storm of a power seldom seen before at sea, and perhaps never experienced before on land. Evacuations were ordered, and people began to stream away from the eastern coasts, where the storm was predicted to land.

The forecasts were right, nearly to the minute. Typhoon Haiyan struck head-on into the Philippines, hitting the islands of Samar and Leyte almost simultaneously, on November 8. By the time it reached land, it had become the fiercest typhoon to have done so in the world's recorded history. When the northern eye wall of the storm struck the village of Guiuan those anemometers that hadn't whirled off scale recorded wind gusts of 196 mph—greater by far than anything previously known.

The physical and human damage was terrifying—although the warnings and the accuracy of the forecasts helped keep down the total of human casualties. Some six thousand people were killed, 27,000 were injured, more than a thousand were missing. Whole cities were flattened, every building reduced to debris as if by an earthquake or atomic bomb. The city of Tacloban, the biggest in the region, was unrecognizable after being hit first by the full force of the storm. It was then swamped by the seawater of a thirteen-foot storm surge that followed.

There was a coincidence in the Philippines: Haiyan's landfall in 2013 as the most savage of all the world's storms was made along the coast of Leyte Gulf, site in 1944 of the most savage of all the world's naval battles. Two nearby villages were named for Douglas MacArthur, the general being a hero in these parts. His "I Shall Return" promise is commemorated by a bronze statue that depicts the general and his staff striding through ankle-deep waters to resume control of the Philippines; it stands by the beach where it happened, in the small town of Palo. All three of these places, Palo and the two MacArthur villages, were damaged by the typhoon.

American military forces were heavily involved in dealing with Haiyan's violence, seventy years after that great naval battle. Thanks to the accuracy of the forecasts, U.S. Marine and Navy ships were already on standby in Japan and Okinawa, or else they were sheltering out at sea. Once the signal came that the State Department had answered Manila's official request for help, the American-led rescue operation got underway.

Operation Damayan, the $21 million rescue operation, formally began the next morning, November 9. The night before, however, when Tacloban was still crawling out from under the storm's wreckage, a flotilla of helicopters brought in members of a U.S. Special Forces team who were already in-country, secretly helping to deal with a long-running Maoist insurgency.

More than eight hundred marines from the Third Expeditionary Brigade in Okinawa were on the ground in the Philippines that afternoon. A survey ship already working in the gulf was on station next day, later joined by a submarine tender filled with emergency supplies and drinking water. The USS *George Washington*, a nuclear-powered carrier, arrived on November 14 with her attendant strike group of destroyers and frigates. She anchored in the bay for the next eight days, serving as headquarters for a relief operation that ultimately involved 2,200 U.S. military personnel; thirteen warships; twenty-one helicopters;

> *When suffering knocks at your door and you say there is no seat left for him, he tells you not to worry because he has brought his own stool.*
> —*Chinua Achebe, 1964*

and the distribution of two thousand tons of American food, blankets, tents, generators, and, water purifiers.

The sight of the warship, and of the squadrons of lesser vessels anchored around her—which later included two British ships, a destroyer and a carrier—served as a reminder, important in the propaganda wars, that American military influence in the world is not only predicated by war and the projection of hard power. This was "soft power" at its most effective—and once the immediate storm crisis was over and the American carrier had slipped off back into patrolling the China Sea, Washington propagandists pointed out how little the Chinese had done to help. Beijing had initially offered a laughable $100,000. Only when stung by the world's response to their seeming niggardliness did they increase the aid to $1.6 million and send down from Shanghai a new hospital ship on its maiden voyage. It arrived too late to be of much use.

Haiyan, the admiral might have pointed out, was only the latest storm in a sequence of climatological disasters that had started to spiral out of control as much as four decades before. The first in this cycle of catastrophes occurred south of the equator and flattened the Australian city of Darwin on Christmas Day, 1974. It was named Cyclone Tracy, and there has never been a more destructive event in all of Australian history.

Ten thousand of Darwin's houses—80 percent of the city's homes—were destroyed. They were nearly instantly demolished, reduced almost to matchwood and pulverized concrete. The process was identical, house after Christmas-decorated house. First the roof was ripped off its stanchions and whirled away into the rain-soaked night. Then the windows shattered, slicing people with slivers of glass. The walls would next blow out—people would

speak of running in darkness and panic from room to room, locating by feel the bathroom doors and racing inside in the belief that the smallest room would be the strongest—only to find the outside wall gone, exposed to the darkness beyond, a frenzy of gales and rain.

Everything failed. The telephones were out. Electricity was down. Antennas were blown down. Aircraft had been tossed about like chaff, smashed beyond recognition. Ships broke loose in the harbor, and sank or drifted far from their moorings, useless. Scores of people who might have helped were away for the Christmas holiday. The broadcast stations had only skeleton crews and no light or water—though one of them, the local Australian Broadcasting Corporation station, managed to get messages out to an affiliate station in the Queensland outback. This tenuous link provided the only communication Darwin

All Fall Down

The collapse of civilizations, from Joseph Tainter's
The Collapse of Complex Societies.

• Hittite Empire (c. 1200 BC)
Nomadic sea peoples overrun Aegean and eastern Mediterranean. Written records cease; area can no longer sustain urban settlement. Excavated sites are found to have been burned.

• Egyptian Old Kingdom (c. 2181 BC)
Nile floods and famines bring about disintegration. Failure of Egyptian kings—who claim supernatural authority—to maintain proper flood levels leads to reduced legitimacy. With end of Sixth Dynasty, Old Kingdom falls.

• Minoan Civilization (c. 1500 BC)
Nearby volcanic eruption dumps ash; earthquakes destroy inland palaces; tsunami destroys Minoan fleet. Security declines as militarism increases. Minoan civilization gone by 1200 BC.

2200 BC | 1050 BC | 100 BC

Mycenaean Civilization (c. 1200 BC) •
Drought, climate change, and invasion by Dorian Greeks lead to famine and depopulation. By 1050 BC, Mycenaean civilization has disappeared.

• Olmec (c. 400 BC)
Final collapse of Mexico's oldest civilization. At some Olmec sites there is evidence of a violent end: at great effort, basalt monuments are destroyed and buried.

• Harappan Civilization (c. 1750 BC)
Massive extrusions of mud block Indus River, causing flooding and decline in trade. Civilization suffers complete breakdown in civil authority.

• Western Zhou Empire (771 BC)
Last Western Zhou ruler is killed in battle. The Zhou had ruled feudally, but within centuries their control slips and they are overrun by barbarians.

• Third Dynasty of Ur (c. 2000 BC)
Drought and excessive irrigation cause rise of saline groundwater; agriculture fails. Similar collapses occur over next three millennia, from first Mesopotamian empire to Islamic empire. By twelfth century, total occupied land area is 6 percent of level 500 years earlier.

had with the outside world for three days after the catastrophe.

Word got out late on Christmas afternoon. It was then that the rest of Australia came to realize that its most northerly capital city had been flattened by a terrible storm. Ministers in Canberra—and others in Sydney and Melbourne and Brisbane—were roused from turkey- and mince-pie-induced lunchtime slumbers to be told of the devastation thousands of miles away.

And when the first rescuers got there, they all made the same comparison: Hiroshima or Nagasaki. The comparison is invidious, of course: the casualty tolls were incomparable (seventy-one were killed by Tracy, not even 0.1 percent of those who died in Japan). But the physical devastation of Darwin was total, and the images resembled the familiar photographs of the two postnuclear cities. Roads were no more than pathways through scores of square miles of rubble. People were wandering around glassy-eyed, bewildered. Hundreds of dogs, frightened and unfed, emerged from the ruins to forage. There was a threat of typhoid and cholera. Police had to find guns—shotguns, mainly, from nearby sheep stations—to deal with looters.

In the end almost the entire city had to be evacuated. Forty-one thousand of the 47,000 were without home, shelter, water, food, medicine, communication. The government arranged shuttles of aircraft—slowly at first, because the ruined Darwin airport could accommodate only one flight every ninety minutes. Over the next two weeks, more than 35,000 people were flown or driven out of the city, and by the time the year ended, it had been all but emptied. More than half of those who left never came back.

• **Teotihuacán society** (c. 700)
Drought in northern Mexico forces populations south. Teotihuacán abruptly collapses, perhaps from earthquakes and plagues; city center burns; population drops within 50 years to a quarter of its peak. Decline may be due to loss of control over trade networks.

• **Casas Grandes** (c. 1340)
City is burned, corpses left unburied in streets, altars systematically destroyed. Elaborate urban culture south of present U.S.–Mexico border reaches peak in early 1200s, then quickly falls into disrepair; upland drought and arroyo cutting are suspected causes.

• **Lowland Classic Maya** (c. 900)
Political and ceremonial activity comes to abrupt end. Possible causes: soil erosion (perhaps caused by swidden agriculture) and land scarcity, silting of lakes, and decline in water supply.

• **Chacoan society** (c. 1050)
Something goes wrong: trade networks decline; towns are abandoned. Walled stone towns (pueblos) had been connected by roads across the San Juan basin in New Mexico. Last inhabitants leave by 1300.

100

800

1500

• **Western Roman Empire** (476)
Climatic change and overfarming lead to insufficient resources (especially grains) and stimulates barbarian migrations. Empire split in third century into east and west; western provinces increasingly lost to barbarians.

• **Wari and Tiahuanaco empires** (c. 1100)
Tectonic uplift lowers water tables and causes agricultural collapse. Both Andean cultures (characterized by irrigation and terracing) had established major urban centers in central Andes; both cultures fall. All cities of southern highlands are abandoned; populations scatter to countryside.

• **Native tribes of North American Eastern Woodlands** (c. 400) Colder climate ends Hopewell tribal culture. By 1250 exhaustion of resources causes fall of Cahokia, the largest Mississippian city. Region-wide collapse of Woodlands tribes follows.

Hohokam society (c. 1450) •
Agricultural malpractice causes waterlogging and salt buildup in soils. Dwellers in Arizona desert had developed a complex culture characterized by extensive canal irrigation; economic stress leads to sociopolitical collapse.

Between the bookends of these two storms, Tracy and Haiyan, are forty years of statistics that underpin Admiral Locklear's argument. Not that his stated concern over the number of storms that gather within his area of operation was meant to imply that storms in lesser oceans are any less daunting. Notorious monsters like Katrina, Camille, Andrew, Ike, Sandy, Hugo, Wilma, Rita, the Labor Day hurricane of 1935, the Okeechobee hurricane of 1928—all of these were great Atlantic storms of historic proportions, and all were hugely destructive and frightening.

It would be impossible to live for a year without disaster unless one practiced character-reading.
—*Virginia Woolf, 1924*

"Destructive" and "frightening" are not true measurements, however. Nor is the most commonly used metric of a storm's financial cost. In America, Atlantic hurricanes tend to be described by their eventual price—the quoted losses for the insurance companies of $108 billion in and around New Orleans in 2005 have made Katrina come to be seen as the absolute worst storm in American history. But cost can hardly be a neutral descriptor: storms that strike American cities are expensive because they wreck expensive things. Storms like Haiyan that strike isolated cities in the eastern Philippines may cause just as much devastation, but the dollar amounts are much lower. Human damage, of course, is different—but still that is not neutral either, since a typhoon hitting a crowded slum will kill far more than one that sinks ships and swamps atolls in the middle of the ocean.

The key number that the World Meteorological Organization has chosen as a baseline for assessing a storm's strength is 925 millibars. Any storm eye with a pressure measured as less than 925 mb is one for the books, intense enough to be worthy of record. And looking at the Pacific Ocean using that measure alone, it becomes clear that it is beyond any other when it comes to playing host to the number of the world's truly intense tropical storms.

In the Atlantic since 1924, nineteen hurricanes qualified for the list of storms with eye pressures of less than 925 mb. Just one out of five of those—the hurricanes known as Labor Day 1935, Allen, Gilbert, Rita, and Wilma—were super-intense, with eye pressures below 900 mb. Neither Camille and Katrina managed to figure below 900 mb. Hurricane Sandy, infamous in recent New York and New Jersey lore, did not make the WMO cut, registering a comparatively benign 940 mb in its nonspinning center.

The western north Pacific now plays host to the worst of the world's low-pressure storms. Since 1950 there have been fifty-nine fully formed Pacific typhoons north of the equator, and in the western south Pacific and off Australia there have been twenty-five similarly rated cyclones since 1974. In the Atlantic the rate of occurrences of sub-925-mb storms runs at about once every five years. In the western Pacific they are much more numerous, with about one every year. And, eccentrically, a recent Pacific hurricane off western Mexico named Patricia in October 2015 had sustained winds of 200 mph and a minimum pressure of 879 mb. It was small and vicious, but did less harm than feared.

Ultra-low-pressure storms occur five times more often in the Pacific than elsewhere in the world. They are generally much more intense—with thirty-seven of the northwest Pacific's fifty-nine having pressures lower than 900 mb. Typhoon Tip, the deepest of them all, recorded a low pressure of just 870 mb, and it enjoyed the unique distinction of being both the deepest and widest of all tropical storms on record, with an edge-to-edge spread of 1,380 miles—meaning that if superimposed on the United States, it would have extended from the Mexican to the Canadian borders and from Yosemite to the Mississippi River, with its eye directly above Denver.

And why is there this current surge in activity? There is the beginning of an answer. All, insist the forecasters, can be traced to the

Oil tanker *Amoco Cadiz* sinking off the coast of Brittany, 1978. Photograph by Jean Gaumy.

ever-increasing amount of thermal energy absorbed into the Pacific Ocean. Current belief holds that by the end of the twenty-first century the global temperature, and the temperature of the Pacific, will have risen by 3 degrees centigrade—maybe a little less, if all adhere to the recent Paris Agreement. The sea levels in the region will have risen by as much as three feet. And such an increase will inevitably cause islands and low-lying peninsulas to submerge and oceanic storms to intensify and become more numerous.

But will such natural developments—anthropogenically triggered, maybe, but essentially natural developments—present a major security challenge?

Admiral Locklear and his staff clearly believe what they say: that so far as the human population of the Pacific is concerned, danger to life and limb is more urgently at risk these days from cyclones than it is from Chinese saber-rattling, that maritime inundation is more pressing a concern than invasion; and that

countries can be destabilized and civil unrest can be multiplied if the affected nations take no heed of the mayhem set to explode around them in the years ahead.

The admiral's views—revolutionary in comparison with the usual commentaries—have not been properly examined, and probably never will be. His final appearance before the Senate Armed Services Committee was, so far as this issue was concerned, a travesty. Only one member of the committee addressed the issue, and then in the most perfunctory way: Sen. James Inhofe of Oklahoma, author of a book that decries climate-change warnings as no more than a grotesque hoax, had derided the admiral for daring to issue such a warning. The only person who was competent to change the world's climate, he said, was God.

When Locklear attempted to splutter some reasoning behind his own argument, the senator cut him off abruptly. Let's return, he said, to the urgent matter—of China.

Battle on the Bridge, by Arnold Böcklin, 1892.

THE ANOMALY
OF BARBARISM

by John Gray

The rise of ISIS is intensely unsettling to the liberal West, and not just because of the capacity the jihadist group has demonstrated to launch a mass-casualty terrorist attack in a major European city. The group's advance confounds the predominant Western view of the world. For the current generation of liberal thinkers, modern history is a story of the march of civilization. There have been moments of regression, some of them atrocious, but these are only relapses into the barbarism of the past, interrupting a course of development that is essentially benign. For anyone who thinks in this way, ISIS can only be a mysterious and disastrous anomaly.

For those baffled by ISIS, however, it cannot be only ISIS that is mysterious. So too must be much of modern history. ISIS has brought with it many atrocious assaults on civilized values: the sexual enslavement of women and children; the murder of gay men; the targeted killing of writers, cartoonists, and Jews; indiscriminate

John Gray is a political philosopher and author of twenty-six books translated into more than twenty languages. He is an emeritus professor of European thought at the London School of Economics. His most recent book is The Soul of the Marionette: A Short Inquiry into Human Freedom.

slaughter at a rock concert; and what amounted to the attempted genocide of the Yezidi. All of these acts of barbarism have modern precedents, many of them in the past century. The use of sexual violence as a military strategy featured in ethnic cleansing in Bosnia in the 1990s; during Bangladesh's war of independence in 1971; in Nepal, Colombia, Sudan, the Democratic Republic of Congo, and many other conflict zones. The destruction of buildings and artworks, which ISIS has perpetrated at the ancient site of Palmyra among other places, has several twentieth-century precedents. Vladimir Lenin's Bolsheviks razed churches and synagogues in Russia. Mao Zedong demolished large parts of China's architectural inheritance and most of Tibet's, while the Pol Pot regime wrecked pagodas and temples and aimed to destroy the country's cities. In these secular acts of iconoclasm, the goal was to abolish the past and create a new society from "year zero"—an idea that goes back to "year one" of the calendar introduced in France in 1793 to signal the new era inaugurated by the French Revolution. Systematically destroying not only pre-Islamic relics but also long-established Islamic sites, the aim of ISIS is not essentially different.

Nor is ISIS so different in its methodical use of terror as a means of consolidating its power. In his "Hanging Order" telegram of August 11, 1918, Lenin instructed communists to execute refractory peasants by public hanging: "This needs to be accomplished in such a way that people for hundreds of miles around will see, tremble, know, and scream out." From its beginning and throughout much of its existence, the Soviet state relied on fear for its hold on power. The show trials of the 1930s continued a Bolshevik pedagogy that inculcated obedience by way of spectacular terror. Yet the system endured for nearly three-quarters of a century, much of the time commanding a significant following in the West. No doubt the regime had flaws, some hideous, but these were regarded as inheritances from tsarist and Asiatic despotism. A more plausible view would be that Soviet crimes came chiefly from implementing a modern European tradition of using terror to remodel society,

emerging with the Jacobins in the aftermath of the French Revolution, which Lenin avowedly followed. But this view was rarely considered.

For those who find the rise of ISIS baffling, much of the past century can only be retrogression from modern life. Even the regime that committed a crime with no precedent in history must be regarded as an example of atavism: the Nazi state has often been described as having taken Europe back to the Dark Ages. Certainly the Nazis exploited a medieval Christian demonology in their persecution and genocide of Jews, but Nazism also

All men that are ruined, are ruined on the side of their natural propensities.
—Edmund Burke, 1796

invoked a modern pseudoscience of race to legitimate these atrocities. Invoking a type of faux Darwinism, Nazi racism could have emerged only in a time shaped by science. Nazism was modern not just in its methods of killing but also in its way of thinking.

This is not to reiterate the claim—made by Marxian theorists of the Frankfurt School—that modern scientific thinking leads, by some circuitous but inevitable route, to Nazism and the Holocaust. It is to suggest that when it is invoked in politics modernity is a figment. The increase of knowledge in recent centuries is real enough, as is the enlargement of human power through technology. These advances are cumulative and accelerating and, in any realistically likely scenario, practically irreversible. But there have been few, if any, similar advances in politics. The quickening advance of science and technology in the past few centuries has not gone with any comparable advance in civilization or human rationality. Instead, the increase of knowledge has repeatedly interacted with human conflicts and passions to produce new kinds of barbarism.

Using the most advanced technologies to demonstrate its transgression of civilized norms, ISIS is a peculiarly modern form of barbarism. Of course, the group exhibits distinctive features.

The Paris attacks show that, more than any other jihadist group, ISIS has the capacity to meld urban terrorism and guerrilla warfare into a unified strategy. Any setbacks ISIS suffers on the battlefield in Syria and Iraq are likely to evoke further attacks on civilian populations in Western cities. ISIS distinguishes itself from other jihadist groups in publicizing its atrocities through the sophisticated use of electronic media. Applying techniques presented in a handbook, *The Management of Savagery*, published online in 2004, these atrocities implement a carefully planned strategy (one that has provoked criticism from Al Qaeda, from which ISIS emerged as a spinoff). Again, ISIS differs from other jihadist groups in its lack of specific demands. While

It belongs to a nobleman to weep in an hour of disaster. —Euripides, 412 BC

Al Qaeda aimed to force the U.S. to withdraw from the Middle East, ISIS is dedicated to the destruction of the entire existing world order—a goal that suggests the group is more eschatological in its view of the world than its current jihadist rivals. None of these features go any distance toward showing that ISIS is other than modern. A transnational crime cartel, rapidly expanding apocalyptic cult movement, and worldwide terror network, ISIS could have emerged only in modern conditions of globalization.

Theories of modernization have a common form: only one type of society can truly meet the needs of a society based on continual scientific and technological innovation. The trouble is that these theories specify incompatible types of social and political order. The nineteenth-century sociologist Herbert Spencer believed that only laissez-faire capitalism could fit the bill. In contrast, Spencer's onetime disciple, the sociologist Beatrice Webb, came to believe that a type of collectivism prefigured in Stalin's Russia was the next stage in modern development. In our own day, both neoconservatives and progressives have accepted the view propounded by Francis Fukuyama that only "democratic capitalism" can satisfy modern needs—a prognostication that is likely to prove no better founded. Modernity in politics is a species of phantom, constantly elusive because it is continuously mutating.

A pursuit of this ghost has shaped the ruinous "war on terror." The course of the Iraq war illustrates some of the consequences. The effects on the West, which included a colossal waste of resources and the rehabilitation by the Bush administration of the barbarous practice of torture, are by now well known. Less well understood is the fact that disaster in Iraq flowed not only from mistakes in policy (grotesque as some of these were) but also from the attempt to remake the country as a democracy. The state of Iraq was built by the British from provinces of the Ottoman Empire by applying a divide-and-rule strategy that meant Iraq's governance could never be democratic. One of the state's chief architects, the British colonial officer, archaeologist, and scholar Gertrude Bell, wrote: "I don't for a moment doubt that the final authority must be in the hands of the Sunnis, in spite of their numerical inferiority. Otherwise you'll have a mujtahid-run theocratic state, which is the very devil." Formulated some eighty years before the American-led attack, Bell's analysis has been amply confirmed by events.

The invasion that toppled Saddam Hussein in April 2003 destroyed the state of Iraq. Partly this was because of the policies of the occupying power, such as disbanding the Iraqi army in May 2003, a bizarre exercise that had far-reaching consequences. A more fundamental reason was the fact that the integrity of the state rested on Sunni hegemony, which the occupation undid. Iraq was a multiethnic and multisectarian state held together principally by force. Self-government for "the Iraqi people" was impossible, since nothing of the kind had ever existed. The only realistically imaginable outcome of regime change was the violent disintegration of the state.

Since the American-led invasion, three new states have emerged in Iraq: the Islamic

Barbarians Marching to the West, by Max Ernst, 1937.

State (as the territorial unit of ISIS is sometimes called), which is ruled according to ISIS's extreme interpretation of Sunni Islam; a de facto Kurdish state in the north of the country; and a Shia state headquartered in Baghdad that operates in an expanded zone of Iranian influence in what remains of the historic state of Iraq. Of the three, only that of the Kurds can claim to be anything like the modern secular democracy that regime change was supposed to install. In most of Iraq, the result of attempting to install democracy has been to empower theocracy—just as Bell predicted.

Saddam's Iraq was ruled according to the ideology of Baathism, a secular and modernizing creed in which a revolutionary vanguard uses the state to effect progress in society. Clear links can be traced between the destruction of Baathist Iraq and the rise of ISIS. Disbanding the army provided a source of recruitment for ISIS commanders, while the ensuing breakup of the state created zones of anarchy into which ISIS could expand. Without the American-led invasion of Iraq, ISIS would most likely not exist. The effect of regime change in Iraq was to destroy a modern secular despotism and empower a type of theocracy that is also modern. ISIS's ideology is a version of Wahhabism, a highly repressive type of Sunni fundamentalism that developed during the eighteenth century in a region of what is now Saudi Arabia. Fundamentalism looks to the lost purity of an imaginary past; but in that they thrive in societies whose traditions are in disarray because of an encounter with new technologies and economic forces, fundamentalist movements are themselves essentially modern. Adopted as the official religion when the present Saudi state was founded in 1932 and promoted throughout the world in recent decades using the kingdom's oil wealth, Wahhabist ideas have been a powerful means of recruitment to jihadist groups in societies where inherited patterns of life have been disrupted.

Drawing on the apocalyptic traditions of medieval Islam, ISIS exhibits many affinities with the millenarian movements that ravaged Europe in the late Middle Ages. That does not make ISIS a rerun of medieval beliefs and values, for modern history abounds with movements driven by apocalyptic myths. As Norman Cohn argued in his seminal study *The Pursuit of the Millennium*, twentieth-century totalitarian movements were fueled by secular versions of end-time myths. Cohn applied his analysis chiefly to Communism and Nazism, but later events suggest it can be applied more widely. From American flying-saucer cults

Our sympathy is cold to the relation of distant misery. —Edward Gibbon, 1788

to the bioterrorist Aum Shinrikyo cult in Japan, there have been many examples of movements that have reframed apocalyptic beliefs in ersatz-scientific terms. Though its eschatological beliefs are explicitly religious, ISIS is the latest example of a recurring modern phenomenon.

While much remains unknown, there is nothing mysterious in the rise of ISIS. It is baffling only for those who believe—despite everything that occurred in the twentieth century—that modernization and civilization are advancing hand in hand. In fact, now as in the past some of the most modern movements are among the most barbaric. But to admit this would mean surrendering the ruling political faith, a decayed form of liberalism without which Western leaders and opinion formers would be disoriented and lost. To accept that liberal societies may not be "on the right side of history" would leave their lives drained of significance, while a stoical response—which is ready to fight while being doubtful of ultimate victory—seems to be beyond their powers. With mounting bewilderment and desperation, they cling to the faith that the normal course of history has somehow been temporarily derailed.

It is chiefly this faith that has driven the West's interventions in countries such as Iraq, Libya, and Syria. The decision to topple Muam- mar Qaddafi in 2011 has left Libya an anarchic hellhole fought over by rival jihadist groups, fueling flows of migrants into Europe—some of whom must surely themselves be jihadists. Yet the West has continued its efforts to engineer the overthrow of Bashar al-Assad in Syria—a project that would create anarchy on an even larger scale. Only in the wake of the Paris attacks have Western governments begun to accept that dealing with ISIS may require a coalition of forces that include Assad's army and Russian air power. Even now they continue to insist Syria can be restored to its historic shape while being reconstituted as a democratic polity under the rule of "moderate forces." Yet to the extent that such forces actually exist, they are small in number, divided among themselves, and incapable of fighting ISIS and Assad simultaneously. As in Iraq and Libya, regime change in Syria would inexorably produce the collapse of the state, with ISIS being a beneficiary of the resulting anarchy.

Assessed by reference to any kind of strategic rationality, the West has displayed unfathomable stupidity. To invade a country, dismantle its institutions, create a failed state, exit from the ensuing chaos, and then return with unending bombing campaigns is imbecility of an order that has few historical parallels. To persist in this behavior after so many catastrophes betrays something other than mere imbecility, however extreme. Behavior of this kind looks more like an extreme version of cognitive dissonance—an attempt to expel disastrous facts from the mind. In an obsessive effort to remake the world according to an idealized image of their own societies, Western leaders have renounced a sense of reality. Each attempt only reinforces the fact of their impotence. Obeying a kind of repetition compulsion, they have found themselves returning again and again to the intractable actuality they are so anxious to avoid.

The prevailing mode of liberal thinking filters out any fact that might disturb its tranquility of mind. One such fact is that toppling despots does not of itself enhance freedom. If you are a woman, gay, a member of a religious minority, or someone who professes no religion, are you freer now in Iraq, Libya, or most of Syria than you were under the dictatorship of Saddam, Qaddafi, or Assad? Plainly, you are much less free. Another uncomfortable fact is that tyrants are often popular. According to today's liberals, when large numbers of people flock to support tyranny it cannot be because they do not want to be free. They must be alienated from their true nature as human beings. Born liberals, human beings become anything else as a result of social conditioning. Only cultural and political repression stands in the way of liberal values becoming a universal way of life.

This strange metaphysical fancy lies behind the fashionable theory that when people leave advanced countries to join ISIS they do so because they have undergone a process of "radicalization." But who radicalized the tens of millions of Europeans who flocked to Nazism and fascism in the interwar years? The disaster that ensued was not the result of clever propaganda, though that undoubtedly played a part. Interwar Europe demonstrates how quickly and easily civilized life can be disrupted and destroyed by the impact of war and economic crisis.

Civilization is not the endpoint of modern history, but a succession of interludes in recurring spasms of barbarism. The liberal civilization that has prevailed in some Western countries over the past few centuries emerged slowly and with difficulty against the background of a particular mix of traditions and institutions. Precarious wherever it has existed, it is a way of life that has no strong hold on humankind. For an older generation of liberal thinkers such as Alexis de Tocqueville and Isaiah Berlin, these were commonplaces. Today these truisms are forbidden truths, which can no longer be spoken or in many cases comprehended.

Liberal civilization is not the emerging meaning of the modern world but a historical singularity that is inherently fragile. This is why it is worth preserving. Defending this form of life against ISIS requires a clear perception that the jihadist group is not an atavistic force that—with a little assistance from intensified bombing—

will fade away with advancing modernization. If the threat is to be removed, ISIS will have to be defeated and destroyed.

The simpleminded reasoning that rejects any Western military action on the grounds that earlier interventions were counterproductive fails to take the measure of the challenge that ISIS now poses. The Paris attacks, which appear to have been a response to defeats in the field, show that the state that ISIS has created cannot simply be contained. Nor would containment be enough in ethical terms, since

We've got to live, no matter how many skies have fallen. —D.H. Lawrence, 1928

ISIS has demonstrated a capacity for genocide. But the aim must not be to replace ISIS's theocratic totalitarianism with a replica of liberal democracy—a delusional project that has unleashed the forces by which we are now besieged. A functioning state that enjoyed a reasonable measure of local support and could keep the peace would be a sufficiently challenging objective for Western policy.

Whether the West is up to the task is unclear. The practical difficulties are formidable. After the fiasco in Iraq, putting large numbers of troops on the ground hardly seems possible for any Western government, while the regional powers that need to be part of any concerted military action—Turkey, the Kurds, the Saudis, and Iran—are pursuing their own goals and rivalries. Russia, too, has its own agenda. Everyone is threatened by ISIS, but no one has yet made fighting it their first priority.

The intellectual difficulties are greater, and possibly insuperable. For many in the West, the threat ISIS poses to their view of the world seems a greater disaster than the atrocities ISIS has committed and threatens to repeat. The bafflement with which the West approaches the group is a symptom of the senility of the liberal mind, a condition for which there is no obvious remedy. Perhaps what our culture lacks, in the end, is the ability to understand itself.

Dancers in *The Peaceful City*, detail of the fresco *Allegory of Good and Bad Government*, by Ambrogio Lorenzetti, 1338–1340.

SOLIDARITY AND SURVIVAL

by Garret Keizer

From lightning and tempest; from earthquake, fire, and flood; from plague, pestilence, and famine, Good Lord, deliver us.
—The Great Litany, *Book of Common Prayer*

Earthquake and Fire

My Uncle Howie was a city fireman for much of his working life, and when he finally took his pension and headed for the hills of West Virginia it was in large part to escape the city. He'd had his fill of late-night false alarms and recreational arson and was opting for a simpler life. Like Voltaire's Candide, survivor of the Lisbon earthquake and the Inquisition too, my uncle was going to find solace in cultivating his own garden. He was never going to eat a store-bought potato again.

One day while bouncing along the ridges of Almost Heaven he came upon two sooty-faced children walking listlessly down the road—because, as they explained when he halted his pickup alongside them, their house was burning down. It was the sort of thing that happened now and again in that neck of the woods. There wasn't much a body could do except watch the fire or walk away from it.

Soon my uncle was heading north to barter with his former cronies for various hand-me-downs at the station, used slickers

---

Garret Keizer is the author, most recently, of Getting Schooled. *His last essay for* Lapham's Quarterly *was "No Smoke for Camilo" in the Spring 2014 issue, Revolutions.*

and helmets, cast-off axes, and even an old fire truck, driving them back to his adoptive hollow's first volunteer fire department, of which he was duly elected chief. The moral being that you can turn your back on civilization if you like, but you're not necessarily going to escape the social contract.

Ditto for its bosom buddy, muse, and patron: Disaster. "Like a good neighbor," goes the signature ad for an insurance company, "State Farm is there." Whatever it has to say about the firm, the motto reminds us that neighborhood was the original insurance. There's intuitive sense in the fact that one of the nation's best-known founders, Ben Franklin, also founded a fire department. If the God of the Mosaic Covenant is "a consuming fire," the seal of the secular covenant is a fire extinguished. In their symbolism no less than their bravery, the New York City firefighters who responded to the 9/11 attacks were well-qualified to be popular heroes. The towers fell, crushing some of them, but their presence reassured us that the social contract still stood.

We rightly think of "the discovery of fire" as one of humankind's first significant steps toward civilization; paradoxically, it is civilization that gives fire its full status as calamity. All those close-built, overcrowded houses; all those incendiary livelihoods, the bakery and the forge. A similar paradox informs the way in which conflagrations both underscore and subvert social inequality. The great fires of Rome (64) and London (1666) did their worst among the poor, and when the singed mob wanted scapegoats, it looked first among the margins of the populace: Dutch and French immigrants in London, Christians in Nero's Rome. Mrs. O'Leary's cow, spuriously blamed for starting the Great Chicago Fire (1871) by kicking over a lantern, might have escaped suspicion had Mrs. O'Leary been of Anglo-Saxon stock.

At the same time, and as a runaway blaze will inevitably show, fire is no respecter of persons. No upstart can climb the social ladder faster. At the first outbreak of the Great Fire of London, the Lord Mayor dismissively declared that "a woman could piss it out." No need even for a crew of obliging lads to open their breeches. By the third day of destruction, King Charles II himself was leading the firefighting efforts, most of which involved preemptive demolitions of buildings in the fire's path. Whimsy pictures the Restoration monarch's Cavalier curls cascading from under a fireman's helmet. Still sour from a civil war in which their parliamentarian sympathies had not fared well, Londoners had hitherto looked askance at their sovereign, like dubious West Virginians sizing up the city fellow with his tater patch. Charles looked better to them after the fire. A writer for *The London Gazette* reported how "his Royal Highness never despairing or slackening his personal care wrought so well that day." If only for a short while, King and Commons had been one.

Tempest and Flood

Perhaps a more vivid sense of the ever-looming possibility of disaster would bring us closer to the Beloved Community, would inspire more of what Camus called "our solidarity against death." Flannery O'Connor puts her finger on the possibility better than I can when she has one of her characters recognize, a moment before she is murdered, that even murderers are her children and thus her responsibility. "She would of been a good woman," her killer observes, "if it had been somebody there to shoot her every minute of her life." So, perhaps, would we all.

When my wife and I visited the Netherlands several years ago, it was suggested to us that the country's egalitarian ethos—so deeply ingrained that the Dutch consider it in poor taste to list one's academic titles on a business card and obligatory to shake hands with women and children as well as men—was a byproduct of the nation's centuries-old struggle with the sea. Everyone had to lend a hand in holding back the water; everyone's thumb had to be ready to plug the dike. No room for beautiful people and their private pools. We also heard that a common course for Dutch celebrities is to leave the country before its traditional disgust with ostentation drives them out.

"Here a wretched race is found," Pliny the Elder observed of the Lowlands in the middle of the first century, "inhabiting either the more elevated spots or artificial mounds. When the waves cover the surrounding area they are like so many mariners on board a ship, and when again the tide recedes their condition is that of so many shipwrecked men." So many shareholders in disaster, in other words, so many signatories on the pledge to keep disaster at bay.

By the beginning of the second millennium, population growth in the Lowlands had increased the need for land, and dike-building began in earnest. By 1250 the dikes were connected in vast networks, with each farmer having a prescribed section of earthworks to maintain, the duty nominally dictated by physical proximity to the dike. *Wie het water deert, die het water keert* went the saying, "Whom the water hurts, he the water stops"—an ethical dike, as it were, and one prone to leakage. In a country where two-thirds of the ground is vulnerable to flooding, "whom the water hurts" ultimately equates to "we the people." The contract extends as far as the terrain.

One of the earliest stories of a deluge, the biblical story of Noah and the ark, can be read as an allegory of a broken social contract. God floods the earth because "every inclination of the thoughts of their hearts was only evil continually." Our best contextual clue as to the exact nature of humankind's offending "evil" occurs in verses attributed to Noah's father, Lamech:

Lamech said to his wives, "I have killed a man for wounding me, a young man for striking me. If Cain is avenged sevenfold, truly Lamech seventy-sevenfold."

Secularize the story, remove the punitive God, and the tale of Noah boils down to an implicit proposition: the deterioration of human community is a prelude to disaster. History provides numerous supporting examples. Hurricane Katrina—at least in New Orleans— was as much a man-made calamity as a blow from nature. Substandard construction of the levees and subdemocratic inequalities greatly enhanced the damage of the storm. A guide assured me during a tour of the devastation two years into "the recovery" that in a different social order the city would have suffered much less than it had. "The cleanup would have been a matter of weeks."

In a similar vein, the economic crisis of 2007-2008, a disaster for millions of American families, was the result of a failure to regulate financial institutions—of letting the dikes fall into disrepair, so to speak. The French, Russian, and Chinese revolutions were disastrous not only in terms of the ruthlessness that brought them to birth but also in terms of the unchecked social imbalances that created the conditions for revolt.

Disaster's strong incentives for maintaining the social contract are hardly negated by technological advances. Ironically, our species' progressive ability to avert certain kinds of disaster by harnessing the forces of nature has created the potential for new forms of calamitous destruction. There had always been a danger of flooding in the Low Countries, for instance, but the first attempts at reclaiming the land and pushing back the water made the consequences of any accidental flooding more catastrophic than before. Dam the water, if you must, but woe to you if the dam should break.

Count that as another argument for equality, since much can depend on who owns the dam. The Industrial Revolution's "dark satanic mills" were engines of progress, but as long as profit was their principal driving force, they were also terrariums of disaster. The Triangle Shirtwaist Factory fire of 1911 and the Monongah mining disaster of 1907 exemplify the overall risk to any society when contractual prerogatives work to the advantage of a few elites. We can word the danger more tersely if we like. Nothing poses a greater risk to our collective survival than the metastasized survival instincts of "the fittest."

Triumph of Death, by Félix Nussbaum, 1944.

Plague, Pestilence, and Famine

I suppose if we wanted we could frame Noah as the original survivalist. He has a better claim to deliverance than his neighbors, a clearer sense of the future, a stronger signal from above. He's a can-do guy with the latest gear. He has that big boat. He lays in stores, plans in advance. With the Deluge behind him and the rainbow overhead, he devotes his days to guzzling wine and passing out naked in his tent.

As with the story of Lot and his daughters, surviving the holocaust of Sodom only to indulge in some incestuous hanky-panky in a throwback cave, the Book of Genesis tends to treat the survival of the fittest, even and especially the morally fittest, with what reads like a skeptic's wink. It is not Darwinism so much as social Darwinism that these ancient stories refute. Time and again, the righteous remnant prove less righteous once the danger is past, once there's no one there to shoot them every minute of their life.

Still, most of us would prefer a berth on the ark to a mass burial at sea. There's a trace of the survivalist in us all. We could not be the animals we are otherwise. In his 2002 study of survivalism, *Dancing at Armageddon*, sociologist Richard G. Mitchell recounts an interview with a Key West–based survivalist whose specially equipped sixty-foot "floating survival retreat" stands ready for any plague, pestilence, or explosion in which "the nation's transportation network will be choked with panic-stricken refugees and would-be survivors." But "if you have chosen a water [escape] route," Mitchell's source told him, "you have the option of firing up and cruising off. You could be one hundred miles away from trouble in a matter of hours, safe in some secluded cove, your antenna quivering with bad news." Presumably there'd be some musical space left on the bandwidth for the savvy survivors to dance to.

Mitchell sees the various "shelters, retreats, getaway vehicles" and omnipresent guns as "the symptoms, not the substance, of survivalism." The latter he locates in the desire for "a hypothetical balance between the imagined hazards and hardships ahead and the resources, skills, and knowledge at hand or within reach." Survivalists "want a part in creating the marketplace, in fashioning economic culture, in crafting rituals of appraisal and exchange." In short, they want some kind of meaningful role in a global order that increasingly asks nothing from them beyond acquiescence and passive consumption.

It seems that what many survivalists also want is a distillation of the social contract to something at once more essential and more exclusive, the kind of "purification" that right-wing movements are apt to valorize and thoroughgoing disaster is bound to guarantee. Once the waters start to rise, the cleansing begins. For the hardcore survivalist, the social contract is itself a kind of latent disaster, one that thwarts the harsh benevolence of evolution and reduces dependent humanity to a colony of lab rats. The center cannot hold and was never really the center to begin with. Catastrophe, whenever it

There is no subtler, no surer means of overturning the existing basis of society than to debauch the currency.
—John Maynard Keynes, 1919

comes and whatever form it takes, will sort us into the only two categories that matter in the end: those left standing and the bodies carted off the stage.

Others have construed the human drama in different terms, believing and acting upon the belief that the survival of human beings means little unless a scrap of humanity survives with them. If the social contract breaks down when the levees do, they're prepared to commend their instinct for self-preservation to the flood. The Martyrs of Memphis, thirty-eight nuns, priests, and doctors who chose to remain in—and in some cases, return to—the city of Memphis, Tennessee, during a deadly outbreak of yellow fever in 1878, illustrate the antisurvivalist case. At roughly the same time as two Memphis residents were trampled to death on a railroad platform during a panicked evacuation that would empty half the city, two Anglican nuns named Constance and Thecla were boarding a train from their order's New York

State motherhouse back to Memphis, where they'd nursed the sick during an outbreak of the fever five years before. The 1878 strain proved more virulent, killing as many as five thousand people, the two nuns among them, and cutting the population so drastically that Memphis wasn't reconstituted as a city until 1893. The hagiographic name for Constance and her fellow martyrs is "Constance and Her Companions," though Constance's nonnegotiable point seems to have been that her companions were all the featherless bipeds in the city of Memphis, "Negro" orphans not excluded.

Good Lord, Deliver Us

It's possible to view disaster as Nature's dissent, or Fortune's, or God's if one believes in God and one's God is jealous. Disaster thumbs its nose at Utopia; it's the mud in the eye of every scheme to better the lot of humankind. You can nationalize the railroads but every now and then a passenger train will go off the rails. You can collectivize the farms—historically a disaster in its own right—but you cannot put famine in front of a firing squad and shoot it as a class enemy. You can never be altogether safe.

Sometimes when I am working in my garden, wondering if Candide could have enjoyed pulling carrots even half as much as I do, I think of historical disasters, mostly in the form of invasions. The science-fiction storyline of "alien invaders" is not so much futuristic as atavistic. In the past there were people who stood as blithely in their gardens as I stand in mine. The rhythms of planting and sowing, the customs of marrying and mourning, had gone unchanged for centuries. Most of those people never journeyed farther than a few miles from their homes. Nor did they want to. There were wolves and ogres in the forest, but life in the village was relatively secure. Suddenly, there are dragon ships in the harbor, Huns massed along the hilltops, metal-encased conquistadors crashing through the jungle on the backs of never-seen-before beasts. These guys have social contracts, too, you see, the basic thrust of which is the total annihilation of yours and you.

A knowledge of history does not give the lie to apocalypse. It gives the logic to apocalypse.

And yet, the disasters we tend to fear most are not the apocalyptic cataclysms that even at their worst leave us with companions in our misery, but the personal disasters, the tragedies that isolate us in our fate. The unlocked door that eases a home invasion, the audit that drags your cupidity into the light of day. At the cutting edge of tragic necessity, the wife who turns out to be your mother. The chorus of *Oedipus Rex* stands close to Oedipus, physically and contractually—they are his counselors, he is their king—but he cannot see them, being blind, and they cannot help him, having nothing but words. Any society they might claim to share is purely academic; emotionally it's as useless as the poor man's eyes. The most dreadful disaster that befalls a human being is not eschatological but existential. The messenger we'd most like to kill looks more like Sartre than Genghis Khan.

Mere sociability, even a strong social contract, amounts to an equivocal benefit in tragic straits: whatever support it may tender, it also marks the pale one is poignantly beyond. The friends who come to commiserate with Job in his affliction are also part of his affliction. "Miserable comforters are you all." They purport to bring consolation but all they offer is judgment, not only in the moralistic pronouncements they employ to uphold their sense of a rational universe in which only the wicked suffer while the righteous have a high old time, but also in their alienating personification of the "happy norm." If Job can just hang on till the holidays, Eliphaz and Bildad will send him Christmas cards with rapturous reports of how Chip and Chelsea are acing medical school. *And what about you, Job? What are your kids up to these days?*

None of this is to suggest that the eradicable fact of disaster or the inconsolable nature of tragedy ought to nullify our impulse toward social progress. To my mind they *ratify* the impulse: they give us stronger incentives to achieve the greatest measures of social justice

and human kindness that we can. Tornadoes are bad enough without torture. On moral imperatives Katrina is more eloquent than Kant [*Königsberg*, page 61]. The same possibility of disaster that inspires the survivalist refutes his claim that in a more socialistic society we become weak, aimless, incapable of heroic action and all the rest. Tell that to a tsunami. The true knight need never fear the obsolescence of his chivalrous heart. Raze the castles and there will still be sandbags to pile against the flood. Strike down the corporate leviathans; there will be other dragons to slay.

Or to be slain by. The dragon Disaster may not love the valiant but it hates the glib. It stands ever at the ready to remind us that our covenants are not comprehensive, that insurance policies written to cover "acts of God"

Hegel says somewhere that all great historic facts and personages recur twice. He forgot to add: "Once as tragedy, and again as farce."
—Karl Marx, 1852

may not cover refusals to act on the part of women and men. God promises Noah he will never again flood the earth; he does not promise that Noah's descendants might not succeed in flooding New York. Or that the promise of the rainbow applies to asteroids too. Disaster laughs at every attempt to write its epitaph. Any valedictory words can be undone, rendered moot, turned into a joke by a single fiery sneeze. I imagine some people become violent and cruel as a way of counteracting that vulnerability, as if the best way to avert disaster is to become disaster oneself, to beat it to the punch. Others adopt a defensive humility, like those limber trees Sophocles praises for bending in the gale. Maybe if I stoop low enough, bad luck won't notice I'm here. Still others choose extraordinary compassion, like the aptly named Constance, more constant than disaster if not quite its match. No doubt we would have found all these kinds of people tending their gardens in the backyards of Pompeii.

Conservation rangers and locals evacuating the body of one of four mountain gorillas killed in mysterious circumstances, Virunga National Park, Democratic Republic of Congo, 2007. Photograph by Brent Stirton.

HUMAN ERROR

by Jennifer Jacquet

In September 2014 I gathered at the American Museum of Natural History with scientists, journalists, and museum staff for the unveiling of the taxidermied body of Lonesome George, the last of the Pinta Island giant tortoises. I met George when he was an octogenarian and I was a twenty-year-old volunteer at the Charles Darwin Research Station in the Galápagos. I sometimes fed him leaves in his pen. Now, just a little more than a decade later, as the curators pulled away the cloth covering the display case, I felt queasy and sad. Most people clapped, probably because they didn't know what else to do. George was standing up, legs and head outstretched, looking uncharacteristically ener-

getic. The conversation quickly turned to the taxidermy job. One magazine reporter said her readers wanted "all the gory details."

Lonesome George's death in 2012 marked the end of a long struggle for existence by giant tortoises against humans who had hunted and eaten them, and who had introduced goats to their island, which destroyed their habitat. I searched the room and saw one person crying. It was biologist James Gibbs, who had been the one to courier George's carcass to the museum. We spoke about the Galápagos and the event we had just witnessed. Gibbs said he wished the museum staff had told everyone about the time island fishermen took the tortoise hostage in a successful ploy to increase fishing quotas.

Jennifer Jacquet is an assistant professor of environmental studies at New York University and the author of Is Shame Necessary? New Uses for an Old Tool.

I wished the museum staff had said something about how difficult it is to be a member of the species that bears the responsibility for the Pinta tortoise's demise.

When he was alive, Lonesome George was a captive reminder of biodiversity loss. One 2006 book called him "the only one of his kind left on earth—a symbol of the devastation man has wrought to the natural world in the Galápagos and beyond." After his death, Washington Tapia, a researcher with the Ecuador National Park Service, told the *New York Times* it was like losing his grandparents. But even for people less intimate with him did his life and demise serve as a reminder of the mass extinction of species currently underway—the sixth in earth's history but the only one caused by humans.

It was said more than once at the museum as well as in media coverage of his death that the tortoise had failed to reproduce. Placing blame on animals is part of the balm we apply to our uneasy consciences about extinction. In 1887 zoologist Leonhard Stejneger noted in an article on the Steller's sea cow that "there is nothing surprising in the speedy extermination of this clumsy animal, which could not dive, and which had actually no means of defense or escape." A 2014 *Audubon* article about Martha, the last passenger pigeon, which had died in the Cincinnati Zoo one hundred years earlier, noted, "Not once in her life had she laid a fertile egg."

The question of infertility, however, is only a distraction from the sorrow of extinction. In 1947, when the Wisconsin Society for Ornithology erected a monument to the passenger pigeon, ecologist Aldo Leopold read a eulogy for the animal. "There will always be pigeons in books and in museums, but these are effigies and images, dead to all hardships and to all delights," he said. "Book-pigeons cannot dive out of a cloud to make the deer run for cover, or clap their wings in thunderous applause of mast-laden woods. Book-pigeons cannot breakfast on new-mown wheat in Minnesota, and dine on blueberries in Canada. They know no

urge of seasons; they feel no kiss of sun, no lash of wind and weather; they live forever by not living at all."

Leopold also noted the existential crisis posed by extinction: the guilt extinction elicits is both contemporary and ours alone bear. "The Cro-Magnon who slew the last mammoth thought only of steaks," he said. "The sailor who clubbed the last auk thought of nothing at all. But we, who have lost our pigeons, mourn the loss. Had the funeral been ours, the pigeons would hardly have mourned us."

Leopold's oration joined a litany of uneasiness about humanity's impact on nature. In 1847 conservationist George Marsh [*Rutland, VT,* page 57] noted in an address that climate was being "gradually changed and ameliorated or deteriorated by human action." By 1864 Marsh had come to the conclusion that "of all organic beings, man alone is to be regarded as essentially a destructive power." The idea that we were living in an era marked by humankind's actions was common in the nineteenth century and continued into the twentieth. It picked up steam with a term first used in 1922 by Russian geologist Aleksei Pavlov and later in 2000 by atmospheric chemist Paul Crutzen: the Anthropocene.

There is no real doubt we are living in the human age. The unprecedented increases in the human population and earth-altering substances such as greenhouse-gas emissions, nitrogen runoff, and plastics are not the result of climatic shifts (like those that set the Holocene in motion roughly twelve thousand years ago) or because an asteroid hit the Yucatán (as it did 66 million years ago, putting an end to the Cretaceous Period and non-avian dinosaurs). The current major shocks to the planetary system are caused by human beings.

The more delusional among us see these changes as merely the latest in an ever-changing world, just a bigger cataclysm among earth's many cataclysms. But that's acceding to a temptation similar to that of the radar operator aboard the B-29 that delivered destruction to Hiroshima; he called the atomic bomb "just a bigger bomb." Such incrementalism, pervasive and no doubt of some comfort, denies that the present moment requires a new conception of human responsibility. But humanity (or some faction of it) has become a uniquely powerful force on the planet. As a 2011 editorial in the journal *Nature* suggested, "The first step is to recognize, as the term *Anthropocene* invites us to do, that we are in the driver's seat."

The current array of species disappearances is comparable in rate and size to the five other mass extinctions in earth's 4.5-billion-year history. But only since the second half of the twentieth century—with the creation of international scientific bodies, and databases that tally likely extinct species (to date, nine pages of very small font)—have we come to understand the magnitude. This havoc we have wreaked on earth's biological system feels fundamentally different than that which we have wreaked on its physical system. We feel bad for warming glaciers and making the oceans more acidic, but we feel particularly bad about annihilating wild animals that managed to struggle for their survival alongside us year after year. They struggled against all odds but one.

Dealing with the disaster we have created means finding a way to reckon with our guilt for causing it. "Why stick around to see the last beautiful wild places getting ruined, and to hate my own species, and to feel that I, too, in my small way, was one of the guilty ruiners?" asked Jonathan Franzen in 2006. "The guilt of knowing what human beings have done" is how conservation biologist George Schaller described the feeling he gets when he looks at the Serengeti. In 2008 Schaller made one of the most definitive statements of Anthropocene-inspired self-reproach. "Obviously," he said, "humans are evolution's greatest mistake." And in 2015 Pope Francis joined the chorus of mourners. "Because of us," he wrote in his encyclical *Laudato Si'*, "thousands of species will no longer give glory to God by

their very existence, nor convey their message to us. We have no such right."

In 1961 psychoanalyst William Niederland coined the term *survivor syndrome* after conducting a study of those who survived Nazi concentration camps as well as survivors of natural disasters and car accidents. Niederland noted that among their symptoms were chronic depression and anxiety. Many camp survivors whom the SS had "selected" to live found it difficult to relate to ordinary people and have ordinary feelings. Sigmund Freud [*Vienna*, page 44] had intimated the idea in an 1896 letter in which he discussed his father's death, describing a "tendency toward self-reproach which death invariably leaves." Niederland's findings gave a name to a condition that also afflicted some survivors of the *Titanic*: of the 705 people who survived the ship's sinking, during which more than 1,500 passengers and crew died, at least ten went on to commit suicide. That's a rate more than a hundred times higher than the current U.S. suicide rate. Frederick Fleet, the *Titanic* lookout who first spotted the iceberg that sank the ship, was the last. He hanged himself only a few years after Niederland published his study.

The psychiatrist Arnold Modell expanded the concept of survivor guilt to include less traumatic events, including the guilt some feel when they believe they are better off than others in their family. He pointed to "an unconscious bookkeeping system" operating in mental life. When "other members of the family do not survive," he wrote in 1983, "those who achieve upward mobility may do so at the expense of the guilt of leaving other family members behind." Modell suggested that survivor guilt was not an affliction reserved for trauma victims who happened to have survived. People who could be considered agents of destruction also experience it.

One such agent was Claude Eatherly, among the forty-two U.S. Army men directly involved in dropping the atomic bombs on Japan. He had flown over Hiroshima and given the signal. Alone among the forty-two, Eatherly

The Great Deluge

A controversial theory proposed in 1996 by geologists William Ryan and Walter Pitman postulates that a catastrophic flood of the Black Sea inspired the biblical story of Noah's ark, the Sumerian Epic of Gilgamesh, and other myths.

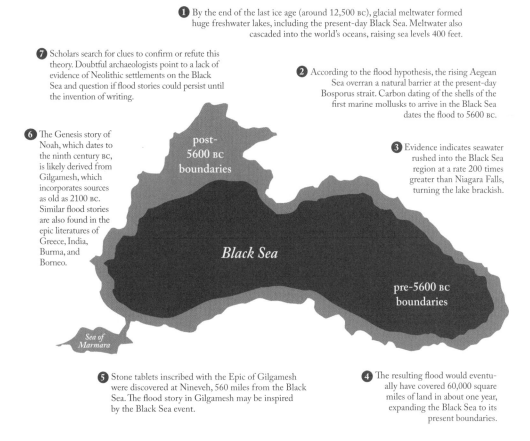

1 By the end of the last ice age (around 12,500 BC), glacial meltwater formed huge freshwater lakes, including the present-day Black Sea. Meltwater also cascaded into the world's oceans, raising sea levels 400 feet.

7 Scholars search for clues to confirm or refute this theory. Doubtful archaeologists point to a lack of evidence of Neolithic settlements on the Black Sea and question if flood stories could persist until the invention of writing.

2 According to the flood hypothesis, the rising Aegean Sea overran a natural barrier at the present-day Bosporus strait. Carbon dating of the shells of the first marine mollusks to arrive in the Black Sea dates the flood to 5600 BC.

6 The Genesis story of Noah, which dates to the ninth century BC, is likely derived from Gilgamesh, which incorporates sources as old as 2100 BC. Similar flood stories are also found in the epic literatures of Greece, India, Burma, and Borneo.

post-5600 BC boundaries

3 Evidence indicates seawater rushed into the Black Sea region at a rate 200 times greater than Niagara Falls, turning the lake brackish.

Black Sea

pre-5600 BC boundaries

Sea of Marmara

5 Stone tablets inscribed with the Epic of Gilgamesh were discovered at Nineveh, 560 miles from the Black Sea. The flood story in Gilgamesh may be inspired by the Black Sea event.

4 The resulting flood would eventually have covered 60,000 square miles of land in about one year, expanding the Black Sea to its present boundaries.

rejected a hero's treatment after his return and instead expressed profound guilt for what he had done. His guilt was off-message, however, and for this and other reasons his reputation was called into question. In 1959 he offered his interpretation. "The truth," he wrote, "is that society simply cannot accept the fact of my guilt without at the same time recognizing its own far deeper guilt."

Eatherly's view anticipated an even broader expansion of guilt by some psychologists, one in which survivor and collective guilt bleed together. This collective form of survivor guilt could be felt throughout a group as the result of perpetrating harm, even if no individual in the group directly contributed to the harm. Examples of this may be construed in the less typical but persistent guilt some feel today about slavery, war, genocide, or white privilege.

Survivor guilt may also exist at the species level. That humans have helped bring on other species' end times is not an easy feeling to deal with. Survivor guilt in the Anthropocene may describe how we respond to harm done by humankind's ever-increasing dominance. Given that we bear responsibility for balancing the interests of human and nonhuman life, it's no surprise that some among us feel we are not doing a satisfactory job.

Guilt, of course, can be debilitating and self-destructive. But philosophers and psychologists have argued it can also motivate people to make reparations for their transgressions—as seemingly was the case with Claude Eatherly, who sought in his own way to prevent the dropping of future atomic bombs. In a 2013 study German university students read an article about how Germany was responsible for harming the climate. Respondents who reported feeling more intense guilt also expressed greater intention to repair the damage.

A complication of survivor guilt in the Anthropocene is that the disaster continues; our guilt is concurrent with it. It's also anticipatory: the burden of guilt applies not only to what we have done but what is yet to come—and what it will mean for our own species' survival. Scientific models can predict how warm the planet will get, what percentage of corals will die, how acidic the oceans will become, how many more species will vanish in the near future. As a result, we are able to question what our future holds. We are now making a decision "on the unconsulted behalf of perhaps 100 trillion of our descendants," wrote

The unleashed power of the atom has changed everything save our modes of thinking and thus we drift toward unparalleled catastrophe.
—Albert Einstein, 1946

British environmentalist Norman Myers, "asserting that future generations"—at least 200,000 of them, lasting twenty times longer than humans have so far been around—"can certainly manage with far less than a full planetary stock of species."

Research into collective guilt has focused mostly on harms committed in the past, but some researchers are now concentrating on the future. For a study published in 2012, nonaboriginal Canadian college students read fictional newspaper articles about a dam project. In one, the project had flooded thousands of acres of aboriginal lands a month prior. In the other, the project would flood thousands of acres a month in the future. Compared to harm in the past, harm in the future induced significantly more guilt.

What sort of amends could we expect survivor guilt at the species level to produce? Some people are now trying to protect land and sea from human impact. Others eliminate invasive species that humans ruinously introduced into native habitats, like the goats on Lonesome George's island of Pinta. There are breeding programs for endangered species in captivity; such a plan resurrected the population of black-footed ferrets in the western Great Plains. Armed bodyguards protect the world's last male northern white rhino in Kenya. And some are relocating species whose habitats we have encroached on in one way or another, a process known as "assisted colonization."

The idea that has garnered the most attention recently is the revival of species, or de-extinction. This is how James Gibbs, courier of Lonesome George's body, appears to be coping with the tortoise's death. He is working to breed tortoises that contain hybrid DNA from Pinta tortoises. If successful, this will eventually produce an animal genetically similar to the original. "You can become paralyzed by extinction," Gibbs has said about the project, "or you can get to work."

The website of Revive & Restore, one of the leading groups advocating for de-extinction, calls the task "the greatest undertaking conservation science has ever attempted" while also claiming it is "simple in principle." Some de-extinction attempts, however, reveal the vast complexity of the enterprise. In early 2015 geneticist George Church and his colleagues inserted fourteen woolly mammoth genes into lab-grown elephant cells, an early step toward reviving the extinct creature. But among the factors that scientists have noted put terrestrial vertebrates at risk of disappearing in the Anthropocene are: a small geographic range (the mammoth's habitat continually shrinks as the tundra warms), low reproductive rates (the mammoth is not a fast breeder), and large body size (repeat: *mammoth*). Revive & Restore's list of criteria for deciding the best candidates for "genetic rescue" includes that the original causes of extinction have been resolved and that new threats can be managed. Regarding the woolly mammoth, the organization can answer only with maybes.

I would love to know woolly mammoths were lumbering across Siberia again. But some proponents of de-extinction act as if existence is the only problem these species face. De-extinction alone does not address the causes of extinction, the condition of habitats, or the quality of species' lives. We cannot refreeze the Arctic tundra, former home of the woolly mammoth, nor can we postpone the arrival of spring, which climate change impels to come earlier every year. We cannot resurrect the cold snap that once prevented the mountain pine beetle from destroying northern forests. There is no satisfactory way to wipe the record clean.

Built as it is from the Greek *anthropos*, the term *Anthropocene* implicates all of humanity. This could be a dangerous way of seeing ourselves. Studies of the placebo effect have long shown that if we believe an inert pill to be real, some will experience suggested benefits. But there is also the so-called nocebo effect, in which some will experience suggested negative side effects of a placebo. Naming the Anthropocene might work the same way, bringing to bear an alarming fait accompli: human destruction could be exacerbated if we believe that destruction is what we do—that environmental destruction is a byproduct of human nature. Call it the anthropocebo effect.

Belief in determinism can be a powerful force in guiding behavior. In one study, students who read a text that explained how free will is an illusion because genetics and environment determine behavior cheated to a significantly greater degree in a follow-up experiment than students who read a text that stated a contrary view. Similarly, framing the Anthropocene in a deterministic way may lead us to accept humans as an inevitably destructive geologic force. A sense of inescapable complicity could lead us to forget that humans are capable of acting differently.

History further complicates the term. Many argue that casting the whole species together in such a way is imprecise because only some humans—specific societies coupled with certain economic systems and technologies—are to blame. In this context, the Anthropocene's start date may be taken as an indicator of who is responsible—and therefore who might be obligated to act. Proposed dates have included the beginning of farming eleven thousand years

ago or its rise eight thousand years ago; the year 1500 (based on an opaque calculation involving human population, affluence, and available technologies); the year 1610 (when an exchange of species between the Old and New World caused a drop in human population and farming, leading to a regeneration of forests and a concurrent decline in atmospheric carbon dioxide); the Industrial Revolution of the late eighteenth century; a period after World War II known as the Great Acceleration; and various years related to the detonation of nuclear weapons, including 1945, 1952, and 1964.

Of this list, nuclear-weapons testing stands out. While radioactive fallout did not fundamentally change the functioning of the earth's biological system, it did leave a well-defined

Out of the experience of an extraordinary human disaster that lasted too long must be born a society of which all humanity will be proud.
—Nelson Mandela, 1994

signature in the geologic record. The date is also compelling for social reasons: nuclear technology left a ready marker in the stratification of our collective psyche—it was the moment we realized we were a hazard to ourselves.

The Anthropocene may also help us acknowledge our sense of what we've done and what we still might do. The term's official adoption into the geological timescale could take place this fall when it comes to vote at the International Geographical Congress. But the vote itself is largely academic: our geological moment is here. As with nuclear weapons, its most interesting questions relate not to what to build or resurrect but to what we can undo and prevent. Survivor guilt in the Anthropocene could be put to good use if we view our social identity as malleable rather than fixed and can recognize that humans are in the driver's seat before the coming planetary wreck. It might be our chance to believe we can steer away from ultimate disaster—that we have not simply been a great evolutionary mistake.

CONVERSATIONS

PLATO OTTO FRIEDRICH

Critias, 360 BC

O Solon, you Hellenes are never anything but children, and there is not an old man among you. In mind you are all young; there is no old opinion handed down among you by ancient tradition, nor any science that is hoary with age. And I will tell you why. There have been, and will be again, many destructions of mankind. The greatest have been brought about by fire and water. There is a story that Phaethon, the son of Helios, having yoked the steeds in his father's chariot, burned up all that was on the earth, and was himself destroyed by a thunderbolt. This has the form of a myth, but really signifies a great conflagration on the earth.

Just when you are beginning to be provided with letters and the other requisites of civilized life, the stream from heaven, like a pestilence, comes pouring down, and leaves only those of you who are destitute of letters and education. So you have to begin all over again like children, and know nothing of what happened in ancient times. You remember a single deluge only, but there were many previous ones. You do not know that there formerly dwelled in your land the fairest and noblest race of men that ever lived, and that you and your whole city are descended from a small seed or remnant of them that survived. And this was unknown to you, because for many generations the survivors of that destruction died, leaving no written word.

The End of the World: A History, 1982

Many of the natural catastrophes that seem to threaten us are not really natural but rather man-made assaults, distortions, and perversions of the balance of nature. Faust is at large again in the form of the scientist who asks too much of God's universe. This moral element connects still more closely the possibilities of nuclear war and natural cataclysm. Either way, the prophecies imply, the end of the world will be the fault of sinning mankind, the repudiation of God's covenant with Noah after the great flood. We no longer believe in Noah, of course, but we do believe in the metaphor of a covenant that gives meaning to our existence, and in the danger of its repudiation. The end of the world is, in a way, a pun. The end can mean not only the conclusion but also the purpose of the world. Just as it has been said that a man's life can be understood only at the moment of his death, so the end of the world, the destruction of the world, seems to imply that there is some higher purpose in the world's existence. Thus, the end of the world makes manifest the end of the world.

Most of us have been trained to believe only the evidence of our senses, so we believe only in the world that we can see around us, and the end that we dread in our prefigurings of World War III is really nothing more than an extension of our own death, the prospect that the city where we now live will suddenly be reduced to a heap of radioactive rubble. The idea that life might continue at the edges of the rubble seems small consolation.

BERNARD DE MANDEVILLE ···················· ANGELINA JOLIE

Fable of the Bees, 1723

The nearer the object is the more we suffer, and the more remote it is the less we are troubled with it. To see people executed for crimes, if it is a great way off, moves us but little, in comparison to what it does when we are near enough to see the motion of the soul in their eyes, observe their fears and agonies, and are able to read the pangs in every feature of the face. When we hear that three or four thousand men, all strangers to us, are killed with the sword, or forced into some river where they are drowned, we say and perhaps believe that we pity them. It is humanity bids us have compassion with the sufferings of others, and reason tells us that whether a thing be far off or done in our sight, our sentiments concerning it ought to be the same, and we should be ashamed to own that we felt no commiseration in us when any thing requires it. But when men talk of pitying people out of sight, they are to be believed in the same manner as when they say that they are our humble servants. Those who have a strong and lively imagination, and can make representations of things in their minds, as they would be if they were actually before them, may work themselves up into something that resembles compassion; but this is done by art, and often the help of a little enthusiasm, and is only an imitation of pity; the heart feels little of it, and it is as faint as what we suffer at the acting of a tragedy, where our judgment leaves part of the mind uninformed.

Speech at the Academy of Motion Picture Arts and Sciences Governors Awards, 2013

I came into this business young and worried about my own pain. And it was only when I began to travel and look and live beyond my home that I began to understand my responsibility to others. And when I met survivors of war and famine and rape, I learned what life is like for most people in this world. And how fortunate I was to have food to eat, a roof over my head, a safe place to live, and the joy of having my family safe and healthy. I realized how sheltered I had been, and I was determined never to be that way again. We are all, everyone in this room, so fortunate. I have never understood why some people are lucky enough to be born with the chance I had, to have this path in life, and why across the world there's a woman just like me, with the same abilities and the same desires, same work ethic and love for her family, who would most likely make better films and better speeches, only she sits in a refugee camp, and she has no voice. She worries about what her children will eat, how to keep them safe, and if they'll ever be allowed to return home. I don't know why this is my life and that's hers. I don't understand that, but I will do the best I can with this life to be of use.

MISCELLANY

Accounts varied of the Great Famine of 1315–22, during which more than 10 percent of Europe's population died. In Flanders: "Parents killed their children and children killed parents, and the bodies of executed criminals were eagerly snatched from the gallows." In France: "There was no wine in the whole kingdom."

In order to halt or slow the advance of glaciers, the Tlingit tribe of the northwest coast of North America used to sacrifice dogs and slaves by throwing them into the glacier's crevasses in the hopes of appeasing the ice spirit.

Opening night of Henry James' *Guy Domville*, on January 5, 1895, was "an unmitigated disaster," James wrote in a letter, "hooted at, as I was hooted at myself, by a brutal mob, and fruitless of any of the consequences for which I have striven." The play's reception, he wrote, "has completely sickened me with the theater and made me feel, at any rate for the present, like washing my hands of it forever."

Astrologers of the Ayyubid Empire predicted in 1186 that the world would end September 16 of that year; a dust storm, stirred up by planetary alignment, would scour the earth of life. Sultan Saladin criticized the "feeble minds" of believers and planned an open-air, candlelit party for that evening. "We never saw a night as calm as that," an attendee later remarked.

Arthur Schopenhauer referred to insurance as "a public sacrifice made on the altar of anxiety."

The first known legal use of the phrase *act of God* was in a 1581 English case concerning property inheritance. It referred, in that instance, to death, declared by the judge to be among "those things which are inevitable by the act of God, which no industry can avoid, nor policy prevent."

In 1919 a steel storage tank burst in Boston and spilled 2.3 million gallons of molasses, creating a twenty-five-foot-high wave that killed twenty-one people and tore buildings from foundations. The tank had leaked since its installation, but the company had, in response to complaints, merely painted it a concealing brown.

Sixteenth-century "father of mineralogy" Georgius Agricola critiqued "the attacks, which are so annoying," of those protesting the extermination of animals and the poisoning of brooks and streams. "With the metals that are melted from the ore," he explained, "birds without number, edible beasts, and fish can be purchased elsewhere and brought to these mountainous regions."

"Pompeii like any other town," Herman Melville wrote in his journal during an 1867 visit. "Same old humanity. All the same whether one be dead or alive. Pompeii comfortable sermon. Like Pompeii better than Paris."

According to sixth-century-BC Greek poet Hipponax of Colophon, in times of drought, famine, or plague an ugly or deformed person was chosen by the community to be *pharmakós*, or scapegoat. After being fed figs, barley cake, and cheese, he would be struck on the genitals with the bulbs and twigs of wild plants, led on a procession accompanied by flute, and burned on a pyre. His ashes were thrown into the sea. It is believed that Hipponax, whom Pliny the Elder once called "notoriously ugly," may have been exaggerating the ritual.

A 1959 *Chicago Daily Tribune* article about Robert Frost, who had recently proclaimed his confidence in humanity's resilience in the face of missile threats, ran with the headline: HUMAN RACE BOMB PROOF, POET BELIEVES.

Hatches of Rocky Mountain locusts (*Melanoplus spretus*) in 1874 and 1875 brought swarms up to 1,800 miles long and 110 miles wide across the Great Plains. Numbers were estimated in the trillions. Farmers risked starvation. The swarm is believed to have been the largest mass of living insects ever witnessed by modern man—but within thirty years the species disappeared. "I can't believe *M. spretus* is extinct," said ecologist Dan Otte in 2014. "But where to look for it?"

The destruction of Sodom and Gomorrah may have been caused by an earthquake that occurred through the Great Rift Valley around 1900 BC. The "brimstone and fire" described in the Bible would have been due to petroleum and gases present in the area igniting the cities.

From 108 BC to 1911, there were 1,828 famines in China—nearly one every year.

"Thank the good God we have all got through and the only family that did not eat human flesh," wrote fourteen-year-old Virginia Reed, a surviving Donner Party member, in an 1847 letter. "Don't let this letter dishearten anybody and never take no cutoffs and hurry along as fast as you can." Reed reported being "pleased with California, particularly with the climate."

Portuguese priest João dos Santos described in 1609 a former custom of royals in the Sofala kingdom: "to commit suicide by taking poison when any disaster or natural physical defect fell upon them, such as impotence, infectious disease, the loss of their front teeth," or any other deformity or affliction.

When Albert Einstein visited Beno Gutenberg, a seismologist at Caltech, in 1933, the two strolled around the Pasadena campus while Gutenberg explained earthquake science. Suddenly their wives arrived to inform them there had been a massive earthquake. "We had become so involved in seismology," recalled Gutenberg later, "that we hadn't noticed."

Bibliophilic bishop Richard de Bury lamented the burning of the Library of Alexandria. "Who would not shudder at such a hapless holocaust, where ink is offered up instead of blood," he wrote in 1344, "where the devouring flames consumed so many thousands of innocents?"

The first mass extinction on earth occurred around 2.5 billion years ago, when a photosynthesizing bacterium appeared and released so much oxygen into the atmosphere that anaerobic life was largely wiped out. This is often called the Great Oxygenation Event, the Oxygen Catastrophe, or the Oxygen Holocaust.

The opening of a particle accelerator at Brookhaven National Laboratory in 2000 inspired fears that high-speed collisions might launch a chain reaction that could turn the earth into a hyperdense sphere about one hundred meters across. A risk calculation determined this to be unlikely; if the collider were to run for ten years, the chance was no greater than 1 in 50 million. "The word *unlikely*, however many times it is repeated," wrote concerned scientists, "just isn't enough to assuage our fears of this total disaster."

Plutarch related that news of the Athenians' brutal defeat at Syracuse during the Peloponnesian Wars first came from a stranger who told the story at a barbershop "as if the Athenians already knew all about it." When the barber spread the news, city leaders branded him a liar and an agitator. He was "fastened to the wheel and racked a long time." Official messengers later came with the "actual facts of the whole disaster," and the barber was released.

A scientific study found that hurricanes given feminine names tend to be deadlier than those given masculine names; people consider them less risky and take inadequate precautions. "Changing a severe hurricane's name from Charley to Eloise," the study notes, "could nearly triple its death toll."

Silvana Mangano and Franco Citti, production still for *Oedipus Rex*, directed by Pier Paolo Pasolini, 1967.

KATASTROFA

by Aleksandar Hemon

My father likes to talk to people, ask them questions, tell them stories. More than once, if I found myself reading, or watching TV, or just silently staring into space, he'd sit next to me and order: "Talk!" I'd bristle, but then I'd talk, of course. It's not just that he cannot stand silence, or endure the thought that people have nothing to say to each other. It's also his voracious curiosity—everyone, he assumes, has some story to tell, not least his professionally storytelling son. He expects other people to reveal themselves to him by way of stories. Silence is the death of narration, and thus of love.

Once, we were visiting my wife Teri's parents in Pensacola Beach, Florida, and my parents came from Canada (where they have lived for the past twenty-three years) to join us for Christmas.

Teri and I had married earlier that year, which was when my parents had encountered her parents and got splendidly along. Now, in Pensacola Beach, my parents spent time with her extended family, which, like my family, frequently gets together and features untold numbers of cousins and friends who have been absorbed into the kinship. My parents saw that the essential structure and practices of an African American family are very much like those of our Bosnian one. But one thing was somewhat lacking, however—Teri's family didn't do much of what my family did (and does still): they didn't tell stories the way we did. Their history, for whatever reason, was not entirely available by way of public narration.

Thus, as we walked one balmy day along the splendid white-sand beach, seabirds coasting

Aleksandar Hemon was born in Sarajevo in 1964. In 1992, while Hemon was in a journalist exchange program in Chicago, war broke out in Bosnia. He became a political refugee, living for the past twenty-four years in Chicago. Hemon is the author of six books, most recently the novel The Making of Zombie Wars.

over our heads, clouds scarce and meringue, my father said to my wife: "Teri, tell me about your family. What bad happened?"

Teri was gracious but could not satisfy his curiosity. Apart from the general calamity of being black in America—applicable to an entire population, even if not necessarily equally—there were few family disasters to talk about. My father found that perplexing, even a bit disappointing—for if nothing bad had happened, it was hard to imagine how any stories could be forthcoming. If nothing bad happened, what do we have to talk about?

Teri knew, of course, that my parents had ended up as refugees in Canada, escaping the siege of Sarajevo. She knew that bad things had happened in our family, the baddest one being the war in Bosnia. But this was one of those moments when I felt compelled to interfere and explain my parents to my wife, to establish and introduce the theoretical foundations of their thought system, to instruct her—and anyone willing to submit and listen—on the ways in which trauma alters the very structure of the world and reality. For I understood instantly why my father would ask a question like that. I recognized his compulsion. The "what bad happened" was a shorthand (or longhand) for catastrophe. He asked her to lead him into the history of her family by way of outlining the catastrophes that defined it—for that's how he would tell the story of our family: the wars, displacements, losses, struggles. There is no history without catastrophe; to outline a history one had to narrate its catastrophes. And what could not be narrated could not be understood. A family—or a world, or a life—without a catastrophe was incomprehensible, because it was an impossible proposition. If catastrophe (according to the theory of tragedy) is the dramatic event that initiates the resolution of the plot, then its absence suggests a possibility that the tragic plot will never be resolved. A catastrophe, in other words, might be a trap, but it also allows for a narrative escape. If you were lucky enough to have survived the catastrophic plot twist, you get to tell the story—you *must* tell the story.

I'm of a staunch belief that anything that can be said and thought in one language can be thought and said in another. The words might have a different value or interpretative aura, but there is always more than enough overlapping not to dismiss the project of translation, which is essential not only to the project of literature, but to the project of humanity as well.

But then there is the Bosnian word *katastrofa*, which, most obviously, comes from the same Greek word (*katastrophe* [καταστροφή], meaning *overturning*) as its English counterpart *catastrophe*. But in Bosnian—or at least in the language my family uses—*katastrofa* has a substantially different value and applicability than *catastrophe* has in English. We use it all the time, deploying it in the contexts that would be less appropriate in English. My mother would thus reprimand my father by saying, "*Ti si, ćale, katastrofa!*" (translatable as: *You, Pop, are a catastrophe!*) because he left a trail of dirty socks all the way to the bedroom. Or my father, in his report on a pipe bursting in their house wall, would use katastrofa to refer to the necessity of digging through said wall to find the source of the leak. My sister, who lives in London, would describe the leaden January skies depressingly looming over England and her head as katastrofa. And I could apply katastrofa to, say, the inability of Liverpool FC to defend corner kicks, or to the realization that I'm in the bathroom without toilet paper and the nearest roll is a hallway away. One of the few Bosnian words Teri understands is katastrofa, mainly by way of hearing me bemoan various unfortunate turns of events.

None of this suggests that we don't take the possibility of catastrophe seriously. On the contrary, the ease with which the word katastrofa is applied is related to its very ubiquity. Rather than existing exclusively in magnanimous, tragic dimensions, katastrofa is everywhere, its particles always shimmering like shrapnel on a sunny day.

Against their will, despite their desires, my parents are experts on katastrofa. I called them not so long ago to discuss their theoretical positions on the idea.

Without a doubt the most recent war was the greatest catastrophe in their lifetimes. (World War II was part of their childhood, but they were less traumatized by it, because their youth turned out to be pretty good.) My mother hadn't expected the war to come, so it crashed into her life like a meteorite, and she still remembers the shock: the shelling, the curfew, the dissolution of her routines, her inability to fit the fact of war into the structure of reality within which she operated, saying to me, who called her from Chicago in the spring of 1992: "It's going to stop soon, they're already shooting less than yesterday." And she remembers how everything they had worked for was erased overnight, not only being rendered meaningless, but also irreversibly destabilizing the very possibility of any structural permanence in their subsequent life. After the experience of war, she couldn't sustain her belief in the inertia of reality—in the force that makes things continue as they are. She claims that her mind now rejects the possibility of another war, but the unnatural rupture made any kind of stability suspect. Back before the war, she, like many, was protected by the unimaginability of the unimaginable—a comfortable, if false, assumption that what cannot be imagined cannot happen, or even be happening. Now, she would hide behind the unimaginable, but what has already happened is always necessarily imaginable, and thus has that screen been shredded. To her, being old or sick is not a katastrofa—for that is, she says, natural—so she's not afraid of it. It's not that she fears war either—what she fears is that something will rupture her newly acquired (very Canadian) stability, that something might undo that particular reality.

My father was also traumatized by the war, but what he experienced as a katastrofa—a very personal one, he says—was primarily the rupture in the continuity of human nature. Before the war, he could believe in the stable goodness (or not-goodness) of people—they were who they were and you knew who they were; you avoided the bad ones, liked the good ones. What catastrophically shocked him was the abrupt shift he saw among some of his friends and acquaintances from neighbors into haters, from good to bad, from decent people into killers—that was the unimaginable for him, that *overturning* of human nature. When I ask him if he spends time expecting another katastrofa, as yet unimaginable, he says, "We're old. There might be a katastrofa, but we won't be around, so we don't care."

As for my sister, who has switched career paths in her forties to become a psychotherapist, she appears clear-eyed about the whole thing. "Katastrofa is the imaginary (and sometimes real) actualization of the worst possible outcome of a given situation," she wrote to me. "The situation could vary from a missed bus or burned lunch to death and war." She went on: "Katastrofa is the state of expectation of the worst, as well as preparation for avoidance, for the struggle against or the managing of the outcome. That state is sometimes conscious, but it is permanently subconscious." She also thinks—and I agree—that there is some cultural determination to this perpetual expectation. We both remember the slogan, attributed to Comrade Tito himself and repeated to all the children and citizens of Yugoslavia for decades before the war: "We must live as though peace will last for a hundred years, and be ready as though war will start tomorrow." (And the war did start tomorrow.) My father recalls his father (Ivan) firmly believing that it was impossible to live for fifty years without experiencing war—Grandpa Ivan himself had experienced two world wars. And if scientists are right in claiming that trauma can alter the genetic code, which can then be passed to ancestors, then katastrofa is inscribed in my genes.

I also asked my parents what the opposite of katastrofa would be. "Normal life," they said, in unison. To them, *normal life* is a self-evident category—it's a life that is normal. After I pressed them, they expounded: normal life requires stability, always dependent on the stability of the state, which allows for

Little Hope, by Paul Klee, 1938.

raising, educating, and empowering children, as well as for an overall sense of progress. Normal life, my father clarified, also has nuances, and it's improved (though the exact translation of the word he used would be *beautified*) with things like skiing, sports, singing, children, beekeeping, etc. At which point I realized that normal life was in fact the life they had before the war, what they had lost. Normal life is therefore simultaneously a nostalgic and utopian project, both irretrievable and unachievable.

Which is to say that normal life is delimited and defined by catastrophe—it's the life ruptured, the life made both unavailable and visible by katastrofa. And, inversely, katastrofa is whatever ruptures life, what makes its stability, its necessary biological and emotional inertia, impossible. Much as catastrophe in tragedy necessitates the resolution of the plot, katastrofa necessitates a narrative of *normal life*, which we can perceive only through the catastrophic screen dividing our life into before and after.

As for me, I have a confession to make: my mind is linguistically obsessive, ever relentlessly and involuntarily generating wordplay and verbal distortions. There has to be a diagnosis related to that kind of constant chatter, or to the fact that, every day of my normal life, I talk to myself in Bosnian, usually in a voice of a Sarajevo street thug—cursing, threatening, insulting, mainly myself (or rather the part that is not a Sarajevo thug). Well, that language-obsessed mind has spontaneously come up with the name of Sergei Katastrofenko—an imaginary Slav, probably Ukrainian—who flickers as a possibility of a character, or a joke, or a catastrophe. The name Sergei Katastrofenko often bounces around my head as I scan the world for the ripples of disaster, even as he hasn't quite acquired a full voice, let alone a body. But when he does acquire it—and when that happens, I'll be losing my mind—he'll become a perfect embodiment of katastrofa, of the idea that no reality—or the narrative of it—is possible without catastrophe.

GLOSSARY

Abaddon: Hebrew name for a place of destruction. In Revelation 9:11 Abaddon is king of the locusts and angel of the abyss. By 3rd cent. the name is used for the devil.

accident: "It is fate misnamed." —Napoleon Bonaparte

al-Nakba: Arabic for "the disaster." Now refers specifically to displacement of Palestinians after Israel's independence in 1948.

annihilate: To cause to cease to exist; especially, to kill. From Latin *annihilatus*, past participle of *annihilare*, to reduce to nothing. First known use, 1388.

apada: आपदा Hindi for disaster, calamity.

apocalypse: A great disaster; a sudden and bad event that causes fear, loss, or destruction. From Greek *apokalypsis*, *apokalyptein*, to uncover, per original use to describe the revelations of John of Patmos.

calamity: From French *calamité*, Latin *calamitas*, damage, disaster, adversity. Associated with *calamus*, straw or cornstalk, in ref. to crop damage from hail or mildew. Also, *calamity-howler*, a person who makes dismal predictions of impending disaster.

cataclysm: A great flood of water, a deluge; esp. the Noachian deluge.

catastrophe: As defined by the insurance industry, a natural or man-made disaster that causes a certain dollar amount—currently set at $25 million—in insured damage.

clusterfuck: A disastrously mishandled situation or undertaking. Also, *charlie foxtrot*, phonetic alphabet for *clusterfuck*.

crash: The action of falling to ruin suddenly and violently; spec. sudden collapse or failure of financial undertaking or of mercantile credit.

debacle: Great disaster or complete failure. From French *débâcle*, to unbar, a breakup of ice in a river. Hence, figurative meaning of a sudden breaking up, downfall, confused rout, or stampede.

doomer: A judge; enforcer of laws or judgments, esp. in Anglo-Saxon England. From Old English *dóm*, Old Germanic *dōmo*, statute, ordinance, lit. that which is put or set up.

embuggerance: A set of circumstances due partly to unavoidable natural problems, partly to human error. Used by UK Royal Engineers during Falklands War. Also, *hobart*, from *highly organized buggering about regardless of time*.

emergency man: In Irish usage, a person employed in special service, such as evictions.

famine bread: Bread made from lichen (e.g., *Umbilicaria arctica*); in Finland, bread made from the bark of a pine tree (*pettuleipä*).

fiasco: A complete failure. French, from Italian, *fare fiasco*, lit. to make a bottle. First known use, c. 1854. The fig. use of *far fiasco*, in the sense "to break down or fail in performance," is of obscure origin.

force majeure: French, superior strength. An event or effect that cannot be reasonably anticipated or controlled; an act of God.

Götterdämmerung: German, twilight of the gods; a collapse (as of a society or regime) marked by catastrophic violence and disorder.

malefactor: "The chief factor in the progress of the human race."— Ambrose Bierce, *Devil's Dictionary*

maxipok: Any outcome that avoids existential disaster; from *maxi*mize the *p*robability of an *ok*ay outcome.

murrain: A plague; a highly contagious disease in cattle and sheep. "There shall be a very grievous murrain."—Exodus 9:3

obliteration bombing: Heavy bombing intended to destroy a target completely; the opposite of *precision bombing* (1943).

panic: Collective flight caused by a hysterical belief. From Pan, god of the wild, whose angry voice was so frightening it caused panic (*panikon deima*) to those who heard it. Also, *panolepsia*, possessed by an excess of violent emotion.

peril: A state of being exposed to imminent injury, loss, or destruction. "Glory is the fair child of peril." —Tobias Smollett

ruin: A state of complete destruction. From Middle English *ruine*, Latin *ruina*, *ruere*, to rush headlong, fall, collapse. First known use, 12th cent. "Mine is the ruin of the lofty hall,/The falling down of tower and of wall."—Geoffrey Chaucer, *Canterbury Tales*

scapegoat: One who is blamed or punished for the sins of others. Erroneously coined in 1530 by William Tyndale to express what he believed to be the literal meaning of Hebrew *ăzāzel*, mentioned in Leviticus in

Portmanteaus of *Armageddon* used by media outlets in the past ten years:

carmageddon, swarmageddon, shawarmageddon, snowmageddon, eurogeddon, Obamageddon, Romneygeddon, courtmageddon, debtmageddon, gaymageddon, Goremageddon, heatmageddon, birdmageddon, wordmageddon.

connection to the sacrifice of a goat on the Day of Atonement.

shock: First adopted as military term; encounter of an armed force with the enemy in a charge or onset; also, encounter of two jousters charging one another. From Middle Dutch *schocken*, to jolt.

snafu: Acronym of "situation normal, all fucked up." (*OED* offers *fouled up*.) British Army used OMFU (ordinary military) and IMFU (imperial military). Also *fubar*, *f*ucked *u*p *b*eyond *a*ll *r*epair or *r*ecognition.

tempest: A violent storm of wind, usually accompanied by rain, hail, snow, or thunder. From Old French *tempeste*, for Latin *tempestās*, season, weather, storm.

terror: "No passion so effectually robs the mind of all its powers of acting and reasoning as fear." —Edmund Burke

tornado: Probably a bad adaptation (perhaps a blundered spelling) of Spanish *tronada*, thunderstorm (*tronar*, to thunder); may derive from an attempt to improve by treatment as derivative of Spanish *tornar*, to turn, return; compare *tornado* participle, returned.

trainwreck: (*Med.*) A very sick patient who has several medical problems simultaneously and is usually comatose.

Disaster

The unfavorable aspect of a star; "an obnoxious planet." From French *désastre* (1564), a misfortune, calamity; *des*, privative sense implying removal, negation, and *astre*, "a Starre, a Planet; also, destinie, fate, fortune, hap" (Randle Cotgrave's 1611 *Dict. of French and English Tongues*); Latin *astrum*, Greek ἄστρον, star. Compare Provençal *benastre*, good fortune, and *malastre*, ill fortune, and English *ill-starred*.

tsunami: The first American use of the word appeared in the September 1896 issue of *National Geographic*, in a description of a tsunami that struck the northeast coast of Hondo. From *tsu* plus *nami*, harbor plus waves. Hiroshima survivors use the word to describe the atomic catastrophe, as if it were a natural disaster.

typhoon: A violent storm or tempest. One possible form (like Portuguese *tufão*, *tufõe*) is Urdu (Persian and Arabic) *tūfān*, a violent storm, hurricane, tornado, referred to Arabic *tāfa*, to turn round, but possibly an adoption of Greek τῡφῶν. Another form is from Chinese *tai fung*, common dialect forms (as in Cantonese) of *ta*, big, and *fĕng*, wind.

Unfallneurose: Accident neurosis. A syndrome whose diagnosis entitled patients to insurance benefits in 1884; this so-called traumatic neurosis spread to almost epidemic proportions throughout Wilhelmine German society until it was legislated out of existence in 1926.

washout: A complete failure (1873).

wēijī: 危机 Mandarin for crisis; a widespread misconception (repeated by John F. Kennedy, Richard Nixon, and Condoleezza Rice) is that the two ideograms represent *danger* and *opportunity*.

wreck: What remains of something that has suffered ruin, demolishment, waste; the dilapidated, disorganized, or disordered residue or remainder of anything. From Anglo-Norman *wrec*, *wrech*, *wrek*; Old Norse *wrec*, *wrek*, from the stem of *wrekan*, to drive, in the sense of a sea vessel broken by being driven onto rocks.

What Happened to Mishap?

Uses per 15,000 words

3

2

1

1800 1820 1840 1860 1880 1900 1920 1940 1960 1980 2000 2010

Based on Google News Viewer, the frequency of the word mishap *in sources printed between 1800 and 2008, from a database of over 5 million books.*

Sources

p. 25, Greenland Kolbert, Elizabeth. *Field Notes from a Catastrophe*. New York: Bloomsbury USA, 2015. Copyright © 2015 by Elizabeth Kolbert. Used with permission of Elizabeth Kolbert.

p. 28, Luoyang Fan Ye. *Science and Civilization in China*, Vol. 3. Translated by Joseph Needham. Cambridge: Cambridge University Press, 1995. Copyright © 1959 by Cambridge University Press. Used with permission of Cambridge University Press.

p. 31, Attica Lucian. *Selected Satires of Lucian*. Translated by Lionel Casson. New York: W. W. Norton & Co., 1968. Copyright © 1962 by Lionel Casson.

p. 32, Walnut Grove, MN Wilder, Laura Ingalls. *On the Banks of Plum Creek*. New York: HarperCollins, 2004. Copyright © 1965 by Little House Heritage Trust. Used with permission of the estate of Laura Ingalls Wilder.

p. 34, Gila River Valley *American Indian Myths and Legends*. Edited by Richard Erdoes and Alfonso Ortiz. New York: Pantheon, 1984. Copyright © 1984 by Richard Erdoes and Alfonso Ortiz.

p. 36, Russia Chekhov, Anton. *Plays by Anton Chekoff*. Translated by Marian Fell. New York: Charles Scribner's Sons, 1916.

p. 38, Japan Nichiren. *The Creed of Half Japan*. Translated by Arthur Lloyd. New York: E.P. Dutton & Company, 1912.

p. 40, Buenos Aires Borges, Jorge Luis. *Collected Fictions*. Translated by Andrew Hurley. New York: Penguin Books, 1999. Copyright © 1998 by Maria Kodama. Translation copyright © 1998 by Penguin Putnam Inc. Used with permission of Viking Books, an imprint of Penguin Publishing Group, a division of Penguin Random House LLC.

p. 41, New York City Schell, Jonathan. *The Fate of the Earth*. London: Jonathan Cape, 1982. Copyright © 1982 by Jonathan Schell. Used with permission of the estate of Jonathan Schell.

p. 44, Vienna Freud, Sigmund. *Civilization and its Discontents*. Edited by Peter Gay. New York: Norton, Year. Copyright © 1961 by James Strachey.

p. 46, Paris Virilio, Paul. *Politics of the Very Worst*. Translated by Michael Cavaliere. New York: Semiotext(e), 1999. Copyright © 1999 by Semiotext(e). Used with permission of Semiotext(e).

p. 47, Warsaw Kaplan, Chaim. *Scroll of Agony*. Translated by Abraham I. Katsh. Bloomington: Indiana University Press, 1999. Copyright © 1973 by Abraham I. Katsh.

p. 50, Britain Shakespeare, William. *The Tragedy of King Lear*. Edited by Jay L. Halio. Cambridge: Cambridge University Press, 2012.

p. 52, Patmos *The Bible*. Edited by David Norton. London: Penguin Classics, 2006. Copyright © 2005 by Cambridge University Press.

p. 53, Kansas City, MO Connell, Evan S. *Mrs. Bridge*. London: Penguin Classics, 2012. Copyright © 1987 by Evan S. Connell.

p. 56, Rome Aelian. *On the Characteristics of Animals*. Translated by Alwyn Faber Scholfield. Cambridge: University of Harvard

Press, 1958. Copyright © 1958 by the President and Fellows of Harvard.

p. 57, Rutland, VT Marsh, George P. *Address Delivered Before the Agricultural Society of Rutland County*. Rutland: Rutland County Agricultural Society, 1848.

p. 59, Brigham City, UT Zwerdling, Daniel. "Thiokol Engineers Warned NASA About Cold," NPR's *Morning Edition*, February 20, 1986. Copyright © 1986 by National Public Radio, Inc. Used with permission of NPR. Any unauthorized duplication is strictly prohibited.

p. 61, Königsberg Kant, Immanuel. *Natural Science*. Edited by Eric Watkins. Cambridge: Cambridge University Press, 2013. Copyright © 2012 by Cambridge University Press. Used with permission of Cambridge University Press.

p. 62, Hekla Herbert of Clairvaux. *Eruption of Hekla 1947-1948*. Edited by Sigurður Þórarinsson. Reykjavik: H.F. Leiftur, 1967. Copyright © 1967 by Sigurður Þórarinsson.

p. 64, Turin Levi, Primo. *Collected Poems*, translated by Jonathan Galassi; from *The Complete Works of Primo Levi*, edited by Ann Goldstein. New York: Liveright, 2015. Copyright © 1984 (*Ad ora incert*) by Garzanti Editore S.p.A., Milano and 1997 (*Opere II*) by Giulio Einaudi editore S.p.A., Torino. English translation copyright © 2015 by Jonathan Galassi. Used with permission of W.W. Norton & Company, Inc.

p. 65, Rome Seneca. *Ad Lucilium Epistulae Morales*, Vol. 1. Translated by Richard M. Gummere. London: William Heinemann, 1917.

p. 67, Fort Irwin, CA Bissell, Tom. *Harper's Magazine*, Febuary 2003. Copyright © 2003 by Tom Bissell. Used with permission of Tom Bissell.

p. 70, Paris Stein, Gertrude. *Reflection on the Atomic Bomb*. Edited by Robert Bartlett Hass. Los Angeles: Black Sparrow Press, 1973. Copyright © 1973 by the estate of Gertrude Stein.

p. 73, North Africa Orosius. *Seven Books of History Against the Pagans*. Translated by Roy J. Deferrari. Washington: Catholic University of America Press, 1981. Copyright © 1964 by Catholic University of America Press, Inc. Used with permission of Catholic University of America Press.

p. 74, Hiroshima Toyofumi Ogura. *Letters from the End of the World*. Translated by Kisaburo Murakami and Shigeru Fujii. Tokyo: Kodansha International Ltd., 2001. Copyright © 1997 by Kodansha International Ltd.

p. 76, Calicut Ibn Battuta. *The Travels of Ibn Battutah*. Translated by Hamilton Gibb and C.F. Beckingham. London: Picador, 2003. Copyright © 2000 by the Hakluyt Society. Used with permission of the Hakluyt Society.

p. 78, Atlantic Ocean Bride, Harold. "Thrilling Tale of Titanic's Surviving Wireless Man," *New York Times*, April 28, 1912.

p. 82, Nigeria Menkiti, Ifeanyi. *Voices from Twentieth-Century Africa*. Edited by Chinweizu. London: Faber & Faber, 1988. Copyright © Ifeanyi Menkiti. Used with

permission of Ifeanyi Menkiti.

p. 83, Auvergne Gregory of Tours. *The History of the Franks*. Translated by Lewis Thorpe. London: Penguin Classics, 1974. Copyright © 1974 by the Estate of Lewis Thorpe. Used with permission of Penguin Books Ltd.

p. 85, Paris Budiansky, Stephen. *Her Majesty's Spymaster*. New York: Penguin Books, 2006. Copyright © 2005 by Stephen Budiansky. Used with permission of Viking Books, an imprint of Penguin Publishing Group, a division of Penguin Random House LLC.

p. 87, Combles Jünger, Ernst. *Storm of Steel*. Translated by Michael Hofmann. New York: Penguin Classics, 2004. Copyright © 1961 by J.G. Cotta'sche Buchhandlung Nachfolger GmbH, Stuttgart. Translation copyright © 2003 by Michael Hofmann. Used with permission of Penguin Classics, an imprint of Penguin Publishing Group, a division of Penguin Random House LLC.

p. 88, Medina *The Koran*. Translated by N.J. Dawood. London: Penguin Classics, 2006. Copyright © 2006 by N.J. Dawood.

p. 92, India *The Bhagavad-Gita*. Translated by Barbara Stoler Miller. New York: Bantam Books, 1986. Copyright © 1986 by Barbara Stoler Miller.

p. 95, Portugal Saramago, José. *Blindness*. Translated by Juan Sager. San Diego: Harcourt, Inc., 1999. Copyright © 1997 by Juan Sager.

p. 98, Akkad *The Literature of Ancient Sumer*. Translated by Jeremy Black, Graham Cunningham, Eleanor Robson, and Gabor Zolyomi. Oxford: Oxford University Press, 2006. Copyright © 2004 by the estate of Jeremy Black, Graham Cunningham, Eleanor Robson, and Gabor Zolyomi.

p. 100, England Knighton, Henry. *The Portable Medieval Reader*. Translated by Mary Martin McLaughlin. New York: Penguin Books, 1977. Copyright © 1976 by James Bruce Ross and Mary Martin McLaughlin. Used with permission of Viking Books, an imprint of Penguin Publishing Group, a division of Penguin Random House LLC.

p. 101, Burlington, VT Carruth, Hayden. *Brothers, I Loved You All*. New York: Sheep Meadow Press, 1978. Copyright © 1978 by Hayden Carruth. Used with permission of Sheep Meadow Press.

p. 102, Khwarezm Ibn al-Athir. *The Chronicle of Ibn al-Athir for the Crusading Period*. Translated by D.S. Richards. Aldershot: Ashgate, 2006. Copyright © 2005 by D.S. Richards.

p. 104, Tokyo Haruki Murakami. *Underground*. Translated by Alfred Bimbaum and Philip Gabriel. New York: Vintage Books, 2001. Copyright © 2000 by Haruki Murakami.

p. 107, Rome Tacitus. *Annals*. Translated by Michael Grant. New York: Penguin Classics, 1996. Copyright © 1996 by Michael Grant Publications. Used with permission of Penguin Books Ltd.

p. 109, London Hyde, Edward. *The Life of Edward, Earl of Clarendon*, Vol. 3. Oxford: Clarendon Press, 1827.

p. 112, Madrid Darío, Rubén.

Selected Writings. Translated by Andrew Hurley, Greg Simon, and Steven F. White. New York: Penguin Classics, 2005. Copyright © 2005 by Andrew Hurley, Greg Simon, and Steven F. White. Used with permission of Penguin Books, an imprint of Penguin Publishing Group, a division of Penguin Random House LLC.

p. 113, Prague Čapek, Karel. *War with the Newts*. Translated by Ewald Osers. North Haven: Catbird Press, 1990. Copyright © 1936 by Karel Čapek. Translation copyright © 1999 by UNESCO. Used with permission of Catbird Press.

p. 116, Hanyang Yun Hoe. *Sources of Korean Tradition*, Vol. 1. Edited by Peter H. Lee and William Theodore de Bary. New York: Columbia University Press, 1997. Copyright © 1997 by Columbia University Press. Used with permission of Columbia University Press.

p. 119, Syria "Black Flags from the Islamic State," The Investigative Project on Terrorism, accessed on February 10, 2016, http://investigativeproject.org/documents/misc/864.pdf

p. 121, Constantinople Ducas. *Decline and Fall of Byzantium to the Ottoman Turks*. Translated by Harry J. Magoulias. Detroit: Wayne State University Press, 1975. Copyright © 1975 by Wayne State University Press.

p. 123, Chicago Repa, Helen. *Western Electric News*, August, 1915.

p. 126, Wessex Hardy, Thomas. *Far From the Madding Crowd*. New York: Henry Holt & Company, 1874.

p. 129, San Bernardino County Watkins, Claire Vaye. *Gold Fame Citrus*. New York: Riverhead Books, 2015. Copyright © 2015 by Claire Vaye Watkins. Used with permission of Riverhead, an imprint of Penguin Publishing Group, a division of Penguin Random House LLC.

p. 132, Paris Cuvier, Georges. *A Discourse on the Revolutions of the Surface of the Globe*. Philadelphia: Carey & Lea, 1831.

p. 136, Glasgow Smith, Adam. *The Theory of Moral Sentiments*. London: A. Millar: 1761.

p. 137, Middletown, CT Dillard, Annie. *For the Time Being*. New York: Vintage Books, 2000. Copyright © 1999 by Annie Dillard. Used with permission of Alfred A. Knopf, an imprint of the Knopf Doubleday Publishing Group, a division of Penguin Random House LLC. All rights reserved.

p. 139, Egypt *Ancient Egyptian Literature*, Vol. 1. Translated by Miriam Lichtheim. Berkeley: University of California Press, 2006. Copyright © 2006 by the Regents of the University of California Press.

p. 141, Palo Alto, CA James, William. "On Some Mental Effects of the Earthquake." *Youth's Companion*, June 7, 1906.

p. 145, Port Royal Heath, Emmanuel. *Kirby's Wonderful and Eccentric Museum; or, Magazine of Remarkable Characters*, Vol. 2. London: R.S. Kirby, 1820.

p. 147, Yellowstone Solotaroff, Paul. *Men's Journal*, April 2011. Copyright © 2011 by Paul Solotaroff.

p. 149, Mexico Motolinia, Toribio de Benavente. *History of the Indians of New Spain*. Translated by

Elizabeth Andros Foster. Westport: Greenwood Press, 1973. Copyright © 1973 by Elizabeth Andros Fostert.

p. 152, **Slateford War Hospital** Sassoon, Siegfried. *Sherston's Progress*. New York: Penguin Classics, 2013. Copyright © 1964 by Siegfried Sassoon. Used with permission of Penguin Books, an imprint of Penguin Publishing Group, a division of Penguin Random House LLC.

p. 154, **Lake Ladoga** Malaparte, Curzio. *The Volga Rises in Europe*. Translated by David Moore. Edinburgh: Birlinn Limited, 2000. Copyright © 1951 by the Estate of Curzio Malaparte.

p. 157, **Columbia, SC** Chesnut, Mary. *A Diary From Dixie*. Edited by Isabella D. Martin & Myrta Lockett. New York: D. Appleton and Company, 1906.

p. 158, **Pripyat** Alexievich, Svetlana. *Voices from Chernobyl: The Oral History of a Nuclear Disaster*. Translated by Keith Gessen. Victoria: Dalkey Archive Press, 2005. New York: Picador, 2006. Copyright © 1997 by Svetlana Alexievich. Translation copyright © 2005 by Keith Gessen. Used with permission of Dalkey Archive Press.

p. 160, **Greenland** Johnson of Skardso, Björn. *Early Voyages and Northern Approaches 1000-1632*. Translated by Tryggvi Oleson. Toronto: McClelland & Stewart, 1963. Copyright © 1963 by Tryggvi Oleson.

p. 164, **Rome** Shelley, Mary Wollstonecraft. *The Last Man*, Vol 2. Philadelphia: Carey, Lea & Blanchard, 1833.

p. 167, **South Pole** Scott, Robert Falcon. *Scott's Last Expedition*, Vol. 1. New York: Dodd, Mead & Co., 1913. "Scott of the Antarctic's final letter." *The Telegraph*, January 11, 2007.

p. 170, **Alexandria** Cavafy, C.P. *Collected Poems*. Translated by Daniel Mendelsohn. New York: Alfred A. Knopf, 2009. Copyright © 2009 by Daniel Mendelsohn. Used with permission of Alfred A. Knopf, an imprint of the Knopf Doubleday Publishing Group, a division of Penguin Random House LLC. All rights reserved.

p. 171, **Ghana** Armah, Ayi Kwei. *West Africa*, September 24, 1984. Copyright © 1984 by Ayi Kwei Armah.

p. 172, **Bucharest** Bernhard, Thomas. *The Voice Imitator*. Translated by Kenneth J. Northcott. Chicago: University of Chicago Press, 1997. Copyright © 1997 by the University of Chicago Press. Used with permission of the University of Chicago Press.

p. 177, **St. Louis, MO** *The American Law Review*, Vo. 23. St. Louis: Review Publishing Co., 1889.

p. 178, **Rome** Lucretius. *On the Nature of Things: De rerum natura*. Translated by Anthony M. Esolen. Baltimore: Johns Hopkins University Press, 1995. Copyright © 1995 by Johns Hopkins University Press.

p. 180, **Hampstead** Canetti, Elias. *Crowds and Power*. Translated by Carol Stewart. New York: Farrar, Straus and Giroux, 1984. Copyright © 1960 by Claassen Verlag, Hamburg. Translation copyright ©

1973 by Victor Gollancz Ltd.

p. 182, **Halifax** Solnit, Rebecca. *A Paradise Built in Hell*. New York: Penguin Books, 2010. Copyright © 2009 by Rebecca Solnit. Used with permission of Viking Books, an imprint of Penguin Publishing Group, a division of Penguin Random House LLC.

p. 212 Plato. *The Dialogues of Plato*, Vol. 2. Translated by Benjamin Jowett. Oxford: Clarendon Press, 1871.

p. 212 Friedrich, Otto. *The End of the World: A History*. New York: Coward, McCann & Geoghegan, 1982. Copyright © 1982 by Otto Friedrich.

p. 213 Mandeville, Bernard de. *The Fable of the Bees*. London: J. Tonson, 1724.

p. 213 Jolie, Angelina. "Angelina Jolie receives the Jean Hersholt Humanitarian Award at the 2013 Governors Awards," YouTube video, from 2013 Governers Awards televised by on November 16, 2013, https://www.youtube.com/watch?v=2ATgxOp31oI

p. 220-221 Sources include the *Oxford English Dictionary* and Merriam-Webster; illustration from *Alchemy & Mysticism*, by Alexander Roob, p. 532.

Art

Cover, © RMN-Grand Palais / Art Resource, NY

IFC, © National Gallery of Art, Washington, DC / Bridgeman Images

p. 5, © Larry Schwarm, courtesy the artist

p. 6, © The Metropolitan Museum of Art, www.metmuseum.org; gift of John Taylor Johnston, 1881

p. 8–9, © Pictures from History / Bridgeman Images; © Leemage / Bridgeman Images; © Paul Virilio / Photo © Louis Monier / Bridgeman Images; Photo © PVDE / Bridgeman Images; © Ernst Jünger / Photo © Louis Monier / Bridgeman Images; © De Agostini Picture Library / Bridgeman Images; Annie Dillard photo © Phyllis Rose

p. 12, © Akademie der Bildenden Künste, Vienna / Bridgeman Images

p. 15, © Daily Mirror Gulf Coverage / Mirrorpix / Getty Images

p. 18, © Manchester Art Gallery / Bridgeman Images

p. 22, © The Metropolitan Museum of Art, www.metmuseum.org; Gilman Collection, Museum Purchase, 2005

p. 24, © David LaChapelle, courtesy the artist

p. 27, © Jun Fujita / Chicago History Museum / Getty Images

p. 29, © AFP / AFP / Getty Images

p. 32, © Chris Johns / National Geographic Creative

p. 35, © Collegiata, San Gimignano / Bridgeman Images

p. 38, © USAF / HIP / Art Resource, NY

p. 40, © François Guenet / Art Resource, NY

p. 41, © British Library Board / Robana / Art Resource, NY

p. 42, © John Brosio, courtesy the artist and Arcadia Contemporary, Santa Monica, CA

p. 45, © Fox Photos / Hulton Archive / Getty Images

p. 47, © Paula Bronstein / Reportage Archive / Getty Images

p. 51, © Gianni Dagli Orti / The Art Archive at Art Resource, NY

p. 53, © Erich Lessing / Magnum Photos

p. 54, © RMN–Grand Palais / Art Resource, NY

p. 57, © Raghu Rai / Magnum Photos

p. 59, © Gianni Dagli Orti / The Art Archive at Art Resource, NY

p. 63, © RMN-Grand Palais / Art Resource, NY

p. 65, Image © The Metropolitan Museum of Art; image source: Art Resource, NY

p. 66, © The Philadelphia Museum of Art / Art Resource, NY; art © Estate of Ben Shahn / Licensed by VAGA, New York, NY

p. 69, photo © Edward Burtynsky, courtesy Nicholas Metivier Gallery, Toronto

p. 71, © Scala / Art Resource, NY

p. 73, © Cunjamá, Manuel; photo © Schalkwijk / Art Resource, NY

p. 74, © Marco Di Lauro / Reportage Archive / Getty Images

p. 77, © Cameraphoto Arte, Venice / Art Resource, NY

p. 78, © Mitch Dobrowner, courtesy the artist

p. 83, © John Moore / Reportage Archive / Getty Images

p. 84, © National Gallery, London / Art Resource, NY

p. 87, © Kharbine-Tapabor / The Art Archive at Art Resource, NY

p. 89, © Liset Castillo, courtesy the artist

p. 92, Image copyright © The Metropolitan Museum of Art; image source: Art Resource, NY

p. 95, © Hiroshi Hamaya / Magnum Photos

p. 96, © William Kentridge, courtesy the artist

p. 99, © The Metropolitan Museum of Art, www.metmuseum.org; gift of Zimmerman Family Collection, 2012

p. 103, © STR / AFP / Getty Images

p. 104, © British Library Board / Robana / Art Resource, NY

p. 107, © Tammam Azzam, courtesy the artist and Ayyam Gallery

p. 108, © Erich Lessing / Art Resource, NY

p. 111, © Jim Goldberg / Magnum Photos

p. 113, © Mitchell Krog / Barcroft USA / Getty Images

p. 114, © The Metropolitan Museum of Art, www.metmuseum.org; bequest of Harry G. Sperling, 1971

p. 117, © The Metropolitan Museum of Art, www.metmuseum.org; Fletcher Fund, 1925

p. 119, © Lori Nix, courtesy the artist and Clamp Art Gallery, NYC

p. 120, © Eugene Richards; photo © Addison Gallery of American Art, Phillips Academy, Andover, MA / Art Resource, NY

p. 123, Image © The Metropolitan Museum of Art; image source: Art Resource, NY; © 2016 Delaware Art Museum / Artists Rights Society, New York

p. 124, © Steve McCurry / Magnum Photos

p. 127, © HIP / Art Resource, NY

p. 128, © Culver Pictures / The Art Archive at Art Resource, NY

p. 130, © Edward Kinsman / Science Source / Getty Images

p. 133, © LACMA; from the Nasli and Alice Heeramaneck Collection,

Museum Associates Purchase, www.lacma.org

p. 134, © Erich Lessing / Art Resource, NY

p. 137, © Recorded Pic-Cineventure-Asahi / Oshima / The Kobal Collection

p. 139, © Buffalo Bill Center of the West / The Art Archive at Art Resource, NY

p. 140, © John Vink / Magnum Photos

p. 143, Digital image © The Museum of Modern Art / Licensed by SCALA / Art Resource, NY; gift of the Farm Security Administration

p. 144, © Dreamworks / Paramount / The Kobal Collection

p. 146, © The Trustees of the British Museum / Art Resource, NY

p. 149, © Daniel Berehulak / Getty Images News / Getty Images

p. 150, © Snark / Art Resource, NY

p. 153, © Rina Castelnuovo, courtesy Andrea Meislin Gallery

p. 155, © The Metropolitan Museum of Art, www.metmuseum.org; Rogers Fund, 1912

p. 159, © The Art Archive at Art Resource, NY

p. 161, © National Army Museum / The Art Archive at Art Resource, NY

p. 162, © bpk, Berlin / Neue Residenz, Bamberg / Art Resource, NY

p. 165, © Edouard Elias / Getty Images News / Getty Images

p. 166, © The Metropolitan Museum of Art, www.metmuseum.org; Rogers Fund and Edward S. Harkness Gift, 1913

p. 168, © British Library Board / Robana / Art Resource, NY

p. 171, © Richard Mosse, courtesy the artist and Jack Shainman Gallery

p. 173, © Private Collection / Waterhouse & Dodd, London / Bridgeman Images

p. 176, © The Philadelphia Museum of Art / Art Resource, NY

p. 179, © Gilles Mermet / Art Resource, NY

p. 181, © Look and Learn / Bridgeman Images

p. 182, © Bridgeman-Giraudon / Art Resource, NY

p. 185, © Album / Art Resource, NY

p. 186, © NASA; image courtesy Jeff Schmaltz, Lance / Eosdis Modis Rapid Response Team at NASA GSFC; caption by Adam Voiland

p. 193, © Jean Gaumy / Magnum Photos

p. 194, © Erich Lessing / Art Resource, NY

p. 197, © Hamburger Kunsthalle, Hamburg / Bridgeman Images; © 2016 Artists Rights Society, New York / ADAGP, Paris

p. 200, © De Agostini Picture Library / G. Dagli Orti / Bridgeman Images

p. 203, © bpk, Berlin / Art Resource, NY; © 2016 Artists Rights Society, New York

p. 206, © Brent Stirton Images / Reportage Archive / Getty Images

p. 216, © Arco Film / The Kobal Collection

p. 219, © The Metropolitan Museum of Art, www.metmuseum.org; the Berggruen Klee Collection, 1984

IBC, © Steve McCurry / Magnum Photos

LAPHAM'S
QUARTERLY

*Everyone, deep in their hearts, is waiting for the end
of the world to come.*

— *Haruki Murakami, 2009*

World Trade Center, New York City, September 11, 2001. Photograph by Steve McCurry.